SUPERFOODS

*150 superfood recipes to inspire
health & happiness*

This edition published by Parragon Books Ltd in 2016
and distributed by

Parragon Inc.
440 Park Avenue South, 13th Floor
New York, NY 10016
www.parragon.com/lovefood

LOVE FOOD is an imprint of Parragon Books Ltd

ISBN 978-1-4748-3807-8

Printed in China

Project managed by Annabel Hampshire
Additional text by Judith Wills
Cover photography by Max and Liz Haarala Hamilton
Designed by Karli Skelton

⟶ ⟫ NOTES FOR THE READER ⟪ ⟵

This book uses standard kitchen measuring spoons and cups. All
spoon and cup measurements are level unless otherwise indicated.
Unless otherwise stated, milk is assumed to be whole, eggs are
large, individual vegetables and fruits are medium, and pepper is
freshly ground black pepper. A pinch of salt is calculated as $\frac{1}{16}$ of
a teaspoon. Unless otherwise stated, all root vegetables should be
peeled prior to using.

Garnishes, decorations, and serving suggestions are all optional and
not necessarily included in the recipe ingredients or method. Any
optional ingredients and seasoning to taste are not included in the
nutritional analysis.

The times given are only an approximate guide. Preparation times
differ according to the techniques used by different people and the
cooking times may also vary from those given. Optional ingredients,
variations, or serving suggestions have not been included in the time
calculations.

While the publisher of the book and the original author(s) of the
recipes and other text have made all reasonable efforts to ensure
that the information contained in this book is accurate and up to
date at the time of publication, anyone reading this book should note
the following important points:

Medical and pharmaceutical knowledge is constantly changing
and the author(s) and the publisher cannot and do not guarantee
the accuracy or appropriateness of the contents of this book;
In any event, this book is not intended to be, and should not be
relied upon, as a substitute for appropriate, tailored professional
advice. Both the author(s) and the publisher strongly recommend
that a physician or other healthcare professional is consulted before
embarking on major dietary changes;

For the reasons set out above, and to the fullest extent permitted
by law, the author(s) and publisher: (i) cannot and do not accept
any legal duty of care or responsibility in relation to the accuracy or
appropriateness of the contents of this book, even where expressed
as "advice" or using other words to this effect; and (ii) disclaim any
liability, loss, damage, or risk that may be claimed or incurred as a
consequence—directly or indirectly—of the use and/or application of
any of the contents of this book.

For best results, use a food thermometer when cooking meat. Check
the latest government guidelines for current advice.

CONTENTS

INTRODUCTION

We all want to live a long and healthy life—and one of the major keys to that is to eat well. Picking up pieces of information here and there can be complicated and time-consuming but help is on hand. This is the only reference you need for choosing the foods and ingredients that will help you achieve your goal.

Eating well can help you in so many ways. A healthy diet can give you protection against all the major diseases, including cardiovascular diseases, cancers, diabetes, arthritis, and dementia, as well as offer protection against health problems, such as asthma, eczema, tiredness, insomnia, gum disease, and many more. It can also boost your general sense of well-being—for example, helping you to feel more alert and aiding your concentration and memory—and it can make you look better too, improving your skin, hair, and eyes. Finally, a healthy diet also gives you the best chance of maintaining a healthy bodyweight and avoiding weight gain and obesity throughout your life.

WHAT IS A HEALTHY DIET?

The traditional definition of a healthy diet is one that provides you with a good balance of all the major nutrients—carbohydrates, fats, and protein—that your body needs to function well. It also provides the right number of calories to give you energy and maintain a suitable weight, as well as dietary fiber and fluids to keep your digestive system working well. It should also provide all the micronutrients—vitamins and minerals needed in tiny amounts—that are vital for health and well-being.

A healthy diet also involves choosing mostly natural, unprocessed, or minimally processed foods and beverages—a "whole-food" diet. In recent years, scientists have found that to be truly healthy, our bodies also need a range of chemicals and compounds found in high quantities in this type of whole, natural food diet. From flavonoids to anthocyanins, there are thousands of these that help keep us in optimum health. We also need a regular supply of different types of bacteria, not only for digestive health but for a host of other benefits, scientists are now discovering, and a natural diet is key to obtaining these bacteria.

WHAT IS A SUPERFOOD?

The foods that can give you the best amount or range of these major, macro, and "new" chemicals and bacteria that are most often in short supply in the average diet are often labeled "superfoods." No one food on its own can give you everything you need from food for a perfect diet, so it is important to eat a range of foods to get everything you need for the healthiest possible diet for you. For example, one food may be a particularly good source of vitamin C, plant chemicals, and antioxidants, while another may be especially rich in soluble fiber and a vitamin B and is known to promote beneficial bacteria. Superfoods work together to make a "super" diet. In this book, we've brought together 150 of the foods that are probably most deserving of the label "superfoods."

OUR RECIPES

The ideal plan is to enjoy meals and recipes that include a variety of superfoods and other staple healthy foods, so that you easily get everything your body needs for good health. What you'll find within this book, as well as detailed descriptions of the superfoods and what they can do for you, are hundreds of tips for their use, as well as 150 exciting recipes using each superfood—plus a wide range of other healthy foods—which together will give you a diet that can keep you healthy for life.

FRUIT

BLUEBERRIES

These berries are the richest of all fruits in antioxidant compounds,
which protect us from cancers and several other diseases.

MAJOR NUTRIENTS PER ⅓ CUP BLUEBERRIES

29 cal	TRACE	7.2g	1.2g	0.4g	5mg	2.4mg	34mcg	40mcg	39mg
CALORIES	TOTAL FAT	CARBS	FIBER	PROTEIN	VITAMIN C	VITAMIN E	FOLATE	LUTEIN/ ZEAXANTHIN	POTASSIUM

The wild blueberry has become one of the most popular berries.
They are the third highest plant food on the ORAC scale, so just a
handful of berries a day can offer protection from some diseases.
The compound pterostilbene, which is found in the fruit, could be as
effective as commercial drugs in lowering cholesterol and may also help
prevent diabetes and some cancers. Blueberries are a good source of
anthocyanins, which can help prevent heart disease and memory loss.
They are high in vitamin C and fiber and also appear to help fight urinary
tract infections.

- Contain a cholesterol-lowering compound.
- Can help prevent coronary heart disease, diabetes, and cancers.
- Help beat urinary tract infections.
- Appear to help protect against intestinal upsets, including food
  poisoning.
- Their carotene, in the form of lutein and zeaxanthin, helps keep
  eyes healthy.

DID YOU KNOW?

*Blueberries should be stored in a
nonmetallic container—contact
with metal can discolor them.*

PRACTICAL TIPS

Blueberries are sweet so can be eaten raw, which helps to preserve their
vitamin C content. They can also be lightly cooked in a small amount
of water and eaten with the juices. Blueberries can boost the nutrient
content of muffins, cakes, crisps, pies, and fruit salads. The berries freeze
well and lose few of their nutrients.

ACAI POWER BOWL

This is a great way to make quick, healthy dairy-free ice cream. You could even eat this for breakfast, it's so healthy. Acai berries are high in vitamin A, calcium, fiber, and iron.

SERVES 4 • PREP TIME: 8 MINS, PLUS FREEZING & COOLING • COOK TIME: 8–10 MINS

PER SERVING:	279 cal	4.5g	0.9g	58g	25.9g	10.1g	5.6g	TRACE
	CALORIES	FAT	SAT FAT	CARBS	SUGAR	FIBER	PROTEIN	SODIUM

INGREDIENTS
2 bananas, sliced
2½ cups raspberries
1 cup rolled oats
2 tablespoons dried cranberries
1 tablespoon sunflower seeds
3 tablespoons maple syrup
½ cup nondairy milk
1 tablespoon acai powder
⅔ cup blueberries

1. Place the banana slices and 1⅔ cups of the raspberries in a single layer on a tray and freeze for at least 2 hours.

2. Preheat a broiler to medium–hot. Mix the oats, cranberries, sunflower seeds, and maple syrup together and spread over a baking sheet.

3. Cook under the preheated broiler for 8–10 minutes, turning frequently, until golden (watch them carefully, because they can suddenly burn). Let cool.

4. Meanwhile, put half the frozen banana into a food processor with half the frozen raspberries and half the milk. Process until broken down. With the machine running slowly, add the acai powder and the remaining banana, raspberries, and milk, adding enough milk to produce an ice cream consistency.

5. Divide the ice cream among four bowls, top with the blueberries, and sprinkle with the maple-toasted oats.

HINT
Almond, coconut, soy, oat, and rice milk are all fantastic nondairy milks that would work well here.

AVOCADOS

The avocado is a rich source of monounsaturated fats for heart health and is packed with important nutrients.

240 cal	3g	12.8g	5g	22g	9mg	3mg	728 mg
CALORIES	TOTAL FAT	CARBS	FIBER	PROTEIN	VITAMIN C	VITAMIN E	POTASSIUM

Avocados are high in fat, but this fat is mostly monounsaturated. The oleic acid contained in monounsaturates can lower the risk of breast cancer, and monounsaturates can help to reduce "bad" blood cholesterol levels. Avocados also have a large range of nutrients, including vitamins C, E, and B6, folate, iron, magnesium, and potassium, and antioxidant plant chemicals beta-sitosterol, which can also help lower blood cholesterol, and glutathione, which protects against cancer.

- High vitamin E content boosts the immune system, keeps skin healthy, and helps prevent heart disease.
- Lutein content helps protect against eye cataracts and macular degeneration.
- High monounsaturated fat content helps lower cholesterol.
- Good source of magnesium for a healthy heart.

DID YOU KNOW?

Extra virgin avocado oil is now available—use it for roasting or drizzling over salads, or serve as a dip with crusty bread.

PRACTICAL TIPS

Choose avocados that have unblemished skins without soft spots, which suggest bruising. They're ready to eat if the flesh yields slightly when pressed with the thumb. To hasten ripening, put them into a paper bag with a banana. To prepare, cut lengthwise down to the pit and twist to separate the two halves. Pierce the pit with the tip of a knife, then pull it out. Use lemon juice, vinegar, or vinaigrette to prevent discoloration.

AVOCADO CHOCOLATE MOUSSE

Avocados add creaminess and richness to this delicious mousse, while
chocolate is decadent and flavorsome—simply wonderful.

SERVES 4 • PREP TIME: 10 MINS • COOK TIME: NONE

PER SERVING:

151 cal	11.8g	2.1g	15.0g	2.7g	7.5g	3.0g	160mg	
CALORIES	FAT	SAT FAT	CARBS	SUGAR	FIBER	PROTEIN	SODIUM	

INGREDIENTS

2 ripe avocados, peeled, pitted, and
coarsely chopped
⅓ cup unsweetened cocoa powder
2 tablespoons rice malt syrup
1 teaspoon vanilla extract
small pinch of sea salt
2 tablespoons unsweetened almond milk

1. Put all the ingredients into a blender or food processor and process until combined. Scrape down the sides and process for an additional minute, or until the mousse is airy. If it is still too thick, add a splash more almond milk and process again briefly.

2. Spoon the mousse into small teacups or serving bowls and serve immediately, or cover and chill in the refrigerator for up to 4 hours.

STRAWBERRIES

Extremely rich in vitamin C, strawberries boost the immune system
and contain chemicals that offer cancer protection.

MAJOR NUTRIENTS PER ⅔ CUP STRAWBERRIES

32 cal	0.3g	7.7g	2g	0.7g	59mg	24 mcg	26 mcg	153mg
CALORIES	TOTAL FAT	CARBS	FIBER	PROTEIN	VITAMIN C	FOLATE	LUTEIN/ ZEAXANTHIN	POTASSIUM

Strawberries rank high in antioxidant activity. They are extremely rich in vitamin C (an average portion contains the entire recommended daily amount for an adult), which helps to boost the immune system and aid wound healing, prevent arterial damage, promote iron absorption, and strengthen blood vessel walls. They also contain other antioxidant phenolic plant chemicals, such as anthocyanins and ellagic acid, which can block cancer cells and help prevent some cancers. Finally, they contain good amounts of fiber, folate, and potassium.

- Excellent source of vitamin C.
- Contain ellagic acid, a compound with anticancer and antioxidant properties.
- Contain anthocyanins, which can help lower "bad" blood cholesterol.
- Useful source of fiber and soluble fiber, potassium, and folate, and zeaxanthin for healthy eyes.

DID YOU KNOW?

Once washed, strawberries will spoil quickly—don't wash them until immediately before serving.

PRACTICAL TIPS

Choose strawberries that look plump and glossy; dull ones are usually past their best. Smaller strawberries tend to have higher levels of ellagic acid, concentrated in the outer layer, and have more flavor. Store in a container with air holes, in a refrigerator, for up to three days, but bring them to room temperature before using.

LAYERED AVOCADO & STRAWBERRY SOUP

Chilled soups are wonderfully refreshing. This creamy avocado-and-watercress version is lightly cooked and pureed, then layered with raw pureed strawberries.

SERVES 4 • PREP TIME: 20 MINS, PLUS COOLING & CHILLING • COOK TIME: 10 MINS

PER SERVING:	196 cal	14.4g	2.3g	18.8g	7.2g	8.1g	3.2g	440mg
	CALORIES	FAT	SAT FAT	CARBS	SUGAR	FIBER	PROTEIN	SODIUM

INGREDIENTS

1 teaspoon avocado oil
4 scallions, sliced
12 sprigs watercress
1 cup vegetable broth
1 avocado, halved, pitted and flesh scooped out
1½ cups hulled and halved strawberries
juice of ½ lemon

1. Heat the oil in a saucepan, add the scallions, and cook over medium heat, stirring, for 2 minutes, until soft. Add the watercress and broth and bring to a boil, stirring. Cover and simmer for 3–4 minutes, until the watercress has just wilted. Let cool, then chill well.

2. Puree the chilled watercress mixture with the avocado in a blender or food processor until smooth, then pour into a bowl. Rinse the blender goblet, then puree the strawberries and mix with the lemon juice. Press through a strainer into a bowl.

3. Spoon half the avocado soup into the bottom of four small glasses, spoon over half the strawberry mixture to create two layers in different colors, then repeat.

4. Serve immediately or chill for up to 45 minutes.

VARIATION

If you can't get watercress and want that peppery flavor that complements the strawberries, replace it with arugula.

WATERMELON

Watermelon has beneficial effects on the body's fluid balance, helping prevent water retention and promoting well-hydrated skin.

MAJOR NUTRIENTS PER ⅔ CUP WATERMELON

30 cal	0.15g	7.55g	0.4g	0.61g	8.1mg	303 mcg	4532 mcg	112mg
CALORIES	TOTAL FAT	CARBS	FIBER	PROTEIN	VITAMIN C	BETA-CAROTENE	LYCOPENE	POTASSIUM

Watermelon has long been used in tropical countries to quench thirst, with the supporting effect of helping the body to shed excess fluid, which is often held in the face, hands, ankles, and feet and causes bloating and puffiness. Because watermelon is 92 percent water, its 6 percent of sugar stays well diluted and does not negatively affect blood sugar levels, but instead helps to pull water into the cells. This action keeps skin and organs well hydrated, which is crucial to retaining youthfulness. The bright red color of the flesh is due to the watermelon's high levels of the carotenoid antioxidants beta-carotene and lycopene, which help protect skin from the damage caused by the sun's UV rays.

- Diuretic effect helps clean out the kidneys, thus supporting revitalizing detoxification.
- The amino acid arginine takes sugars out of the bloodstream for use as energy, helping to regulate weight.
- Excellent source of vitamin C for healing all body tissues and keeping skin plump and free of age spots.

DID YOU KNOW?

Cubic watermelons, grown in glass boxes, have been developed in Japan, because they are easier to stack and store than the natural, spherical fruit.

PRACTICAL TIPS

Choose watermelons with skin that looks smooth and dull. They should sound hollow when tapped, and when opened, should reveal strong red flesh inside with no white streaks, as well as dark brown or black seeds. Eat slices of watermelon to cool down on a hot day, or make juice by scooping out the seeds and blending the flesh.

WATERMELON SUNDAES

Colorful and tempting, this refreshing breakfast is a perfect
start to the day when you feel like something light.

SERVES 4 • PREP TIME: 10 MINS • COOK TIME: NONE

PER SERVING:

172 cal	8.3g	1.3g	14.2g	10g	2.1g	12g	80mg
CALORIES	FAT	SAT FAT	CARBS	SUGAR	FIBER	PROTEIN	SODIUM

INGREDIENTS

1 cup low-fat yogurt with live cultures
¾ cup low-fat cream cheese
1 teaspoon stevia granules
¼ cup coarsely chopped pistachio nuts
¼ cup slivered almonds, toasted
1⅓ cups watermelon chunks
3 tablespoons pomegranate seeds

1. In a mixing bowl, thoroughly combine the yogurt, cream cheese, and stevia granules.

2. Stir in half the pistachio nuts and slivered almonds.

3. Divide the watermelon chunks among four serving glasses and spoon one-quarter of the yogurt mixture on top of each.

4. Sprinkle with the remaining nuts, followed by the pomegranate seeds, and serve the sundaes immediately.

APPLES

In recent years, scientific evidence has shown that the old proverb,
"An apple a day keeps the doctor away," may be correct.

MAJOR NUTRIENTS PER AVERAGE-SIZE APPLE

60 cal	TRACE	16g	2.8g	TRACE	5mg	123mg
CALORIES	TOTAL FAT	CARBS	FIBER	PROTEIN	VITAMIN C	POTASSIUM

Although apples don't, with the exception of potassium, contain any particular high levels of vitamins or minerals, they do contain high levels of various plant chemicals, including the flavonoid quercetin, which has anticancer and anti-inflammatory action. They are also a valuable source of pectin, a soluble fiber that can help lower "bad" cholesterol and help prevent colon cancer. Research has found that adults who eat apples have smaller waistlines, less abdominal fat, and lower blood pressure than those who don't—apples may also prevent asthma in children. Apples are also virtually fat free.

- Rich in flavonoids for healthy heart and lungs.
- Ideal snack for dieters as they are low in calories, low on the glycemic index, and can keep hunger at bay.
- Fiber content is rich in pectin, which can improve the blood lipids profile and reduce "bad" cholesterol.
- A good source of potassium, which can prevent fluid retention.

DID YOU KNOW?

Research has found a link between quercetin—found in apples—and protection against Alzheimer's disease.

PRACTICAL TIPS

Don't keep your apples in a light, hot room, because they will rapidly lose their vitamin C content. Instead, keep them in a plastic bag with air holes in the refrigerator, or in a cool, dark cabinet. Try to eat the skin, because it contains up to five times as many plant chemicals as the flesh. When preparing apples, put the cut slices into a bowl of water with 1–2 tablespoons of lemon juice to prevent discoloration.

CHEDDAR & APPLE-STUFFED CHICKEN BREASTS

Apples are seen as a natural companion for pork, but they're also delicious with chicken and any type of hard cheese. This recipe makes the most of this pairing.

SERVES 4 • PREP TIME: 15 MINS • COOK TIME: 25–30 MINS

PER SERVING:	329 cal	17g	6.8g	8g	5.2g	1.5g	35g	840mg
	CALORIES	FAT	SAT FAT	CARBS	SUGAR	FIBER	PROTEIN	SODIUM

INGREDIENTS

1 tablespoon sunflower oil, for oiling
4 thick boneless, skinless chicken breasts, about 7 ounces each
1 tablespoon sunflower oil
1 small onion, finely chopped
1 celery stalk, finely chopped
¼ teaspoon dried sage
1 sweet, crisp apple, cored and diced
¾ cup shredded sharp cheddar cheese
2 tablespoons finely chopped parsley
6 slices prosciutto
salt and pepper (optional)
10½ ounces green vegetables, cooked, to serve

1. Preheat the oven to 375°F and lightly oil a small roasting pan.

2. Put a chicken breast on a cutting board, rounded side up. Use a small, sharp knife to cut a pocket along the length of the breast, cutting as deep as you can without cutting through to the other side or the ends. Repeat with the remaining chicken breasts, then set aside.

3. To make the stuffing, heat the oil in a skillet, add the onion, celery, and sage, and sauté, stirring, for 3–5 minutes, until soft. Stir in the apple and sauté for an additional 2 minutes, until it is soft but not falling apart. Stir in the cheese and most of the parsley and season with salt and pepper, if using.

4. Divide the stuffing among the breast pockets. Wrap 1½ slices of prosciutto around each chicken breast, then rub the tops with a little oil.

5. Transfer to the prepared pan and roast in the preheated oven for 20–25 minutes, or until the chicken is cooked through and the juices run clear when the tip of a sharp knife is inserted into the thickest part of the meat. Remove from the oven, cover with aluminum foil, and let stand for 3–5 minutes before serving with green vegetables. Garnish with the remaining parsley.

CRANBERRIES

These small red fruits have a variety of health benefits
and help to boost the work of the kidneys.

PER 1 CUP RAW CRANBERRIES

46 cal	TRACE	12.2g	4.6g	0.4g	13mg	1.2mg	91 mcg
CALORIES	TOTAL FAT	CARBS	FIBER	PROTEIN	VITAMIN C	VITAMIN E	LUTEIN/ ZEAXANTHIN

Fresh cranberries are too sour and acidic to eat raw, but they have been used for many years as a sauce to serve with turkey. However, since their health-giving properties were discovered, they are now widely found sweetened and dried, in beverages, and in baked desserts and preserves. Their best-known benefit is that they can help to prevent, or alleviate, urinary tract infections. This is partly because they contain quinic acid, which increases the acidity of the urine, and partly because of the tannins they contain, which are antibacterial. The same compounds may also help protect against stomach ulcers and heart disease.

- High soluble fiber content may help reduce "bad" cholesterol.
- May protect against heart disease.
- Help prevent and alleviate urinary tract infections.
- Help prevent digestive disorders and stomach ulcers.

DID YOU KNOW?

People taking warfarin should avoid eating cranberries or drinking cranberry juice—the berry can raise blood levels of this anticoagulant medicine to a high, possibly fatal, degree.

PRACTICAL TIPS

Fresh cranberries should have a smooth, bright skin. It is said that one way to test their freshness is to drop one—if it bounces, it is fresh. Cranberries are rich in pectin and make a valuable addition to preserves made with low-pectin fruit, such as strawberries, to help them set. The sugar content of most cranberry products, such as beverages and dried fruit, means that they are relatively high in calories and so may not be suitable for people on a low-calorie or low-sugar diet.

CRIMSON VITALITY SMOOTHIE

This drink combines cranberries, beet, apples, and ginger for a healthy burst of goodness that can be enjoyed any time of day.

SERVES 1 • PREP TIME: 10–15 MINS • COOK TIME: NONE

PER SERVING:

287 cal	0.9g	0.1g	74.1g	49.5g	3.9g	3g	80mg
CALORIES	FAT	SAT FAT	CARBS	SUGAR	FIBER	PROTEIN	SODIUM

INGREDIENTS

1 beet, halved

1¼ cups cranberries

½-inch piece fresh ginger, peeled

2 apples, quartered

small handful of crushed ice (optional)

chilled water, to taste

1. Feed the beet, followed by the cranberries and ginger, and then the apples, through a juicer.

2. Fill a glass halfway with crushed ice, if using, pour in the juice, top up with water to taste, and serve immediately.

HINT

If your beet has fresh, vibrant leaves instead of tired, limp-looking ones, add them to the juicer, too.

BANANAS

The banana is the ultimate energy snack because it provides quick,
quality fuel. It is perfect for replenishing flagging cells.

MAJOR NUTRIENTS PER AVERAGE-SIZE BANANA

105 cal	0.39g	26.95g	3.1g	1.29g	0.43 mg	10.3 mg	422 mg
CALORIES	TOTAL FAT	CARBS	FIBER	PROTEIN	VITAMIN B6	VITAMIN C	POTASSIUM

Bananas are undeniably high in sugar, but they shouldn't be underestimated for their health-giving anti-aging properties. A ripe banana contains a high amount of fiber, including the prebiotic inulin, which feeds our beneficial (probiotic) digestive bacteria, the first line of defense for the immune system. Keeping your digestive bacteria healthy can help prevent inflammatory conditions, such as eczema, asthma, and arthritis, and support the digestion and absorption of nutrients needed to retain optimal health and keep you looking and feeling young.

- Contain high levels of potassium, vitamin C, and vitamin B_6, which are all important for heart health. Athletes draw on this rich mix to support performance, recovery, and muscle response. Potassium and vitamin C help transport oxygen around the body to renew and revitalize the skin.
- Help kidney function and eliminate fluid retention, reducing puffiness for a more youthful appearance.

DID YOU KNOW?

The name banana comes from the Arabic banan, or "finger"; they grow in clusters of up to 20 fruit known as hands.

PRACTICAL TIPS

The fruit of choice for many people with a sweet tooth, bananas are best eaten when the skin is a solid yellow color, with no bruises. Avoid overripe bananas, because, by this stage, the sugars will have broken down and the fruit will be too sweet. Bananas may not be suitable for people with phlegm and nasal congestion, because they can make these conditions worse.

HEALTHY FRENCH TOAST WITH BANANAS & PECANS

There's no better way to start the day than with this tempting and sustaining banana-and-nut-topped French toast.

SERVES 4 • PREP TIME: 20 MINS • COOK TIME: 12–17 MINS

PER SERVING:

405 cal	19.4g	2.7g	53.4g	17g	7.6g	9.7g	200mg
CALORIES	FAT	SAT FAT	CARBS	SUGAR	FIBER	PROTEIN	SODIUM

INGREDIENTS

½ cup coarsely chopped pecans
2 eggs
4 ripe bananas, chopped
½ teaspoon vanilla extract
½ teaspoon ground cinnamon
4 thick slices whole-wheat bread
1 tablespoon olive oil
½ teaspoon ground cinnamon, for sprinkling

1. Put the pecans into a small, dry skillet and toast over medium heat for 3–4 minutes, tossing regularly until just toasted. Set aside.

2. Put the eggs, 2 bananas, vanilla extract, and cinnamon into a blender and process for 1–2 minutes, or until the consistency is smooth and thick.

3. Pour the mixture into a medium, shallow dish. Place two slices of bread into the mixture and, working quickly, gently press the bread into the liquid, letting it soak up the mixture. Turn the slices over and repeat.

4. Meanwhile, heat half the oil in a large, nonstick skillet over medium–high heat. Using a spatula, remove the soaked bread from the banana mixture and place it in the pan. Cook in batches, for 2–3 minutes on each side, then remove from the pan, set aside, and keep warm. Repeat for the remaining slices, adding the remaining oil, if needed.

5. Top with the pecans and remaining bananas, sprinkle with cinnamon, and serve immediately.

LEMONS

Indispensable in many recipes, lemons are rich in vitamin C
and can help protect us from breast and other cancers.

MAJOR NUTRIENTS PER AVERAGE-SIZE LEMON

17 cal	TRACE	5.4g	1.6g	0.6g	31mg	80mg
CALORIES	TOTAL FAT	CARBS	FIBER	PROTEIN	VITAMIN C	POTASSIUM

The fresh, acidic flavor of lemon juice enhances both sweet and savory foods and dishes, while the peel can be used to add flavor. The acid and antioxidants in lemon juice can help prevent foods from discoloring once peeled or cut. All parts of the lemon contain valuable nutrients and antioxidants. They are a particularly good source of vitamin C. The plant compound antioxidants include limonene, an oil that may help to prevent breast and other cancers and lower "bad" blood cholesterol, and rutin, which has been found to strengthen veins. Lemons stimulate the taste buds and may be useful for people with a poor appetite.

- Rich in vitamin C.
- Contain disinfecting and insecticide properties.
- Rutin content may help to strengthen veins and prevent fluid retention, especially in the legs.
- Help increase appetite.

DID YOU KNOW?

An average lemon contains about 3 tablespoons of juice. The tenderizing acid in lemons makes a useful addition to marinades for meat.

PRACTICAL TIPS

Either wash thoroughly or buy unwaxed or organic lemons, if you want to use the peel. You can get more juice from a lemon if you warm it for a few seconds—in the microwave or in hot water—before squeezing. The heavier the lemon, the more juice it should contain. Lemon juice, thanks to its pectin, helps preserves, such as jams and jellies, to set. It can be used instead of vinegar in salad dressings or added to mayonnaise.

LEMON CHEESECAKE WITH ALMOND CRUST

A crunchy crust with a zesty and creamy cheesecake topping,
this is perfect for when friends come over for dinner.

SERVES 8 • PREP TIME: 20 MINS, PLUS CHILLING • COOK TIME: 1 HOUR 15 MINS

PER SERVING:							
402 cal	35.6g	16.2g	11g	3.7g	2.4g	10.6g	200mg
CALORIES	FAT	SAT FAT	CARBS	SUGAR	FIBER	PROTEIN	SODIUM

INGREDIENTS

½ tablespoon butter, for greasing
1½ tablespoons butter
1 cup ground almonds (almond meal)
½ cup finely chopped almonds
2 tablespoons sugar-free smooth almond butter
2 tablespoons quinoa flour
2 tablespoons stevia

TOPPING

1 cup mascarpone cheese
1¼ cups cream cheese
2 extra-large eggs
finely grated zest and juice of 1 large unwaxed lemon
1 tablespoon quinoa flour
¼ cup stevia

1. Preheat the oven to 350°F. Lightly butter an 8-inch round nonstick springform cake pan and line the bottom with parchment paper.

2. To make the crust, melt the butter in a small saucepan over medium–low heat. Pour it into a large bowl and add the ground almonds, chopped almonds, almond butter, quinoa flour, and stevia, then mix well. Spoon the batter into the prepared pan and, using the back of a fork, press down into an even layer. Bake in the preheated oven for 25 minutes, then remove from the oven and reduce the oven temperature to 250°F.

3. To make the topping, put the mascarpone cheese and cream cheese into a large bowl and beat until loose. Beat for an additional 30 seconds, then add the eggs, one at a time, beating between each addition. Add the lemon zest and juice, quinoa flour, and stevia, then whisk again until well mixed.

4. Pour the topping over the crust. Bake for 50 minutes, or until the sides are set and the middle still has a slight wobble. Let cool, then cover and chill in the refrigerator for 1–2 hours.

KIWI

The kiwi has an unusual amount of healthy omega-3 oils for a fruit. This, combined with its high vitamin C content, helps maintain youthful heart function.

46 cal	0.39g	11.06g	2.26g	0.85g	69.9 mg	1.10 mg	22.66 mg	0.10 mcg	31.75 mg	235 mg	25.64 mg
CALORIES	TOTAL FAT	CARBS	FIBER	PROTEIN	VITAMIN C	VITAMIN E	CALCIUM	COPPER	OMEGA-3 OILS	POTASSIUM	ZINC

Eating the edible seeds of fruits is extremely beneficial, and the seeds of the kiwi are particularly easy to swallow. As well as fiber and zinc, seeds contain all the nutrients and enzymes needed for a plant to grow, and taking them into our bodies means we are able to grow and rejuvenate, too. Kiwi seeds contain on average 62 percent alpha-linoleic acid, the omega-3 oil that helps protect the heart and decrease inflammation, inside and outside the body, so preventing the diseases associated with aging. Kiwi is also a good source of copper, needed for collagen production, which promotes healthy skin, nails, and muscles.

- Comparable to a banana in terms of high potassium content, keeping kidneys healthy so they can remove aging toxins.
- Contains more vitamin C than oranges, as well as vitamin E and rehydrating omega-3 oils for a skin-nourishing combination.
- Vitamin C works with copper to produce collagen, keeping skin renewed and firm.

DID YOU KNOW?

Studies have shown that kiwi may relieve symptoms of respiratory conditions, such as asthma and coughs. Healthy breathing is crucial for rejuvenation and staying youthful throughout life.

PRACTICAL TIPS

Kiwi can be eaten whole like an apple; eating the skin means you don't skip on the vitamin C that lies just beneath the skin, and it vastly increases the fruit's insoluble fiber and antioxidant content. To test if a kiwi is ripe, press it. You should be able to depress the skin slightly. Dried kiwi slices make healthy snacks; they can be bought in health food stores and supermarkets.

SKIN-SOOTHER SMOOTHIE

Packed with healing vitamin C from the fruit, skin-protecting vitamin E
from the peanut butter, and essential fatty acids (EFAs) from the flaxseed,
this spectacular striped drink might just be your skin's new best friend.

SERVES 1 • PREP TIME: 10 MINS • COOK TIME: NONE

PER SERVING:	466 cal	13.4g	2.1g	87.5g	51.1g	15.7g	10.1g	TRACE
	CALORIES	FAT	SAT FAT	CARBS	SUGAR	FIBER	PROTEIN	SODIUM

INGREDIENTS

BANANA LAYER

1 banana, peeled and coarsely chopped
1 tablespoon smooth peanut butter
1 tablespoon soy yogurt

BLUEBERRY LAYER

1 cup blueberries
juice of ½ lemon

KIWI LAYER

3 kiwi, peeled and coarsely chopped
1 tablespoon milled flaxseed

1. Put all the ingredients for the banana layer into a blender and blend until smooth. Transfer to a bowl and rinse the blender goblet.

2. To make the blueberry layer, put the blueberries and lemon juice into the blender and blend until smooth. Transfer to a separate bowl and rinse the blender goblet.

3. To make the kiwi layer, place the kiwi in the blender with the flaxseed and blend until smooth. Layer the three smoothie mixtures into a large glass and serve immediately.

FIGS

Fresh and dried figs are rich in fiber and high in iron,
boosting energy and promoting healthy blood.

MAJOR NUTRIENTS PER FRESH FIG

47 cal	TRACE	12.3g	1.9g	0.5g	1.3 mg	54 mcg	22 mg	11 mg	148 mg
CALORIES	TOTAL FAT	CARBS	FIBER	PROTEIN	VITAMIN C	BETA-CAROTENE	CALCIUM	MAGNESIUM	POTASSIUM

Figs are usually available dried, because fresh figs are easily damaged and have a short shelf life. This delicious fruit contains good amounts of fiber, most of it soluble, which helps protect against heart disease. Figs are also a good source of several minerals and vitamin B$_6$, with small amounts of a range of the B vitamins, folate, and several other vitamins and minerals. Dried figs are a concentrated source of potassium and are rich in calcium, magnesium, and iron. They are, however, also high in calories, so they are best eaten in moderation.

- Contain sterols, which help to lower blood cholesterol.
- Good source of natural energy and sugars.
- Good source of potassium to help prevent fluid retention.
- Dried fruit is an excellent source of iron, for healthy blood, and of calcium, for bone density.

DID YOU KNOW?

The leaves of the fig tree are edible. Fig-leaf liquid extract has antidiabetic properties, reducing the amount of insulin needed by some people with diabetes.

PRACTICAL TIPS

Fresh figs deteriorate quickly and so should be eaten the day they are bought or picked. They are best eaten as they are, but they are also delicious with ham, served as an appetizer, or as part of a dessert. Some varieties of fig have edible skin while others need to be peeled.

MACHE & CUCUMBER SALAD WITH FIGS

This unusual salad combination gets much of its flavor from the zesty dressing.
The walnut oil is the perfect complement to the sweetness of the figs.

SERVES 4 • PREP TIME: 5 MINS • COOK TIME: NONE

PER SERVING:	231 cal	20.6g	2.2g	13.7g	9.8g	2.2g	1.3g	TRACE
	CALORIES	FAT	SAT FAT	CARBS	SUGAR	FIBER	PROTEIN	SODIUM

INGREDIENTS

2 cups mache
½ cucumber, diced
4 ripe figs

DRESSING

1 small shallot, finely chopped
¼ cup walnut oil
2 tablespoons extra virgin olive oil
2 tablespoons apple cider vinegar
½ teaspoon honey
salt and pepper (optional)

1. Put all the dressing ingredients into a screw-top jar, with salt and pepper, if using, and shake well to mix.

2. Put the mache and cucumber into a bowl and pour over half the dressing. Toss well to coat evenly, then divide among four serving plates.

3. Cut the figs into quarters and arrange 4 quarters on top of each portion. Drizzle the remaining dressing over the top and serve the salads immediately.

RASPBERRIES

Packed with vitamin C and antioxidants to protect the heart, raspberries are one of the most nutritious fruits.

MAJOR NUTRIENTS PER ¾ CUP RASPBERRIES

52 cal	0.6g	12g	6.5g	1.2g	26 mg	0.6 mg	0.8 mg	25 mg	21 mcg	0.7 mg	151 mg	0.4 mg
CALORIES	TOTAL FAT	CARBS	FIBER	PROTEIN	VITAMIN C	VITAMIN B3	VITAMIN E	CALCIUM	FOLATE	IRON	POTASSIUM	ZINC

Raspberries are the seventh-highest fruit on the ORAC scale and are, therefore, an extremely desirable fruit. They are best eaten raw, because cooking or processing destroys some of these antioxidants, especially anthocyanins. Anthocyanins are red and purple pigments that have been shown to help prevent both heart disease and cancers, and they may also help prevent varicose veins. Raspberries also contain high levels of ellagic acid, a compound with anticancer properties. In addition, they are high in vitamin C and fiber, as well as contain good amounts of iron, which the body absorbs well because of the high levels of vitamin C.

- High antioxidant activity.
- May help to prevent varicose veins.
- One portion contains approximately half a day's recommended intake of vitamin C.
- High in fiber to help control high "bad" cholesterol.

DID YOU KNOW?

Raspberries consist of numerous smaller fruits called drupelets, which are clustered around a centered stalk core. Each drupelet contains a seed, which is why raspberries are so high in fiber.

PRACTICAL TIPS

The berries do not keep for long, so they should be picked only when ripe. They do freeze well, however, if packed in containers instead of bags. Never wash raspberries before storing unless absolutely necessary—their structure is easily destroyed. The healthy soluble fiber in raspberries is pectin, which means they make excellent, easy-to-set preserves.

RASPBERRY & MASCARPONE ICE CREAM

Fresh raspberries and extra creaminess from the mascarpone mean you will be fighting people off the last scoops of this classic ice cream.

SERVES 8 • PREP TIME: 20 MINS • COOK TIME: 10 MINS, PLUS FREEZING

PER SERVING:

| 285 cal CALORIES | 28.6g FAT | 16.5g SAT FAT | 3.9g CARBS | 1.2g SUGAR | 0.8g FIBER | 4.2g PROTEIN | 40mg SODIUM |

INGREDIENTS

1 extra-large egg
4 extra-large egg yolks
2½ tablespoons stevia
⅓ cup mascarpone cheese
1 teaspoon vanilla extract
1¾ cups heavy cream
⅔ cup raspberries, halved

1. Crack the egg into a large heatproof bowl, add the yolks and stevia, and whisk with a handheld electric mixer for 30 seconds. Place over a saucepan of gently simmering water, making sure the bowl doesn't touch the water, and whisk until the mixture is pale and airy. This cooks the eggs and makes a sweet custard. Be careful not to overcook them.

2. Pour cold water into a large, wide bowl and place the custard bowl in it, with the bottom of the bowl in the water, to cool. Continue to whisk the eggs for 2 minutes, then lift the bowl out of the water and set aside.

3. Put the mascarpone cheese and vanilla extract into a separate large bowl and beat briefly until loose. Pour in the cream and beat again until it holds soft peaks.

4. Using a metal spoon, gently fold the custard into the cream mixture, preserving as much air as possible. Carefully stir in the raspberries.

5. Pour the mixture into a freezerproof container, cover with a lid, and freeze for 4 hours, or until set. Take the ice cream out of the freezer 10 minutes before serving to let it soften. Scoop it into glasses or small bowls and serve.

MANGOES

The mango is a nutritional superstar among fruits, being particularly rich in antioxidants and vitamins C and E.

MAJOR NUTRIENTS PER AVERAGE-SIZE MANGO

114 cal	0.3g	28g	5.2g	1.4g	74mg
CALORIES	TOTAL FAT	CARBS	FIBER	PROTEIN	VITAMIN C

Mangoes are grown throughout the tropics. Their orange flesh contains more antioxidant beta-carotene, which can protect against some cancers and heart disease, than most other fruits. They are high in vitamin C—one fruit can contain more than your body uses in a day—and in fiber. Unlike most other fruits, they also contain a significant amount of the antioxidant vitamin E, which can boost the body's immune system and maintain healthy skin. Their medium–low glycemic index also means they are a good fruit for dieters, because they help regulate blood sugar levels.

- High levels of pectin—a soluble fiber that helps reduce "bad" blood cholesterol.
- Rich in potassium (320 mg per fruit) for regulating blood pressure.
- Valuable source of vitamin C.

DID YOU KNOW?

Mangoes contain a special enzyme that can be a soothing digestive aid—it can also tenderize meat.

PRACTICAL TIPS

If you buy unripe mangoes, put them in a paper bag in a dark place and they will ripen within a few days. Eat ripe mangoes raw for maximum vitamin C content, or eat them with a little fat, such as yogurt or in a salad dressed with olive oil, to better absorb their carotenes.

LAYERED POWERBOWL SMOOTHIE

This colorful smoothie, rich in antioxidants from the fruits, with additional protein from the chlorella powder, almonds, and sesame seeds, is a great breakfast.

SERVES 2 • PREP TIME: 10–15 MINS • COOK TIME: NONE

PER SERVING:

 303 cal CALORIES

 6.4g FAT

 1.1g SAT FAT

 61.3g CARBS

 44.2g SUGAR

 7.1g FIBER

 6.4g PROTEIN

 TRACE SODIUM

INGREDIENTS

1 large mango, pitted, peeled, and chopped
2 kiwis, peeled and chopped
½ teaspoon chlorella powder
2 watermelon wedges (about ⅛ of watermelon), peeled (leave the seeds in for vitamin E)
1 tablespoon ground almonds (almond meal)
1 teaspoon sesame seeds
2 tablespoons granola
¼ teaspoon ground cinnamon

1. Put the mango into a small blender and process until smooth. Divide between two glass bowls. Rinse the blender.

2. Put the kiwi and chlorella powder into the blender and process until smooth. Spoon it over the mango. Rinse the blender goblet.

3. Put the watermelon into the blender and process until smooth. Add the ground almonds and sesame seeds and process briefly to combine. Spoon it over the kiwi mixture.

4. Sprinkle with the granola and cinnamon and serve.

MELONS

The juicy flesh of the melon is rich in vitamin C and is a great source of potassium, which helps prevent fluid retention.

MAJOR NUTRIENTS PER AVERAGE-SIZE CANTALOUPE

28 cal	TRACE	6.3g	1.5g	1g	39mg	2647 mcg	315 mg
CALORIES	TOTAL FAT	CARBS	FIBER	PROTEIN	VITAMIN C	BETA-CAROTENE	POTASSIUM

A melon contains more than 92 percent water, which can help keep the kidneys working well. The orange varieties are a great source of beta-carotene and are also high in vitamin C, although amounts vary according to variety. All melons are rich in vitamin B6 and potassium, and several varieties are high in the bioflavonoid group of plant chemicals, which have anticancer, antiheart disease, and anti-aging properties. Melons are also rich in soluble fiber.

- High potassium content helps prevent fluid retention and balances sodium in the body.
- Soluble fiber content helps arterial health and can help lower "bad" blood cholesterol.
- Beta-carotene content of orange varieties is one of the highest of all fruits and vegetables.

DID YOU KNOW?

If you buy half or a quarter of a melon, it should be stored in the refrigerator, well wrapped in plastic wrap, to prevent other foods absorbing its strong odor.

PRACTICAL TIPS

Unlike many fruits, melons don't ripen once picked, so choose one with a rich fragrance, which indicates it is ripe. If it has wrinkles, it is overripe. Store melons at cool to moderate room temperature.

CRUNCHY GREEK YOGURT MELON CUPS

Refreshingly tangy and low in fat but also surprisingly filling and high in protein, these pretty cups are a perfect quick breakfast and ideal for a weight-loss diet, too.

SERVES 4 • PREP TIME: 15 MINS, PLUS CHILLING • COOK TIME: NONE

PER SERVING:

234 cal	6.3g	0.7g	28.3g	18.5g	2.6g	17.2g	40mg
CALORIES	FAT	SAT FAT	CARBS	SUGAR	FIBER	PROTEIN	SODIUM

INGREDIENTS

4 cups Greek-style yogurt
1 teaspoon vanilla extract
1¾ cups (½-inch) cantaloupe cubes
2⅓ cups (½-inch) watermelon cubes
1 tablespoon sunflower seeds
1 tablespoon pumpkin seeds
2 tablespoons chopped almonds
½ cup oat granola

1. Beat together the yogurt and vanilla extract. Set half of the yogurt mixture aside. Divide the remaining yogurt mixture among four small glasses or serving dishes.

2. Spoon half the cantaloupe and half the watermelon evenly over the yogurt.

3. Mix the seeds, almonds, and granola together in a small bowl. Spoon the seed mixture evenly over each yogurt cup. Stir in the reserved yogurt. Chill for 30 minutes before serving.

ORANGES

Vitamin C, the antioxidant vitamin that boosts the immune system and protects from the signs of aging, is found in abundance in oranges.

MAJOR NUTRIENTS PER AVERAGE-SIZE ORANGE

65 cal	TRACE	16g	3.4g	1g	64mg	61mg	182 mcg	238 mg
CALORIES	TOTAL FAT	CARBS	FIBER	PROTEIN	VITAMIN C	CALCIUM	LUTEIN/ ZEAXANTHIN	POTASSIUM

Oranges are one of the least expensive sources of vitamin C, which protects against cell damage, aging, and disease. The fruit is also a good source of fiber, folate, and potassium, as well as calcium, which is vital for bone maintenance. They contain the carotenes zeaxanthin and lutein, both of which can help maintain eye health and protect against macular degeneration. Oranges also contain rutin, a flavonoid that can help slow down or prevent the growth of tumors, and nobiletin, an anti-inflammatory compound. All these plant compounds also help vitamin C to work more effectively.

- Can help prevent infections, and the severity and duration of colds may be lessened by increasing intake of vitamin C.
- Oranges are one of the few fruits that are low on the glycemic index, so they are a useful food for dieters and diabetics.
- Good content of soluble fiber pectin, which helps control blood cholesterol levels.
- Anti-inflammatory, so may help reduce incidence of arthritis.
- Blood oranges contain even higher levels of antioxidants in red anthocyanin pigments, which are linked with cancer prevention.

DID YOU KNOW?

You should eat some of the white pith of the orange as well as the juicy flesh, because it contains high levels of fiber, useful plant chemicals, and antioxidants.

PRACTICAL TIPS

Buy oranges that feel heavy to hold compared with their size—this means they should be juicy and fresh. Store them in the refrigerator to retain their vitamin C. Orange peel contains high levels of nutrients, but should be scrubbed and dried before use.

RICH ORANGE CREPES

These French-style thin pancakes make a great weekend breakfast or brunch, when you have a little more time for preparation. They give a good vitamin C boost at the start of the day.

SERVES 4 • PREP TIME: 15 MINS • COOK TIME: 10 MINS

PER SERVING:

| 418 cal CALORIES | 22.6g FAT | 13.4g SAT FAT | 46.1g CARBS | 15g SUGAR | 2.8g FIBER | 8.4g PROTEIN | 120mg SODIUM |

INGREDIENTS
1¼ cups all-purpose flour
1 cup milk
3 tablespoons fresh orange juice
1 extra-large egg
2 tablespoons butter, melted
2 oranges, divided into sections
2 teaspoons butter, melted, for frying

ORANGE BUTTER
4 tablespoons unsalted butter
finely grated zest and juice of 1 orange
1 tablespoon sugar

1. To make the crepes, put all the ingredients (excluding the orange sections) into a mixing bowl and whisk until smooth. Alternatively, process in a food processor until smooth.

2. Heat a crepe pan until hot, lightly brush with butter, and pour in a small ladleful of batter, swirling to thinly coat the surface of the pan.

3. Cook the crepes until golden underneath, then turn and cook the other side. Remove from the pan and keep warm while you cook the remaining batter.

4. To make the orange butter, melt the butter in a small saucepan, add the orange zest and juice and the sugar, and stir until the sugar has dissolved. Simmer, stirring, for 30 seconds, then remove from the heat.

5. Serve the crepes folded over, with the orange sections and the orange butter poured over the top.

VARIATION
You could replace the orange butter with lemon butter, preparing it with 1 lemon and 2 tablespoons sugar.

PINEAPPLES

A special compound found within pineapples can help ease the
pain of arthritis and may help prevent strokes.

MAJOR NUTRIENTS PER AVERAGE-SIZE PINEAPPLE SLICE

40 cal	TRACE	10.6g	1.2g	0.5g	30 mg	10 mg	97 mg
CALORIES	TOTAL FAT	CARBS	FIBER	PROTEIN	VITAMIN C	MAGNESIUM	POTASSIUM

Pineapples have long been used as a medicinal plant in various parts of the world, particularly the Americas. Apart from being a good source of vitamin C and various other vitamins and minerals, including magnesium, the pineapple contains an active substance known as bromelain. This protein has been proven to ease the inflammation associated with arthritis and joint pain, and may also help to reduce the incidence of blood clots, which can lead to heart attacks and strokes. Unfortunately, the inedible stem is the richest source of bromelain, but there is also a little in the fruit.

- May aid digestion and limit pain from arthritis and joint conditions.
- Can help to reduce the risk of blood clots.
- Good source of the antioxidant vitamin C.
- Good source of ferulic acid, which can help prevent cancer.

PRACTICAL TIPS

A pineapple is ripe to eat when a leaf is easily pulled from the top. To prepare, cut off the leafy top and a small layer of the bottom, and then slice off the tough skin and "eyes." Once cut into slices, remove the tough core in the center. Avoid using fresh pineapple in gelatin—the bromelain enzyme prevents it from setting. Canned pineapple contains no bromelain but retains much of its vitamin C. Pineapples are delicious simply served fresh, chopped with cereal or yogurt for breakfast, or try them cooked in brown sugar and a little butter for a tasty warm dessert.

DID YOU KNOW?

*The bromelain in pineapples
is an effective meat tenderizer—
use a few spoonfuls of juice and
add to meat-base stews.*

PINEAPPLE & MINT ICED TEA

This refreshing iced tea is infused with soothing ginger and fresh mint and delivers a bounty of vitamins and minerals, providing a fresh and rejuvenating thirst-quenching drink.

MAKES 1 CUP • PREP TIME: 20–25 MINS • COOK TIME: 45 MINS, PLUS STEEPING

PER 1 CUP:

 810 cal CALORIES

 1.2g FAT

 0.1g SAT FAT

 206.8g CARBS

 177.1g SUGAR

 13.5g FIBER

 5.3g PROTEIN

TRACE SODIUM

INGREDIENTS

1 pineapple
4¼ cups water
1¼ cups fresh mint sprigs
2-inch piece fresh ginger, finely sliced
½ cup agave syrup
crushed ice
2 tablespoons mint leaves, to decorate

1. Prepare the pineapple by slicing off the bottom and leaves with a sharp knife. Rest the pineapple on its bottom and slice off the peel until you reveal the flesh. Slice the fruit in half and remove the woody core from the center. Cut the remaining flesh into ¾-inch cubes.

2. Pour the water into a large saucepan and add the pineapple, mint, and ginger. Stir in the agave syrup and place the saucepan over medium–high heat. Simmer for 45 minutes, or until the liquid has reduced by half.

3. Remove from the heat and let the tea cool completely and steep. This will take 4–5 hours. Using a slotted spoon, remove the mint sprigs and ginger.

4. Empty the crushed ice into a large pitcher and add the mint leaves. Pour over the cooled tea and stir. Serve immediately.

HINT

A jar is an interesting way to serve this tea, but you could also serve it in cocktail glasses or other attractive glasses.

BLACKBERRIES

Juicy blackberries are small powerhouses of health that are rich
in antioxidants to protect us from cardiovascular diseases.

MAJOR NUTRIENTS PER ⅔ CUP BLACKBERRIES

25 cal	TRACE	5g	3.1g	0.9g	15 mg	2.4 mg	41 mg	34 mcg	0.7 mg	160 mg
CALORIES	TOTAL FAT	CARBS	FIBER	PROTEIN	VITAMIN C	VITAMIN E	CALCIUM	FOLATE	IRON	POTASSIUM

In recent years, it has been discovered that these tasty fruits are potent health protectors as well as a delicious fall treat. They rate almost as high on the ORAC scale as blueberries. Their deep purple color denotes that they are rich in several compounds, which can help beat heart disease, cancers, and the signs of aging. These compounds include anthocyanins and ellagic acid. Additionally, blackberries are rich in fiber and minerals, including magnesium, zinc, iron, and calcium. Their high vitamin E content helps protect the heart and keeps skin healthy.

- High in ellagic acid, a chemical known to block cancer cells.
- Rich in antioxidant vitamin E and fiber.
- A good source of vitamin C, which boosts the immune system.
- A useful source of folate for healthy blood.

DID YOU KNOW?

Blackberries contain salicylate, which is related to the active ingredient in aspirin. For this reason, people who are allergic to aspirin may also have a reaction to blackberries.

PRACTICAL TIPS

The freshest blackberries have a shiny, plump appearance. If they look dull, they are probably past their best and the vitamin C content will be lower. The darker the blackberry, the more ellagic acid it is likely to contain. Cooking doesn't destroy ellagic acid, so you can use blackberries to make preserves or in pies and crisps. However, for maximum vitamin C, they are best eaten raw. Blackberries freeze well, so pack them into lidded containers or open-freeze on a tray and then pack into plastic bags.

CARDAMOM WAFFLES WITH BLACKBERRIES & FIGS

Aromatic cardamom adds a wonderful depth of flavor to these fabulous fruit-topped waffles, so dig out your waffle maker and cook up this satisfying weekend family breakfast.

SERVES 6 • PREP TIME: 25 MINS, PLUS RESTING • COOK TIME: 10–17 MINS

PER SERVING:

422 cal	17.3g	7.8g	53.9g	23.7g	7.3g	16.1g	200mg
CALORIES	FAT	SAT FAT	CARBS	SUGAR	FIBER	PROTEIN	SODIUM

INGREDIENTS

5 extra-large eggs, separated
pinch of salt
1 teaspoon ground cardamom
3½ tablespoons unsalted butter, melted and cooled
1 cup low-fat milk
2 cups whole-wheat flour
1 tablespoon olive oil, for brushing
⅔ cup Greek-style plain yogurt
6 ripe figs, quartered
1⅓ cups blackberries
6 tablespoons agave syrup, to serve

1. You will need a waffle maker for this recipe. Put the egg yolks, salt, and cardamom into a bowl and beat well with a wooden spoon. Stir in the melted butter. Slowly beat in the milk until completely incorporated. Gradually add the flour until you have a thick batter.

2. In a separate bowl, whisk the egg whites until they hold stiff peaks and gently fold them into the batter. Let the batter rest for at least 1 hour, but preferably overnight.

3. Heat the waffle maker according to the manufacturers' directions. Brush with a little oil and spoon the batter onto the waffle iron. Cook for 4–5 minutes, or until golden. Keep the waffles warm until you are ready to serve.

4. Serve the waffles with the yogurt, fig quarters, blackberries, and agave syrup.

HINT

To keep the waffles warm, cover them with aluminum foil and put into an oven preheated to 250°F.

APRICOTS

Fresh apricots are highly nutritious and have a low glycemic index,
making them an excellent food for sweet-toothed dieters.

MAJOR NUTRIENTS PER 2 AVERAGE-SIZE FRESH APRICOTS

31 cal	TRACE	7.2g	1.7g	0.9g	6mg	766 mcg	0.5 mg	766 mcg
CALORIES	TOTAL FAT	CARBS	FIBER	PROTEIN	VITAMIN C	BETA-CAROTENE	IRON	POTASSIUM

Fresh apricots contain vitamin C, folate, potassium, and vitamin E. Their high content of beta-carotene, an important antioxidant, helps to prevent some cancers. They are also ideal for weight maintenance, because they are a good source of fiber and are fat-free. The semidried, plumped fruit is a good source of potassium and iron, although the drying process diminishes the vitamin C and carotene content. Fresh apricots, because they contain more water, are, weight for weight, lower in calories than dried ones.

- Contain a range of carotenes: beta-carotene for cancer prevention; lutein and zeaxanthin for eye health; and cryptoxanthin, which may help to maintain bone health.
- High in total and soluble fiber for healthy heart and circulation.
- Excellent source of potassium.

DID YOU KNOW?

Hunza apricots are a form of dried apricot that grows wild in the Hunza Valley in Kashmir, India. The fruits are left on the trees to dry and must be cooked before eating.

PRACTICAL TIPS

Fresh apricots need to be completely ripe to maximize their carotene content, and cooking them helps the carotene and soluble fiber to be better absorbed in the body. Fresh apricots are excellent in fruit crisps or poached in white wine.

ROASTED FRUIT CRISP

A healthy take on an old favorite—gooey soft fruits, with a nutty coconut crumble topping, full of fiber but also rich in antioxidants due to the colorful fruits.

SERVES 4 • PREP TIME: 15 MINS • COOK TIME: 35–40 MINS

PER SERVING:

410 cal CALORIES	22.5g FAT	13.6g SAT FAT	50.7g CARBS	26.7g SUGAR	9.7g FIBER	6.4g PROTEIN	TRACE SODIUM

INGREDIENTS

4 apricots, pitted and quartered
1 tablespoon sugar
1⅔ cups raspberries
1⅓ cups blackberries
½ cup rolled oats
⅓ cup whole-wheat flour
⅓ cup pecans
1 tablespoon sesame seeds
¼ cup firmly packed dark brown sugar
¼ cup coconut oil
coconut yogurt, to serve (optional)

1. Preheat the oven to 350°F. Put the apricot quarters into a roasting pan and sprinkle with the sugar. Roast in the preheated oven for 15 minutes.

2. Spoon the apricots into four ovenproof dishes and sprinkle with the remaining fruit. Put the remaining ingredients into a food processor and process to lumpy crumbs.

3. Spoon the crumble topping over the fruit, place the dishes on a baking sheet, and bake in the oven for 20–25 minutes, until golden and bubbling. Serve with coconut yogurt, if using.

GRAPEFRUIT

An excellent source of vitamin C, eating grapefruit boosts the
immune system and protects our hearts.

30 cal	TRACE	7.5g	1.1g	0.5g	37 mg	127 mg	770 mcg	15 mg	9 mcg
CALORIES	TOTAL FAT	CARBS	FIBER	PROTEIN	VITAMIN C	POTASSIUM	BETA-CAROTENE	CALCIUM	FOLATE

In recent years, the pink-fleshed grapefruit has become as popular as
the white- or yellow-flesh types. It is a little sweeter and contains more
health benefits; the pink pigment indicates the presence of lycopene, the
antioxidant carotene that has been shown to help prevent prostate and
other cancers. Like other citrus fruits, grapefruits contain bioflavonoids,
compounds that appear to increase the benefits of vitamin C, also found
in this fruit in excellent amounts. Grapefruit are low on the glycemic index
and are low in calories, so they are an important fruit for dieters. Because
grapefruit juice can alter the effect of certain medicines (for example, ones
that lower blood pressure), people on medication should check with their
physician before they consume the fruit.

- High in antioxidants, which can help prevent prostate
  and other cancers.
- Rich in vitamin C to boost the immune system.
- Excellent fruit for dieters.
- Help reduce bouts of wheezing in asthma-prone people.

DID YOU KNOW?

*The slightly bitter taste
of some grapefruit is caused
by a compound called
naringenin, which has
cholesterol-lowering properties.*

PRACTICAL TIPS

Grapefruit is delicious halved, sprinkled with raw sugar and broiled for a
short while. Try to eat some of the white pith with your grapefruit, because
it is high in nutrients. Grapefruit, like all citrus fruits, will contain more
juice if they feel heavier.

SMOKED SALMON & PINK GRAPEFRUIT SALAD

Citrus fruit really brings out the flavor of smoked salmon, and the pink grapefruit here adds so much more than a squeeze of lemon juice.

SERVES 2 • PREP TIME: 20 MINS • COOK TIME: NONE

PER SERVING:

 246 cal CALORIES   **17g** FAT   **2.4g** SAT FAT   **16.5g** CARBS   **11.7g** SUGAR   **3.9g** FIBER **9.7g** PROTEIN **680mg** SODIUM

INGREDIENTS

1 pink grapefruit
2½ cups arugula
2 cups frisée
½ fennel bulb, thinly sliced
¼ teaspoon sea salt
1 tablespoon extra virgin olive oil
½ teaspoon white wine vinegar
2¼ ounces smoked salmon
1 tablespoon extra virgin olive oil, for drizzling
pepper (optional)

1. Using a sharp knife, cut a slice from the top and bottom of the grapefruit. Remove the peel and white pith by cutting downward, following the shape of the fruit as closely as possible. Cut between the flesh and membrane of each section and ease out the flesh. Discard the membrane and set aside the flesh.

2. Put the arugula, frisée, and fennel into a bowl. Sprinkle with the sea salt. Gently toss with your hands to distribute the salt. Add the oil and gently toss. Sprinkle with the vinegar, toss again, and divide between two serving plates.

3. Cut the smoked salmon into bite-size pieces and arrange on top of the salad with the grapefruit sections. Drizzle with oil, sprinkle with pepper, if using, and serve.

VARIATION

Smoked salmon works well here but you could also use other types of smoked fish, such as trout.

PASSION FRUIT

Passion fruit is full of antioxidants, such as the healing vitamins A and C,
which take action in the body to slow down the signs of aging.

MAJOR NUTRIENTS PER AVERAGE-SIZE PASSION FRUIT

17 cal	0.13g	4.21g	1.9g	0.40g	229IU	5.4 mg	134 mcg	63 mg
CALORIES	TOTAL FAT	CARBS	FIBER	PROTEIN	VITAMIN A	VITAMIN C	BETA-CAROTENE	POTASSIUM

High in the orange spectrum of antioxidants, the vitamin A and beta-carotene content of passion fruit gives skin a youthful boost. Enjoying this fruit will also protect your skin against the sun and help avoid sun damage, such as pigment changes and lines. Although we need some sunlight for health, especially to enhance mood and encourage restorative sleep cycles and bone health, we are damaged by its UV rays when it hits the skin. Many fruits, especially tropical fruit, such as passion fruit, which receives intense amounts of sunlight, contain vitamin A and carotenoid antioxidants to protect themselves against UV rays as they ripen. By eating these fruits, we reap the same sun-protecting properties, while also satisfying our requirements for high amounts of vitamin C.

- High levels of potassium, fiber, and vitamin C combine to prevent heart disease.
- A highly alkalizing fruit, which helps fluid balance and detoxification, crucial for maintaining a youthful appearance.
- Vitamin C helps knit together the collagen that keeps skin plump and wrinkle-free.

DID YOU KNOW?

The yellow variety of this nutrient-rich fruit has more antioxidant carotenoids and is made into juice, while the purple variety has more vitamin C and is sold as fresh produce.

PRACTICAL TIPS

The seeds of passion fruit are edible, so you can scoop out the entire contents from the skin and enjoy as a delicious snack. When made into juice or to flavor foods, the seeds are usually removed. Keep the ripe fruit in the refrigerator for up to a week.

STRAWBERRY & PASSION FRUIT YOGURTS

If you want a light, sweet-tasting snack, these little jars of
summery freshness will give you an instant boost.

SERVES 4 • PREP TIME: 20–25 MINS, PLUS CHILLING • COOK TIME: 2–3 MINS

PER SERVING:

141 cal	3.5g	2.8g	19.3g	14.6g	3.2g	10.4g	TRACE
CALORIES	FAT	SAT FAT	CARBS	SUGAR	FIBER	PROTEIN	SODIUM

INGREDIENTS

¼ cup dry unsweetened coconut
1⅓ cups hulled strawberries
finely grated zest and juice of 1 lime
1½ cups fat-free Greek-style yogurt
4 teaspoons honey
2 passion fruits, halved
1 tablespoon coarsely chopped dried goji berries

1. Add the coconut to a dry skillet and cook over medium heat for 2–3 minutes, shaking the pan, until light golden in color. Remove from the heat and let cool.

2. Coarsely mash the strawberries and mix with half the lime juice. Add the lime zest, remaining lime juice, the yogurt, and honey to a bowl and stir together.

3. Add three quarters of the cooled coconut to the yogurt, then scoop the seeds from the passion fruits over the top and lightly fold into the yogurt.

4. Layer alternate spoonfuls of strawberry and yogurt in four 1-cup canning jars, then sprinkle with the remaining coconut and the goji berries. Clip down the lids and chill until ready to serve. Eat within 24 hours.

VARIATION

If you don't like coconut, try adding ¼ cup finely chopped hazelnuts instead for a crunchy finish (omitting Step 1).

CHERRIES

Glossy red cherries are one of the best fruit sources of antioxidants, which help prevent many diseases associated with aging.

MAJOR NUTRIENTS PER ½ CUP CHERRIES

50 cal	TRACE	13g	1.7g	0.8g	5.6mg	68 mcg	178 mg
CALORIES	TOTAL FAT	CARBS	FIBER	PROTEIN	VITAMIN C	LUTEIN/ ZEAXANTHIN	POTASSIUM

Although cherries contain slightly smaller amounts of vitamins and minerals than other stone fruits, they are rich in several plant compounds that have definite health benefits. They rank highly—in twelfth place—on the ORAC scale of antioxidant capacity in fruits, and the chemicals they contain include quercetin, a flavonoid that has anticancer and heart-protecting qualities, and cyanidin, which is an anti-inflammatory that minimizes symptoms of arthritis and gout. The soluble fiber contained in cherries is helpful for controlling "bad" blood cholesterol levels, while the fruit is also a good source of potassium and a reasonable source of vitamin C and carotenes.

- High in antioxidants, which help protect the heart and prevent signs of aging.
- Rich in quercetin to help prevent cancers.
- Rich in cyanidin to alleviate arthritis and inflammatory diseases.
- Soluble fiber helps improve blood cholesterol profile.

DID YOU KNOW?

Morello cherries are a sour, instead of sweet, variety of cherry and are usually used in pies and cooking.

PRACTICAL TIPS

Fresh cherries will have green stalks and a glossy skin. The deeper the color, the more antioxidant compounds they contain, so choose red or black instead of yellow cherries. To preserve vitamin C, store them in the refrigerator. Fresh cherries contain higher levels of antioxidants, so they are best eaten raw.

CHERRY AID SMOOTHIE

This deliciously tangy drink has the sweetness of pears, the tartness of cherries, and the innumerable health benefits of chia seeds. It's a great refresher at any time of the day.

SERVES 1 • PREP TIME: 20 MINS • COOK TIME: NONE

PER SERVING:

376 cal	4.8g	0.6g	87.7g	57.1g	4.8g	5.2g	TRACE
CALORIES	FAT	SAT FAT	CARBS	SUGAR	FIBER	PROTEIN	SODIUM

INGREDIENTS

2 pears, halved
1 tablespoon chia seeds
1 cup pitted cherries
½ cup chilled water
small handful of crushed ice (optional)

1. Feed the pears through a juicer.

2. Put the chia seeds into a blender and process until finely ground. Add the pear juice, cherries, water, and crushed ice, if using, and blend until smooth.

3. Pour into a glass and serve immediately.

RHUBARB

Rhubarb has been used as a laxative for thousands of years to prevent the buildup of aging toxins that can make you feel sluggish.

21 cal	0.2g	4.54g	1.8g	0.9g	8mg	29.3 mcg	86 mg	288 mg
CALORIES	TOTAL FAT	CARBS	FIBER	PROTEIN	VITAMIN C	VITAMIN K	CALCIUM	POTASSIUM

Rhubarb roots and stems are rich in anthraquinones. These substances are also found in senna, aloe, and cascara—all used in herbal medicine as natural laxatives. Preparations made from these plants are sometimes harsh on the digestive tract, however, which makes dietary sources, such as rhubarb, preferable. As part of a high-fiber diet, rhubarb will help bowel function by toning the muscle of the intestinal wall and making sure of the removal of aging toxic waste without dehydrating or damaging the digestive tract. Traditionally, rhubarb has been used to promote skin health and maintain a youthful appearance by following this route of cleaning the body and the detoxification pathways from the inside.

- Modulates inflammatory responses, helping restore balance to the immune system and prevent aging diseases.
- Removes excess fats from the bloodstream, helping the circulation to deliver revitalizing oxygen and nutrients to the cells.
- Good source of vitamin K, needed for youthful bone health.

DID YOU KNOW?

Rhubarb has been used for thousands of years by the Chinese for digestive and kidney health— both vital for retaining youth— and is also mentioned in medieval European and Arabic medical texts.

PRACTICAL TIPS

Rhubarb tastes extremely tart on its own, so it always needs sweetening. Although this can have the effect of negating its healthy properties, honey or fruit juice will minimize the damage. Getting used to the tartness of rhubarb as an aspect of its distinctive flavor also reduces the temptation to oversweeten.

PORK TENDERLOIN WITH ROASTED RHUBARB

Young pink rhubarb tempers the pork's natural sweetness and produces deliciously tangy juices. Use a blade-end or center-cut piece of pork for moistness and flavor.

SERVES 4 • PREP TIME: 20 MINS • COOK TIME: 55 MINS–1 HOUR, PLUS RESTING

PER SERVING:

 276 cal CALORIES **8g** FAT **2g** SAT FAT **6.7g** CARBS **4.8g** SUGAR **0.9g** FIBER **42.4g** PROTEIN **80mg** SODIUM

INGREDIENTS

1¾ pounds boneless pork tenderloin
1 tablespoon olive oil
1 teaspoon sea salt flakes
½ teaspoon pepper
10 small fresh rosemary sprigs
½ cup chicken broth
3½ pink rhubarb stalks, trimmed and sliced
diagonally into 1½-inch lengths
1 tablespoon honey

1. Preheat the oven to 375°F. Using the tip of a sharp knife, score the fat, but not the flesh, of the pork at ½-inch intervals. Tie the meat with kitchen twine to make a neat roll. You can ask your butcher to do this.

2. Put the meat into a small roasting pan. Rub with the oil and then with the salt and pepper, rubbing in well. Insert the rosemary sprigs into the slits in the fat. Roast in the preheated oven for 40 minutes.

3. Pour in the broth. Arrange the rhubarb around the meat and drizzle with the honey. Roast for an additional 10–15 minutes, until the rhubarb is tender and starting to color at the edges.

4. Transfer the pork and rhubarb to a warm serving platter, reserving the pan juices. Make a tent over the meat with aluminum foil and let rest in a warm place for 10 minutes.

5. Place the roasting pan on the stove over medium–high heat. Simmer rapidly to reduce the pan juices, including any that have flowed from the meat, for 3–4 minutes, until slightly thickened. Strain into a pitcher and serve with the meat.

PEARS

This fruit—known to be hypoallergenic—is antibacterial, high in fiber, and contains antioxidants to help prevent cancer and gastroenteritis.

MAJOR NUTRIENTS PER AVERAGE-SIZE PEAR

60 cal	TRACE	15g	3.3g	0.5 g	9mg	225 mg
CALORIES	TOTAL FAT	CARBS	FIBER	PROTEIN	VITAMIN C	POTASSIUM

Pear cultivation goes back more than 3,000 years in western Asia, and there has been some evidence of its discovery as far back as the Stone Age. Pears are closely related to apples and there are many varieties. It has been found that, compared to many other fruits, they are less likely to produce an adverse or allergic response, and this makes them particularly useful as a first fruit for young children. They contain a range of useful nutrients and a good amount of fiber, which helps maintain a healthy colon.

- Safe fruit for most children and for people who experience food allergies.
- A good source of a range of nutrients, including vitamin C and potassium.
- Contain hydroxycinnamic acids, antioxidants that are anticancer and antibacterial and may help prevent gastroenteritis.

DID YOU KNOW?

Much of the fiber in pears is contained in the skin, so it is best simply to wash the fruit and not peel it.

PRACTICAL TIPS

Pears don't ripen well on the tree, so store-bought pears tend to be underripe. Place them in a cool to moderately warm room and, once ripe, eat within a day—they tend to spoil quickly. Pears can also discolor easily; to prevent this, sprinkle the cut sides with lemon juice. Although an ideal snack or lunch-box fruit, pears are versatile and can be baked, sautéed, or poached, and can be used in mixed fruit compotes, crisps, and pies.

CRUNCH-TOPPED ROASTED PEARS

Soft, fragrant pears go wonderfully well with crunchy nuts and are
one of the tastiest fruits to roast in the oven.

SERVES 4 • PREP TIME: 10 MINS • COOK TIME: 20 MINS

PER SERVING:	215 cal	5.1g	0.7g	34.4g	20.5g	5.9g	2.9g	TRACE
	CALORIES	FAT	SAT FAT	CARBS	SUGAR	FIBER	PROTEIN	SODIUM

INGREDIENTS

4 dessert pears, such as Comice or Bartlett
1 cup medium white wine
1 tablespoon raw sugar
½ teaspoon allspice
¼ cup toasted mixed nuts, chopped
2½ tablespoons rolled oats
2 tablespoons whole-wheat bread crumbs
2 teaspoons sunflower seeds
8 sprays cooking oil spray

1. Preheat the oven to 375°F.

2. Cut the pears in half lengthwise and remove the cores. Place in a large shallow baking dish. Pour the white wine around the pears and bake in the preheated oven for 10 minutes.

3. Meanwhile, combine the sugar, spice, nuts, oats, bread crumbs, and sunflower seeds in a bowl.

4. Remove the pears from the oven, top each one with some of the nut mixture, then spray with cooking oil spray. Return to the oven for 7–8 minutes, or until the topping is golden. Serve drizzled with any juice left in the dish.

GRAPES

Grapes are rich in polyphenols—which protect our hearts, improve circulation,
and help lower cholesterol—and have antifungal properties.

MAJOR NUTRIENTS PER ⅔ CUP GRAPES

70 cal	TRACE	18g	0.9g	0.7g	10.8 mg	191 mg
CALORIES	TOTAL FAT	CARBS	FIBER	PROTEIN	VITAMIN C	POTASSIUM

All grape varieties contain beneficial compounds, mainly polyphenols, and most of these are found in the skin. Black, purple, and red varieties also contain much higher levels of the flavonoid quercetin and anthocyanins—the dark pigments—and both may help prevent cancer and heart and cardiovascular disease. The antioxidant benefits of paler grapes are mainly from their catechin content. Resveratrol, another antioxidant present in all grapes, has been linked to the prevention or inhibition of cancer and heart disease, degenerative nerve disease, and viral infections, and may also be linked to protection against Alzheimer's disease.

- Rich source of polyphenols, for cancer prevention and a healthy cardiovascular system.
- Quercetin can improve blood cholesterol profile and has an anticlotting action.
- Antiviral and antifungal action.
- Good source of vitamin C.

DID YOU KNOW?

More than 70 percent of world grape production is used for wine, 27 percent for fresh fruit, and 2 percent for dried fruit.

PRACTICAL TIPS

Wash grapes before use—they may have been sprayed with pesticides—and store in the refrigerator or a cool room to preserve vitamin C content and prevent deterioration. If using in a dessert, cut at the last minute to prevent the cut side from discoloring.

GRAPE & LYCHEE SMOOTHIE

This supergreen drink blends fragrant lychees with creamy, smooth avocado and naturally sweet grapes for the perfect pick-me-up to rehydrate and fight fatigue.

SERVES 1 • PREP TIME: 15 MINS • COOK TIME: NONE

PER SERVING:

413 cal	15.6g	2.3g	72.8g	54.6g	8.3g	6.2g	40mg
CALORIES	FAT	SAT FAT	CARBS	SUGAR	FIBER	PROTEIN	SODIUM

INGREDIENTS
2 cups green grapes
2 cups young spinach
½ ripe avocado, pitted and flesh scooped from the skin
5 lychees, peeled and pitted
small handful of crushed ice
½ cup chilled water
slice of avocado to serve (optional)

1. Feed the grapes and spinach through a juicer.

2. Pour the juice into a blender, add the avocado, lychees, and crushed ice, and blend until smooth.

3. Add the water and blend again. Pour into a glass, add the avocado slice, if using, and serve immediately.

PAPAYA

The tropical papaya is extremely high in carotenes, which are linked with cancer prevention and with healthy lungs and eyes.

MAJOR NUTRIENTS PER AVERAGE-SIZE PAPAYA

120 cal	0.4g	30g	5.5g	1.5g	180 mg	780 mg	839 mcg	2313 mcg	228 mcg	30 mg
CALORIES	TOTAL FAT	CARBS	FIBER	PROTEIN	VITAMIN C	POTASSIUM	BETA-CAROTENE	BETA-CRYPTOXANTHIN	LUTEIN/ZEAXANTHIN	MAGNESIUM

The papaya flesh is high in fructose (fruit sugars) and relatively high in calories, so it's good as a hunger-beating snack or dessert. The flesh is also high in carotenes, which can help prevent cancer, and it is a good source of fiber. In addition, it is one of the richest fruits in potassium and is much higher in calcium than most other fruits. Papaya is also extremely high in vitamin C, and it is a reasonable source of magnesium and vitamin E. It contains the enzyme papain, which breaks down protein and tenderizes meat.

- Rich in beta-carotene, which can help prevent prostate cancer.
- A good source of the carotenes lutein and zeaxanthin, which can help protect the eyes from macular degeneration.
- Rich in beta-cryptoxanthin, which can help maintain healthy lungs and may help prevent arthritis.
- Excellent source of vitamin C and fiber.
- High soluble fiber content helps control blood sugar levels by slowing sugar absorption.

DID YOU KNOW?

Papaya seeds can be dried in a low oven and used in the same way as peppercorns.

PRACTICAL TIPS

When a papaya is ripe, its skin is orange instead of green. It can be added to a casserole to tenderize the meat. In a fruit salad, add just before serving—the papain in it can soften other fruits too much. The papain also prevents gelatin from setting, so avoid using it in gelatin-base desserts. Lime juice sprinkled on the fruit brings out its flavor.

CHICKEN, PAPAYA & AVOCADO SALAD

This delicious salad is a powerhouse of valuable nutrients, with peppery greens, avocado, nuts, and quinoa sprouts, not to mention the star of the show—papaya.

SERVES 2 • PREP TIME: 20 MINS • COOK TIME: 10 MINS

PER SERVING:

1,002 cal	87.5g	8.7g	41.6g	21.4g	12g	40.3g	40mg
CALORIES	FAT	SAT FAT	CARBS	SUGAR	FIBER	PROTEIN	SODIUM

INGREDIENTS

2 boneless, skinless chicken breasts, each weighing about 5½ ounces
2 tablespoons olive oil
3½ ounces peppery greens, such as arugula, mizuna, chicory, and watercress
1 large papaya, peeled, seeded ,and thickly sliced
1 ripe avocado, peeled, pitted, and thickly sliced
¼ cup toasted hazelnuts, halved
2 tablespoons red or white quinoa sprouts
salt and pepper (optional)

DRESSING

2 tablespoons lime juice
6 tablespoons hazelnut oil
salt and pepper (optional)

1. Place the chicken breasts on a board. With the knife parallel to the board, slice each breast in half horizontally to make four cutlets in total.

2. Place the cutlets between two sheets of plastic wrap and pound with a rolling pin to a thickness of about ⅜ inch.

3. Heat the oil in a large skillet. Add the chicken and cook over medium–high heat for 3–4 minutes on each side, until golden on the outside and no longer pink in the middle. Transfer to a warm plate and season with salt and pepper, if using.

4. Slice the chicken lengthwise into ¾-inch-wide strips.

5. Divide the salad greens between two plates. Arrange the chicken, papaya, and avocado on top. Sprinkle with the hazelnuts and quinoa sprouts.

6. To make the dressing, whisk together all the ingredients until smooth and creamy. Pour over the salad and serve immediately.

PEACHES

The soft fruit of this member of the rose family makes a nutritional sweet substitute for refined sugars and provides skin-nourishing nutrients.

MAJOR NUTRIENTS PER AVERAGE-SIZE PEACH

58 cal CALORIES	0.38g TOTAL FAT	14.31g CARBS	2.2g FIBER	1.36g PROTEIN	9.9 mg VITAMIN C	4891IU VITAMIN A	243 mcg BETA-CAROTENE	0.38 mg IRON	136 mcg LUTEIN/ ZEAXANTHIN	13.7 mg MAGNESIUM	285 mg POTASSIUM	30 mg PHOSPHORUS

Like most orange fruit and vegetables, peaches are abundant in carotenoid nutrients, the antioxidants that protect fatty areas of the body—in the liver, skin, heart, and other organs, including the brain, which is 60 percent fat. These fatty areas are susceptible to damage, and we rely on fat-soluble antioxidants, such as carotenoids and vitamin A, to slow down degeneration and aging. Peaches are also high in vitamin C, which protects watery areas of the body that are in and between cells and in the bloodstream. The high boron content of peaches has been shown to promote new bone growth and reduce the risk of prostate cancer in men.

- Rich in potassium, vitamin C, and iron, important for circulation and taking oxygen around the body to renew and revitalize the skin.
- Their gentle laxative effect helps maintain bowel regularity, making sure of the removal of aging toxins.
- Contain the minerals magnesium and phosphorus, used by the nervous system for optimum brain and muscle function.

DID YOU KNOW?

Peaches have long been considered a medicinal plant and are recommended during convalescence for those experiencing fatigue or depression.

PRACTICAL TIPS

Choose fruit that is still firm and only just becoming soft, with yellowy cream coloring between the red areas and a velvety skin. Look for bruises, because they spread quickly, and wash only immediately before eating, because any damage to the skin can accelerate spoiling.

CELERIAC, FENNEL & PEACH SLAW

The peach combines well with the slightly licorice undertones of the celeriac and fennel to make an unusually flavored summer side dish.

SERVES 4 • PREP TIME: 10 MINS • COOK TIME: NONE

PER SERVING:
175 cal	10.9g	1.7g	19g	10.6g	4.3g	2.5g	160mg
CALORIES	FAT	SAT FAT	CARBS	SUGAR	FIBER	PROTEIN	SODIUM

INGREDIENTS

¼ cup mayonnaise
1 teaspoon sriracha chili sauce
1 teaspoon horseradish sauce
zest and juice of 1 lemon
½ teaspoon pepper
2 ripe peaches, pitted and sliced
½ head of celeriac, cut into matchsticks
1 fennel bulb, sliced
1 small red onion, sliced

1. In a large bowl, whisk together the mayonnaise, chili sauce, horseradish sauce, lemon zest and juice, and pepper.

2. Add the peaches, celeriac, fennel, and onion to the bowl. Mix well to combine thoroughly, then serve immediately.

VARIATION

This slaw will work well with any soft stone fruit and is great served with pork, chicken, or fish.

PLUMS

Research shows that antioxidants found in plums protect the brain as well as the heart. They are also a good source of iron.

MAJOR NUTRIENTS PER AVERAGE-SIZE PLUM

30 cal	TRACE	7.5g	0.9g	0.5g	6.3 mg	125 mcg	0.4 mcg	48 mcg	104 mg
CALORIES	TOTAL FAT	CARBS	FIBER	PROTEIN	VITAMIN C	BETA-CAROTENE	IRON	LUTEIN/ ZEAXANTHIN	POTASSIUM

Plums come in a variety of colors, from the more common red and purple varieties to yellow and white. The fruits are well known for their health-giving phenolic compounds—neochlorogenic and chlorogenic acids—which are particularly effective at neutralizing the free radicals that contribute to disease and the aging process. They seem to be especially beneficial in their antioxidant action on the fatty tissues in the brain and help prevent damage to the fats circulating in our blood. The red and purple varieties are also rich in anthocyanins, the pigments that help to prevent heart disease and cancers.

- Low glycemic index is useful for dieters and diabetics.
- Good source of carotenes for cancer protection and eye health.
- Rich in phenolic compounds for healthy brain and strong antioxidant action.
- Source of easily absorbed iron for healthy blood and body maintenance.

DID YOU KNOW?

Plums, native to China and Europe, have been eaten for at least 2,000 years. There are also more than 2,000 varieties.

PRACTICAL TIPS

Buy plums that are almost ripe, preferably still with a slight bloom on the skin, and let ripen at room temperature for one to two days—completely ripe plums contain the most antioxidants. Plums bought for cooking should be poached in a little water and eaten with their juices, because some of the nutrients will leach into the water.

RICE PUDDING WITH CINNAMON-POACHED PLUMS

Creamy rice pudding with cinnamon-flavor plum compote is an incredibly
warm and comforting dish that takes us right back to childhood.

SERVES 4 • PREP TIME: 15 MINS • COOK TIME: 50–55 MINS

PER SERVING:

296 cal	7.5g	4.2g	52.6g	33.7g	2.4g	6.3g	40mg
CALORIES	FAT	SAT FAT	CARBS	SUGAR	FIBER	PROTEIN	SODIUM

INGREDIENTS

½ cup short-grain rice
2 tablespoons sugar
1 tablespoon unsalted butter
2 cups milk
1 thinly pared strip of orange zest

COMPOTE

8 red plums, pitted and halved
1 cinnamon stick
2 tablespoons sugar
juice of 1 orange

1. Put the rice, sugar, and butter into a saucepan and stir in the milk and orange zest. Heat gently, stirring occasionally, until almost boiling.

2. Reduce the heat to low, then cover and simmer gently for 40–45 minutes, or according to package directions, stirring occasionally, until the rice is tender and most of the liquid has been absorbed.

3. Meanwhile, to make the compote, put the plums, cinnamon, sugar, and orange juice into a large saucepan. Heat gently until just boiling, then reduce the heat, cover, and simmer for about 10 minutes, or until the plums are tender.

4. Remove the plums with a slotted spoon and discard the cinnamon. Serve the rice pudding warm with the compote.

VARIATION
This delicious fruit compote would work just as well on top of oatmeal or pancakes.

OLIVES

Olives offer the same health benefits as olive oil, but with extra phytosterols, lutein, and vitamins A and E for an added anti-aging boost.

MAJOR NUTRIENTS PER 1 CUP OLIVES

145 cal	15.32g	11.3g	3.84g	3.3g	1.03g	393IU	3.81mg
CALORIES	TOTAL FAT	MONO UN-SATURATED FAT	CARBS	FIBER	PROTEIN	VITAMIN A	VITAMIN E

1215 mg	11,145 mg	231 mcg	510 mcg	176mg	1,556 mg
OMEGA-6 OILS	OMEGA-9 OILS	BETA-CAROTENE	LUTEIN/ZEAXANTHIN	PHYTOSTEROLS	SODIUM

The fatty nature of olives makes them a fantastic carrier of the fat-soluble nutrients that are so important for forming and protecting every single cell membrane in the body. This translates as wrinkle prevention, bone strength, and brain clarity. The valuable oil within the olives moves these nutrients in through the digestive system so that they can be absorbed and used where needed. Taken together, the monounsaturated fats, omega-6 oils, vitamins, and carotenoids in olives provide staunch support for all-round heart health. The only downside of this food is the high sodium content, which needs balancing out with potassium from other foods for the body to retain good blood pressure.

- Contain lutein and vitamin A to protect the eyes from macular degeneration, a condition associated with older age.
- Vitamins A and E keep skin lubricated; dry skin can wrinkle and age more easily.
- Vitamin E may help prevent cancer and keeps blood vessels healthily dilated.

DID YOU KNOW?

The Latin for the olive tree is Olea europaea, which literally translates as "European oil." The fruit of the olive has to be processed in some way—such as curing or fermenting—or it will have a bitter taste.

PRACTICAL TIPS

Olives come in a wide range of varieties, not only green and black. Try sampling some of the different sizes, flavorings, and preparations at a good-quality farmers' market or deli to discover your personal preference, and to find out which go best with other foodstuffs and beverages. Olives with pits retain their flavor better.

CRACKED MARINATED OLIVES

These traditionally flavored olives will up the ante at your next cocktail party.
They will keep in the refrigerator for several weeks.

SERVES 8 • PREP TIME: 30 MINS, PLUS STANDING AND MARINATING • COOK TIME: NONE

PER SERVING:

83 cal	7.8g	1g	4.3g	0.3g	1.9g	0.6g	280mg
CALORIES	FAT	SAT FAT	CARBS	SUGAR	FIBER	PROTEIN	SODIUM

INGREDIENTS

1 pound canned, unpitted large green olives, drained
4 garlic cloves, peeled
2 teaspoons coriander seeds
1 small lemon
4 fresh thyme sprigs
4 feathery fennel stalks
2 small fresh red chiles (optional)
extra virgin olive oil, for marinating
pepper (optional)

1. To let the flavors of the marinade penetrate completely, put the olives onto a cutting board and, using a rolling pin, bang them lightly so that they crack slightly. Alternatively, use a sharp knife to cut a lengthwise slit in each olive as far as the pit. Using the flat side of a broad knife, lightly crush each garlic clove. Using a mortar and pestle, crack the coriander seeds. Cut the lemon, with its zest, into small chunks.

2. Put the olives, garlic, coriander seeds, lemon chunks, thyme sprigs, fennel, and chiles, if using, into a large bowl and toss together. Season with pepper, if using. Tightly pack the ingredients into a glass jar with a lid. Pour in enough oil to cover the olives, then seal the jar tightly.

3. Let the olives stand at room temperature for 24 hours, then marinate in the refrigerator for at least 1 week but preferably 2 weeks. From time to time, gently give the jar a shake to remix the ingredients. Remove from the refrigerator and let reach room temperature, then remove the olives from the oil and serve.

HINT

Serve these marinated olives with plenty of toothpicks to make this tasty snack easier to eat.

POMEGRANATE

Pomegranate juice has been found to contain around three times the protective dose of antioxidant polyphenols of green tea.

MAJOR NUTRIENTS PER MEDIUM POMEGRANATE

234 cal	3.3g	52.7g	11.3g	4.7g	28.8 mg	28mg	107 mcg	0.85 mg	34mg	666 mg	1.4 mcg
CALORIES	TOTAL FAT	CARBS	FIBER	PROTEIN	VITAMIN C	CALCIUM	FOLATE	IRON	MAGNESIUM	POTASSIUM	SELENIUM

Polyphenols are a group of compounds in plant foods that are important nutrients, because of their antioxidant, anti-inflammatory, and anticancer health benefits. Risk of high blood pressure, heart diseases, degenerative diseases of the nervous system, and several types of cancer, including prostate cancer, can all be reduced with the help of a diet rich in polyphenols. Pomegranate seeds and their juice contain such high levels of three major types—tannins, anthocyanins, and ellagic acid—that a study of healthy juices found pomegranate juice came out top, beating both acai and blueberry juice. The fruits are also a good source of iron for healthy blood, and are high in total dietary fiber and soluble fiber to help control blood sugars and reduce LDL cholesterol and total cholesterol levels. Finally, one average fruit contains nearly half of the daily recommended vitamin C intake and a third of the daily vitamin E requirement.

- Rich in polyphenols for a range of health benefits.
- Excellent source of dietary fiber for improved blood cholesterol profile.
- High in vitamins C and E.
- Good source of iron.

DID YOU KNOW?

Pomegranates were the primary symbol of Aphrodite, the Greek goddess of love, who gave her name to "aphrodisiac." An average pomegranate contains about 600 seeds.

PRACTICAL TIPS

The easiest way to extract the seeds from the pith is to halve the fruit and use a small spoon to scoop them out, or a ripe fruit can be halved and squeezed so that the seeds drop out. The seeds are probably best eaten raw and are ideal for sprinkling onto sweet or savory salads, stirred into yogurt, or added to a smoothie.

GINGERED CARROT
& POMEGRANATE SALAD

Turn the humble carrot into an exotic, fresh-tasting salad with a little
Middle Eastern magic with the help of jewel-like pomegranate.

SERVES 4 • PREP TIME: 20–25 MINS • COOK TIME: NONE

PER SERVING: | **166 cal** | **10.9g** | **1.5g** | **16.8g** | **9.9g** | **3.6g** | **1.8g** | **80mg** |
|---|---|---|---|---|---|---|---|
| CALORIES | FAT | SAT FAT | CARBS | SUGAR | FIBER | PROTEIN | SODIUM |

INGREDIENTS

6 carrots, finely grated
2-inch piece fresh ginger, peeled and grated
1 small pomegranate, quartered
1½ cups ready-to-eat seed sprouts,
such as alfalfa and radish sprouts

DRESSING

3 tablespoons light olive oil
1 tablespoon red wine vinegar
1 tablespoon pomegranate molasses
salt and pepper (optional)

1. Put the carrots and ginger into a salad bowl. Flex the pomegranate pieces to pop out the seeds, prying any stubborn ones out with the tip of a small knife, and add to the bowl.

2. To make the dressing, put the oil, vinegar, and pomegranate molasses into a screw-top jar, season with salt and pepper, if using, screw on the lid, and shake well. Drizzle the dressing over the salad and toss gently together. Cover and let marinate in the refrigerator for 30 minutes.

3. Sprinkle the seed sprouts over the salad and serve.

DRIED APRICOTS

Dried apricots are a nutritious and concentrated source of energy, nutrients, and fiber and are low on the glycemic index.

MAJOR NUTRIENTS PER 3 PIECES DRIED APRICOTS

72 cal	TRACE	18.8g	2.2g	1g	TRACE	1,297 mcg	0.8 mg	349 mg
CALORIES	TOTAL FAT	CARBS	FIBER	PROTEIN	VITAMIN C	BETA-CAROTENE	IRON	POTASSIUM

Apricots are rich in the plant compound beta-carotene, and dried apricots are a particularly valuable source. Beta-carotene is an antioxidant that can protect against heart disease and aging and some cancers. It also converts into vitamin A in the body, which is vital to maintain bones and for vision, healthy skin, and the immune system. The good iron content in the dried fruits is another immune system booster. Dried apricots contain catechins, antioxidants with anti-inflammatory action, as well as help to control blood pressure. Containing twice the fiber, weight for weight, of fresh apricots, dried apricots are a good source of heart-friendly soluble fiber, and they are one of the lowest fruits on the glycemic index, at a value of 30, and thus a useful snack for dieters and those with diabetes, because they are only slowly absorbed into the bloodstream.

- Contain high levels of beta-carotene for a variety of important health benefits.
- Low GI fruit is a good aid to weight control.
- High in total fiber and soluble fiber to help protect the heart.
- Excellent source of iron to boost immunity and keep blood healthy.

DID YOU KNOW?

Dried apricots and other dried fruits that are produced commercially are usually preserved with the aid of sulfites, which are thought to trigger asthma in susceptible people. Organic dried fruits do not contain sulfites.

PRACTICAL TIPS

Try poaching dried apricots in a little water until tender. This helps the carotenes and soluble fiber to be absorbed by the body. Dried apricots can be used in savory dishes, such as couscous salad or Moroccan stews. Be careful, however, if you are allergic to aspirin; dried apricots contain salicylate, a natural substance similar to the active ingredient in aspirin.

CHEWY APRICOT & ALMOND ENERGY BARS

These oaty, dairy-free energy bars are great for carrying
with you for a healthy midmorning snack.

MAKES 15 • PREP TIME: 25 MINS • COOK TIME: 30 MINS, PLUS COOLING

PER BAR:	235 cal	14g	7.2g	26.6g	14.6g	3.5g	4.2g	TRACE
	CALORIES	FAT	SAT FAT	CARBS	SUGAR	FIBER	PROTEIN	SODIUM

INGREDIENTS

½ cup coconut oil
⅓ cup firmly packed light brown sugar
¼ cup almond butter or other nut butter
1 crisp, sweet apple, cored and coarsely grated
1⅔ cups rolled oats
¼ cup brown rice flour
½ cup unblanched almonds, coarsely chopped
¼ cup sunflower seeds
1¼ cups diced dried apricots

1. Preheat the oven to 350°F. Line a shallow, 8-inch square cake pan with nonstick parchment paper.

2. Heat the oil and sugar in a medium saucepan over low heat until the oil has melted and the sugar is dissolved. Remove from the heat and stir in the almond butter until melted.

3. Add the apple, oats, flour, almonds, and sunflower seeds, and mix together well.

4. Spoon two-thirds of the batter into the prepared pan and press down firmly. Sprinkle with the apricots and press firmly into the batter, then dot the remaining batter over the top in a thin layer so that some of the apricots are still visible.

5. Bake in the preheated oven for about 25 minutes, until the top is golden brown. Remove from the oven and let cool in the pan until almost cold, then cut into 15 small rectangles. Let cool completely and serve.

HINT

To store, lift the bars out of the pan, separate, and pack into a plastic container. Store in the refrigerator for up to three days.

PRUNES

A prune is any species of dried plum. They are highly concentrated sources of fiber and are effective at flushing aging toxins out of the body.

MAJOR NUTRIENTS PER ½ CUP PRUNES

240 cal	0.38g	63.88g	7.1g	2.18g	43 mg	41 mg	394 mcg	148 mcg
CALORIES	TOTAL FAT	CARBS	FIBER	PROTEIN	CALCIUM	MAGNESIUM	BETA-CAROTENE	LUTEIN/ZEAXANTHIN

The host of antioxidants contained in prunes means that they are high on the ORAC scale. Most of these protective and disease-preventing antioxidants are phenolic compounds, or water-soluble antioxidants, such as vitamin C and rutin, both of which keep your veins healthy and so help prevent bruising and varicose veins, support circulation and heart function, and transport nutrients to the skin for healing. Prunes and prune juice are common home remedies for constipation, partly because of their fiber content; the soluble fiber helps speed up toxic waste elimination, while the insoluble fiber helps to bulk out stools.

- The insoluble fiber in prunes makes you feel full, and thus they regulate appetite to help you maintain weight levels.
- Prunes release their sugars slowly, preventing these sugars from causing accelerated aging of the skin.
- About 60 percent of the soluble fiber in prunes comes from pectin, which helps remove damaging and aging toxic metals, such as lead and mercury, from the body.

DID YOU KNOW?

In recent times, the popularity of prunes as a culinary ingredient has increased. This may be partly due to a campaign in which they have been remarketed as "dried plums."

PRACTICAL TIPS

Make a simple puree by liquidizing prunes and dried apricots with some boiling water and cinnamon. This less sugary alternative to preserves makes a great sweetener for yogurt and oatmeal. Prunes work well in savory dishes, such as Moroccan stews, providing complementary sweet tones to slow-cooked meats.

COMPOTE OF DRIED FRUITS

Made entirely with dried fruit, this compote is a good winter standby. It is also versatile—
eat it on its own as a dessert, or with oatmeal, yogurt, or quark for breakfast.

SERVES 4 • PREP TIME: 5 MINS • COOK TIME: 20 MINS

PER SERVING:

349 cal	0.7g	0.1g	80.5g	73g	8.3g	2.9g	40mg
CALORIES	FAT	SAT FAT	CARBS	SUGAR	FIBER	PROTEIN	SODIUM

INGREDIENTS

1 cup dried apricots, halved
¾ cup prunes
1⅔ cups halved dried apple rings
⅓ cup dried cranberries
2 cups orange juice
2 pieces preserved ginger in syrup,
drained and chopped, 2 tablespoons syrup reserved

1. Put the apricots, prunes, dried apple, and cranberries into a saucepan and pour the orange juice over the fruit.

2. Bring to a boil over medium heat, then stir in the ginger and reserved syrup. Reduce the heat to low, cover, and simmer gently for about 15 minutes, until the fruit is soft.

3. Lift out the fruit with a slotted spoon and place in a serving dish. Simmer the juice, uncovered, for 3–4 minutes, until reduced and slightly thickened. Pour the syrup over the fruit and serve warm or cold.

VEGETABLES & SALADS

KALE

Deep green kale contains the highest levels of antioxidants of all
vegetables and is a good source of vitamin C.

MAJOR NUTRIENTS PER 1½ CUPS KALE

50 cal	0.7g	10g	2g	3.3g	120 mg	1.7 mg	29 mcg
CALORIES	TOTAL FAT	CARBS	FIBER	PROTEIN	VITAMIN C	VITAMIN E	FOLATE

9226 mcg	135 mg	1.7mg	39550 mcg	34 mg	447 mg	0.9 mcg
BETA-CAROTENE	CALCIUM	IRON	LUTEIN/ZEAXANTHIN	MAGNESIUM	POTASSIUM	SELENIUM

Kale is one of the most nutritious members of the Brassica, or cabbage, family. It rates as the vegetable highest in antioxidant capacity on the ORAC scale, and contains more calcium and iron than any other vegetable. A single portion contains twice the recommended daily amount of vitamin C, which helps the vegetable's high iron content to be absorbed in our bodies. One portion also gives about one-fifth of the daily calcium requirement for an adult. Kale is rich in selenium, which helps fight cancer, and it contains magnesium and vitamin E for a healthy heart. The range of nutrients kale provides will keep skin young-looking and healthy.

- Rich in flavonoids and antioxidants to fight cancers.
- Contains indoles, which can help lower "bad" cholesterol and prevent cancer.
- Calcium-rich for healthy bones.
- Extremely rich in carotenes to protect eyes.

DID YOU KNOW?

Kale contains naturally occurring substances that can interfere with the functioning of the thyroid gland—those with thyroid problems may not want to eat kale.

PRACTICAL TIPS

Wash kale before use, because the curly leaves may contain sand or soil. Don't discard the deep green outer leaves—these contain rich amounts of carotenes and indoles. Kale is good steamed or stir-fried and its strong taste goes well with bacon, eggs, and cheese. Kale, like spinach, shrinks a lot during cooking, so make sure you add plenty to the pan.

CRUNCHY PARMESAN & KALE CHIPS

This recipe for kale chips is one of the simplest you'll ever make.
They're deliciously crisp, with a salty kick from the Parmesan.

SERVES 4 • PREP TIME: 10 MINS • COOK TIME: 15 MINS

PER SERVING:

153 cal	10.2g	4.6g	5.8g	0.2g	1g	10.6g	560mg
CALORIES	FAT	SAT FAT	CARBS	SUGAR	FIBER	PROTEIN	SODIUM

INGREDIENTS

3 cups kale (woody stems removed)
1 tablespoon olive oil
pinch of cayenne pepper
1¼ cups finely grated Parmesan cheese
sea salt (optional)

1. Preheat the oven to 350°F. Put the kale and oil into a bowl, season with the cayenne pepper and salt, if using, then toss.

2. Arrange the kale in a single layer on a large baking sheet. Sprinkle the cheese over the kale. Bake in the preheated oven for 10–15 minutes, or until the leaves are dry and crisp but just a little brown at the edges.

3. Let cool for 5 minutes, until crisp, then serve.

MUSHROOMS

The compounds in mushrooms, which boost the immune system, help to prevent cancers, infections, and autoimmune diseases, such as arthritis and lupus.

MAJOR NUTRIENTS PER 3 OUNCES MUSHROOMS

22 cal	TRACE	4.2g	1.3g	2.1g	3.8 mg	7mg	18 mcg	0.5 mg	407 mg	9.2 mcg	0.5 mg
CALORIES	TOTAL FAT	CARBS	FIBER	PROTEIN	VITAMIN B3	CALCIUM	FOLATE	IRON	POTASSIUM	SELENIUM	ZINC

Most of the mushrooms that we buy are the young, white button mushrooms and the older, darker gilled flat mushrooms, but there are several others, such as Chinese shiitake mushrooms, porcini, and wild mushrooms. While the amount of beneficial compounds varies according to their variety and age (older, darker ones have more benefits), most mushrooms are rich in plant chemicals that help boost the immune system. One active component of mushrooms that may be beneficial is glutamic acid, a naturally occurring form of monosodium glutamate. Mushrooms are also a useful source of protein.

• Contain compounds that can help prevent cancers and autoimmune diseases.
• Ideal source of healthy protein for vegetarians and dieters.
• Rich in the anticancer antioxidant mineral selenium.
• Good source of the B vitamins, including folate and niacin, which has cholesterol-lowering properties.

DID YOU KNOW?

You should not pick mushrooms from the wild unless you get them checked for safety by a fungi expert. Several varieties look harmless but are poisonous.

PRACTICAL TIPS

Store mushrooms in the refrigerator in a paper bag instead of a plastic bag to help them breathe. Most mushrooms shouldn't need washing, but if any soil clings to them, gently wipe clean with paper towels. Don't peel or remove the stems—these contain much of their goodness.

ROASTED MUSHROOM & GARLIC SOUP

Large, meaty immune-boosting mushrooms make this soup a real winner
when you're feeling hungry but don't want a meat-base meal.

SERVES 1 • PREP TIME: 20 MINS • COOK TIME: 40–50 MINS

PER SERVING:

 205 cal
CALORIES

 7.7g
FAT

 1.9g
SAT FAT

 26.2g
CARBS

 6.4g
SUGAR

 5.3g
FIBER

 10.1g
PROTEIN

 1,128 mg
SODIUM

INGREDIENTS

2 open-cap mushrooms, wiped clean
2 garlic cloves, peeled
1 slice whole-wheat bread, cut into small cubes
1 teaspoon olive oil
¼ ounce dried porcini
1 cup vegetable broth
1 teaspoon fresh thyme leaves
1 teaspoon Worcestershire sauce
1 teaspoon reduced-fat crème fraîche or
sour cream (optional)
freshly ground black pepper (optional)
1 fresh thyme sprig, to garnish

1. Preheat the oven to 350°F.

2. Loosely wrap the open-cap mushrooms and garlic in
aluminum foil and place in the preheated oven. Bake for
10 minutes, open the foil, and bake for an additional 5 minutes.

3. To prepare croutons, drizzle the bread cubes with the oil,
place on a baking sheet, and bake for 10–15 minutes, or until
golden brown.

4. Meanwhile, put the porcini, broth, and thyme leaves in a
lidded saucepan.

5. When the open-cap mushrooms are cooked, remove from the
oven, slice, and add them to the pan with the Worcestershire
sauce, garlic, mushroom juices, and pepper, if using. Cover and
simmer for 15 minutes over low heat.

6. Let cool slightly, then puree half the soup in a blender for a
few seconds. Return to the pan and reheat gently. Stir in the
crème fraîche, if using, and add pepper to taste, if using.

7. Transfer to a warm bowl, sprinkle with the croutons, garnish
with the thyme sprig, and serve immediately.

RED CABBAGE

This vegetable is rich in compounds that protect us
from cancers and the signs of aging.

31 cal	TRACE	7.4g	2.1g	1.4g	0.4 mg	57mg
CALORIES	TOTAL FAT	CARBS	FIBER	PROTEIN	VITAMIN B3	VITAMIN C

670 mg	45 mg	18 mcg	0.8 mg	329 mcg	243 mg	0.6 mcg
BETA-CAROTENE	CALCIUM	FOLATE	IRON	LUTEIN/ ZEAXANTHIN	POTASSIUM	SELENIUM

A member of the Brassica, or cabbage, family, purple-red cabbage is high in nutrients and has protective plant compounds. These include: indoles, which have been linked with protection against hormone-base cancers, such as breast, uterine, and ovarian; sulforophane, which can help block cancer-causing chemicals; and monoterpenes, which protect body cells from damage by free radicals. Red cabbage is much higher in immunity-boosting carotenes than other cabbages—lycopene is linked with protection from prostate cancer, and anthocyanins may protect against Alzheimer's disease. Red cabbage is also higher in vitamin C than the pale types and is a good source of minerals, including calcium and selenium.

- Contains a variety of cancer-fighting compounds.
- Low in calories, with a low glycemic index—ideal for dieters.
- Rich in the antioxidant vitamin C.
- Anthocyanin content may protect against Alzheimer's disease.

DID YOU KNOW?

Cabbage leaves have natural antiseptic properties and can be applied directly to wounds and bruises to help relieve pain and promote healing.

PRACTICAL TIPS

Thinly sliced red cabbage can be used raw in coleslaw instead of green cabbage. Sprinkle with lemon juice or salad dressing to prevent it from turning gray. Once cut, red cabbage should be used within one to two days. When cooking, steaming is the method that preserves the maximum nutrients, so try not to overcook.

TURKEY STRIPS WITH RED CABBAGE & KALE SLAW

Forget deep-fried chicken; this oven-baked, crispy-coated
turkey version is quick and easy to make—and healthier.

SERVES 4 • PREP TIME: 20 MINS • COOK TIME: 15 MINS

PER SERVING:

 471 cal CALORIES
 27g FAT
 4.2g SAT FAT
 21.3g CARBS
 8.6g SUGAR
 9.2g FIBER
38.4g PROTEIN
720mg SODIUM

INGREDIENTS

⅓ cup flaxseed
⅓ cup sesame seeds
2 eggs
*1 pound skinless, boneless turkey breast,
cut into thin strips*
3 tablespoons virgin olive oil
sea salt and pepper (optional)

RED CABBAGE & KALE SLAW

1¼ cups thinly shredded red cabbage
½ cup thinly shredded kale
1 carrot, shredded
1 sweet crisp apple, cored and coarsely grated
1 teaspoon caraway seeds
¼ cup Greek-style plain yogurt

1. Preheat the oven to 425°F and put a large baking sheet into it to heat.

2. To make the slaw, put the red cabbage, kale, and carrot into a bowl and mix well. Add the apple, caraway seeds, and yogurt, season with salt and pepper, if using, and mix well. Cover and chill in the refrigerator until needed.

3. Put the flaxseed in a spice mill or blender and process until coarsely ground. Add the sesame seeds and process for a few seconds. Transfer the mixture to a plate.

4. Crack the eggs into a shallow dish, season with salt and pepper, if using, and lightly beat with a fork.

5. Dip each turkey strip into the beaten egg, then lift out with a fork and dip both sides into the seed mixture to coat. Brush the hot baking sheet with a little oil, add the turkey strips in a single layer, then drizzle with a little extra oil.

6. Bake the turkey, turning the strips once and moving them from the corners into the center of the baking sheet, for 15 minutes, or until golden brown and cooked through. Cut one of the larger slices in half to check that the meat is no longer pink inside. Any juices that run out should be clear and piping hot with steam rising. Serve the strips with the slaw.

SWEET POTATOES

The orange-fleshed sweet potato is high in carotenes and cholesterol-lowering compounds, and is an ideal food for dieters to ward off hunger with.

MAJOR NUTRIENTS PER AVERAGE-SIZE SWEET POTATO

129 cal	TRACE	30.2g	4.5g	2.4 g	3.6 mg	0.4 mg
CALORIES	TOTAL FAT	CARBS	FIBER	PROTEIN	VITAMIN C	VITAMIN E
12,760 mcg	45 mg	0.9 mg	38 mg	506 mg	0.9 mcg	0.5 mg
BETA-CAROTENE	CALCIUM	IRON	MAGNESIUM	POTASSIUM	SELENIUM	ZINC

Sweet potatoes have a creamy texture and a sweet, slightly spicy flavor. Don't confuse it with yams, which have creamy white flesh—sweet potatoes have orange flesh. The orange-fleshed sweet potato contains the most nutrients. They are richer in nutrients than potatoes and lower on the glycemic index, and so they are beneficial for diabetics and dieters and for regulating blood sugar levels. They also contain plant sterols and pectin that can help lower "bad" blood cholesterol. They are extremely high in beta-carotene as well as being an excellent source of vitamin E, magnesium, and selenium.

- Carotenes have strong anticancer action.
- Sterols and pectin content help reduce "bad" cholesterol.
- Low glycemic index—good for dieters.
- Antioxidants and vitamin E help improve skin conditions.
- High potassium content helps regulate body fluids and prevent fluid retention.

DID YOU KNOW?

Research has found that sweet potatoes are one of the oldest foods in the world, existing since prehistoric times. They contain naturally occurring substances that can crystallize, and people with kidney or gallbladder problems may be advised not to eat them.

PRACTICAL TIPS

Sweet potatoes can be substituted for normal potatoes in many recipes but, unlike potatoes, their skins are often waxed or treated with chemicals and are, therefore, not always suitable for eating. They can be added to stews, pasta, casseroles, and soups; or roasted; mashed with oil; or baked, halved, and served drizzled with oil. The addition of oil helps with the absorption of carotene.

SMOKY PAPRIKA SWEET POTATO FRIES

Starchy and sweet, with crunchy edges and fluffy insides, these fries make
a really satisfying snack. Always use the best paprika you can find.

SERVES 2 • PREP TIME: 10 MINS • COOK TIME: 40 MINS

PER SERVING:	399 cal	28.4g	10.4g	32.8g	8.8g	5g	4g	440mg
	CALORIES	FAT	SAT FAT	CARBS	SUGAR	FIBER	PROTEIN	SODIUM

INGREDIENTS

2 sweet potatoes,
scrubbed and cut into sticks
2 tablespoons olive oil
1 heaping tablespoon smoked paprika
sea salt and pepper (optional)

SOUR CREAM DIP

4 chives, finely snipped
⅔ cup sour cream

1. Preheat the oven to 350°F. Put the sweet potatoes, oil, and paprika into a large bowl, season with salt and pepper, if using, and toss well.

2. Arrange the sticks in a single layer on a large baking sheet. Bake in the preheated oven for 30–40 minutes, or until crisp.

3. To make the dip, put the chives and sour cream in a bowl and mix. Season with salt and pepper, if using, and divide between two small dipping bowls.

4. Line two larger bowls with paper towels. Transfer the fries to the bowls and serve immediately with the dip.

ONIONS

The onion is a top health food, containing sulfur compounds that are natural antibiotics offering protection from cancers and heart disease.

MAJOR NUTRIENTS PER 1 ONION

63 cal	TRACE	15g	2.1g	1.4g	1.5 mg	9.6 mg	33 mg	24 mcg	29 mcg	28 mg	216 mg	0.8 mcg
CALORIES	TOTAL FAT	CARBS	FIBER	PROTEIN	VITAMIN B3	VITAMIN C	CALCIUM	CHROMIUM	FOLATE	MAGNESIUM	POTASSIUM	SELENIUM

Onions are rich in the powerful compound diallyl sulfide, which gives them their strong smell and helps prevent cancer by blocking the effects of carcinogens (cancer-causing particles) in the body. Onions also contain numerous flavonoids, such as quercetin, and these antioxidant compounds help prevent blood clots and protect against heart disease and cancer. The vegetable also has anti-inflammatory and antibacterial action and can help minimize the nasal congestion of a cold. In addition, onions are rich in chromium, a trace mineral that helps cells respond to insulin, and are a good source of vitamin C and other trace elements.

- Can help protect against several cancers, including lung cancer.
- Help protect the heart and circulatory system and may increase "good" blood cholesterol.
- Anti-inflammatory, which may help symptoms of arthritis.
- Antibacterial and may help control colds.
- Can help regulate insulin response.

DID YOU KNOW?

If you cook onions quickly at a high heat, you destroy a large percentage of the beneficial sulfide compounds that they contain.

PRACTICAL TIPS

Stored in an airy, dry, cool place without touching each other, most onions will last for several months, although the vitamin C content will diminish over time. To cook, onions should be gently sautéed in oil to retain maximum nutrients. Mild onions can be thinly sliced and eaten raw.

SWEET ROOTS BOWL

Root vegetables are full of starch and sugar, so they're great for giving your energy levels a long-term boost. Using tahini in dressings increases your intake of protein and essential fats.

SERVES 4 • PREP TIME: 12 MINS • COOK TIME: 35–40 MINS

PER SERVING:

 402 cal CALORIES   **18.4g** FAT   **2.3g** SAT FAT   **54.2g** CARBS   **11.8g** SUGAR **9.5g** FIBER   **10.1g** PROTEIN **120mg** SODIUM

INGREDIENTS

2 sweet potatoes, cut into chunks
2 beets, cut into chunks
2 red onions, cut into wedges
2 tablespoons olive oil
2 teaspoons cumin seeds
⅓ cup brown rice
¼ cup tahini
juice of 1 lemon
½ teaspoon pepper
½ teaspoon honey
3 cups shredded kale
2 tablespoons slivered almonds, toasted

1. Preheat the oven to 400°F. Put the sweet potatoes, beets, and onions into a bowl with the oil and cumin seeds and toss together to coat with the oil.

2. Transfer to a roasting pan and roast in the preheated oven for 35–40 minutes, until tender.

3. Meanwhile, cook the rice according to the package directions. Whisk together the tahini, lemon juice, pepper, and honey.

4. Stir the kale into the root vegetables 10 minutes before the end of the roasting time.

5. Drain the rice and divide among four warm bowls. Toss the vegetables with the dressing and serve on top of the rice, sprinkled with the toasted almonds.

VARIATION

Instead of rice, try serving the root vegetables over protein-packed quinoa.

TOMATOES

Tomatoes are one of the healthiest foods, because they contain lycopene, which offers protection from prostate cancer, and compounds to help prevent blood clots.

MAJOR NUTRIENTS PER SMALL–MEDIUM TOMATO

18 cal	0.2g	3.9g	1.2g	0.9g	12.7 mg	123 mcg	2,573 mcg	237 mg
CALORIES	TOTAL FAT	CARBS	FIBER	PROTEIN	VITAMIN C	LUTEIN/ ZEAXANTHIN	LYCOPENE	POTASSIUM

Tomatoes are our major source of dietary lycopene, a carotene antioxidant that fights heart disease and may help to prevent prostate cancer. Tomatoes also have an anticoagulant effect, because of the salicylates contained in them, and they contain several other antioxidants, including vitamin C, quercetin, and lutein. Tomatoes are low in calories but high in potassium, and they contain useful amounts of fiber.

- Excellent source of lycopene, which helps prevent prostate cancer.
- One medium tomato contains nearly one-quarter of the day's recommended intake of vitamin C for an adult.
- Rich in potassium to help regulate body fluids.
- Quercetin and lutein content helps prevent cataracts and keep eyes and heart healthy.
- Contain salicylates, which have an anticoagulant effect.

DID YOU KNOW?

Lycopene is actually more active in processed tomato products, such as ketchup, tomato paste, and tomato juice, than it is in the raw tomato.

PRACTICAL TIPS

The riper and redder the tomato, the higher its lycopene content. Vine-ripened tomatoes also contain more lycopene than those ripened after picking. The tomato skin is richer in nutrients than the flesh and the central seed part is high in salicylates, so avoid peeling and don't seed unless necessary. The lycopene in tomatoes is better absorbed in your body if it is eaten with something that contains oil, such as a salad dressing.

SLOW-COOKED TOMATO PASTA SAUCE

This is the traditional Italian tomato-base pasta sauce. The flavors deepen during the slow simmering, so resist the temptation to rush this stage.

MAKES 3 CUPS • PREP TIME: 20 MINS • COOK TIME: 1 HOUR 40 MINS

PER 3 CUPS:	805 cal CALORIES	53.3g FAT	7.3g SAT FAT	79.2g CARBS	49.3g SUGAR	20.6g FIBER	15.7g PROTEIN	80mg SODIUM

INGREDIENTS

¼ cup olive oil
1 onion, chopped
5 garlic cloves, finely sliced
2 tablespoons coarsely chopped fresh flat-leaf parsley
2 tablespoons coarsely chopped fresh basil
13 tomatoes (about 3¼ pounds), coarsely chopped
1 teaspoon packed brown sugar
1 tablespoon red wine vinegar
salt and pepper (optional)

1. Heat the oil in a heavy saucepan over medium heat. Add the onion and sauté gently until soft and almost golden. Add the garlic and herbs and sauté for 30 seconds before carefully pouring in the chopped tomatoes, including the seeds and skin.

2. Stir in the sugar and vinegar. Season with salt and pepper, if using, then reduce the heat to medium–low and simmer the sauce, uncovered, for 1½ hours, or until the tomatoes have broken down and the sauce has thickened. Stir occasionally to prevent anything from catching on the bottom of the pan.

3. Let cool slightly and serve mixed into pasta or spaghetti, or as required.

ARTICHOKES

Globe artichokes are low in calories and ideal for dieters, and their
cynarin content helps maintain liver health.

MAJOR NUTRIENTS PER AVERAGE-SIZE ARTICHOKE

60 cal	TRACE	13.4g	6.5g	4.2g	12 mg	54 mg	65 mcg	1.5 mg	557 mcg	425 mg	72 mg
CALORIES	TOTAL FAT	CARBS	FIBER	PROTEIN	VITAMIN C	CALCIUM	FOLATE	IRON	LUTEIN/ ZEAXANTHIN	POTASSIUM	MAGNESIUM

A delicious delicacy, globe artichokes are the unopened flowers of a large perennial plant. The whole vegetable can be served as an appetizer, but only the tender leaf bases and more nutritious central heart are edible. Artichokes are one of the richest vegetable sources of a range of minerals, including calcium, iron, magnesium, and potassium. They are high in fiber, and contain cynarin, which is said to boost liver function.

- Rich source of minerals, including calcium, iron, and the antioxidant mineral magnesium for bone and heart health.
- High in fiber, with a high proportion of soluble fiber for healthy blood cholesterol.
- Good source of vitamin C and folate.
- Low in calories and low on the glycemic index.

DID YOU KNOW?

Iron, copper, and aluminum cookware will cause artichokes to oxidize and discolor, so use stainless steel, glass, or enamel.

PRACTICAL TIPS

Small baby artichokes can be eaten whole but, when using larger ones, snap off the stem, cut off the top third of the artichoke, and remove the tough outer leaves individually by hand. Simmer in boiling water containing a little lemon juice for 20 minutes, or until the leaves are easy to remove. Eat only the creamy bases of each leaf. Once the leaves are removed, the bristly choke should be pulled out to reveal the tender heart, which is delicious served hot with a dressing, cold in a salad, or with pasta.

AVOCADO, ARTICHOKE & ALMOND SALAD

This beautiful salad is full of healthy ingredients, giving you loads of heart-friendly monounsaturated fats and a huge boost of fiber.

SERVES 4 • PREP TIME: 15 MINS • COOK TIME: NONE

PER SERVING:

| 364 cal CALORIES | 24g FAT | 3g SAT FAT | 31g CARBS | 4.1g SUGAR | 13.4g FIBER | 9g PROTEIN | 560mg SODIUM |

INGREDIENTS

1 red mini romaine lettuce, tough outer leaves discarded

6 canned artichoke hearts in water, drained and patted dry

1 small yellow bell pepper, seeded and thinly sliced

2 ripe avocados, peeled, pitted, and sliced

2 cups mache

⅓ cup slivered almonds

4 radishes, finely chopped

8 dark rye crispbreads, to serve

DRESSING

3 tablespoons balsamic vinegar

1 tablespoon olive oil

½ teaspoon salt

pepper (optional)

1. Cut ⅝ inch from the bottom of the romaine lettuce. Peel off the outer leaves and reserve. Cut the heart lengthwise into eight pieces and arrange on a serving platter with the reserved leaves.

2. Halve the artichoke hearts and add to the serving platter with the yellow bell pepper and avocados.

3. Sprinkle with the mache, slivered almonds, and radishes.

4. To make the dressing, combine the vinegar, oil, salt, and pepper, if using, whisking together thoroughly, then drizzle the dressing over the salad.

5. Serve immediately with the crispbreads.

VARIATION
For a more substantial meal, this salad would go well served with some salmon, chicken, or pork.

CAULIFLOWER

Cauliflower contains the same potent cleansing and rejuvenating sulfur compounds
as the other members of the Brassica, or cabbage family, such as Brussels sprouts.

MAJOR NUTRIENTS PER ⅔ CUP CAULIFLOWER

25 cal	0g	5g	2.5g	2g	0.65 mg	0.22 mg	46 mg	57mg
CALORIES	TOTAL FAT	CARBS	FIBER	PROTEIN	VITAMIN B5	VITAMIN B6	VITAMIN C	FOLATE

One of these compounds, sulforaphane, has been found to help prevent adult-onset diabetes and destroy invading microbes, such as bacteria and viruses. It can also work as an antioxidant through enzymes produced in the liver, helping repair areas of the body that have been damaged. Research has shown that this wonder substance helps prevent cancer and the progression of tumors by stopping cancer cells from spreading and actively killing them off. Another sulfur compound in cauliflower, indole-3-carbinol, appears to lower estrogen, thereby helping to prevent cancers of the breast and prostate as well as regulating female hormones, keeping women youthful post menopause.

- Source of vitamin B6, used to unlock energy from the food we eat, for skin and bone renewal.
- Vitamin C helps the liver remove damaging, aging toxins.
- Vitamin C and vitamin B5 support the adrenal glands and so help us cope with stress, an important factor in staying young.

DID YOU KNOW?

A purple cauliflower variety, called Purple Cape, has recently been developed so that fans of cauliflower can take on beneficial proanthocyanidins, the antioxidants also found in purple baby broccoli.

PRACTICAL TIPS

Serve raw florets with dips or use in a salad. Remove the outer leaves and steam a whole cauliflower for about 10 minutes or separate into florets and steam for about 6 minutes. While cooking, test regularly with a knife to make sure it doesn't overcook. Overcooked cauliflower evokes memories of horrible school meals, but cooked properly it is crunchy and delicious.

BASIL & LEMON
CAULIFLOWER RICE

Raw cauliflower is pulsed in a food processor to resemble rice grains, then
pan-fried with celery and garlic to make this nutritious side dish.

SERVES 4 • PREP TIME: 20–25 MINS • COOK TIME: 15–20 MINS

PER SERVING:

182 cal	14.4g	1.3g	11.4g	3.7g	4.7g	5.7g	40mg
CALORIES	FAT	SAT FAT	CARBS	SUGAR	FIBER	PROTEIN	SODIUM

INGREDIENTS

⅔ cup coarsely chopped unskinned hazelnuts
1 small head of cauliflower
1 tablespoon olive oil
2 celery stalks, coarsely chopped
3 garlic cloves, coarsely chopped
¾ cup coarsely chopped fresh basil
zest and juice of 1 lemon
2 cups chopped watercress
or other peppery greens
salt and pepper (optional)

1. Add the chopped hazelnuts to a large, dry skillet and toast over medium heat until golden. Remove from the pan and set aside.

2. Remove the core from the cauliflower and divide up the florets. Put into a food processor and pulse until the cauliflower resembles rice grains. Put into a bowl and set aside.

3. Add the oil to a skillet over medium heat and sauté the celery and garlic for 5–6 minutes, or until soft.

4. Add the cauliflower rice to the skillet and stir to combine. Cook, stirring occasionally, for 8–10 minutes. Remove from the heat and let cool for a few minutes before adding the basil, lemon zest and juice, hazelnuts, and watercress. Season with salt and pepper, if using, and serve immediately.

HINT
*Cauliflower rice can be used as a substitute for traditional rice
in other recipes—experiment with flavor combinations.*

GARLIC

Valued as a health protector for thousands of years, garlic bulbs are a useful antibiotic, and can also reduce the risk of both heart disease and cancer.

MAJOR NUTRIENTS PER 2 GARLIC CLOVES

9 cal	TRACE	2g	TRACE	0.4g	2mg	11 mg	24 mg	1 mcg
CALORIES	TOTAL FAT	CARBS	FIBER	PROTEIN	VITAMIN C	CALCIUM	POTASSIUM	SELENIUM

Although often used only in small quantities, garlic can still make an impact on health. It is rich in powerful sulfur compounds that cause its strong odor but are the main source of its health benefits. Research has found that garlic can help minimize the risk of both heart disease and many types of cancer. It is also a powerful antibiotic and inhibits fungal infections, such as athlete's foot. It also appears to minimize stomach ulcers. Eaten in reasonable quantity, it is also a good source of vitamin C, selenium, potassium, and calcium. Garlic should be crushed or chopped and left to stand for a few minutes before cooking.

- May prevent formation of blood clots and arterial plaque and help prevent heart disease.
- Regular garlic consumption may significantly reduce the risk of colon, stomach, and prostate cancers.
- Natural antibiotic, antiviral, and antifungal.
- Can help prevent stomach ulcers.

DID YOU KNOW?

Cooking meat at high temperatures, as when broiling or grilling, can have a carcinogenic effect, but when garlic is used with the meat, it reduces the production of the cancer-promoting chemicals.

PRACTICAL TIPS

Choose large, firm undamaged bulbs and store in a container with air holes, in a dark, cool, dry place. Peel the garlic by lightly crushing the clove with the flat side of a cleaver or knife and just lightly cook—long cooking destroys its beneficial compounds.

GARLIC & HERB
BREAD SPIRAL

A delicious alternative to the garlic bread often served as an accompaniment to pizza. The inclusion of parsley will help neutralize any strong odors.

SERVES 6 • PREP TIME: 30 MINS, PLUS RISING • COOK TIME: 20–25 MINS

PER SERVING: 488 cal CALORIES | 20.3g FAT | 8.9g SAT FAT | 60.6g CARBS | 0.9g SUGAR | 2.5g FIBER | 14.8g PROTEIN | 720mg SODIUM

INGREDIENTS

1 tablespoon vegetable oil, for greasing
3⅔ cups white bread flour
2¼ teaspoons active dry yeast
1½ teaspoons salt
1½ cups lukewarm water
2 tablespoons vegetable oil
1 tablespoon white bread flour, for dusting
6 tablespoons butter, melted and cooled
3 garlic cloves, crushed
2 tablespoons chopped fresh parsley
2 tablespoons snipped fresh chives
1 egg, beaten, for glazing
sea salt flakes, for sprinkling (optional)

1. Brush a large baking sheet with oil. Combine the flour, yeast, and salt in a mixing bowl. Stir in the water and half the oil, mixing to a soft, sticky dough.

2. Turn out the dough onto a lightly floured surface and knead until smooth and no longer sticky. Return to the bowl, cover, and let rest in a warm place for about 1 hour, until doubled in size.

3. Meanwhile, preheat the oven to 475°F. Mix the butter, garlic, herbs, and remaining oil together. Roll out the dough to a 13 x 9-inch rectangle and spread the herb mix evenly over the dough to within ½ inch of the edge.

4. Roll up the dough from one long side and place on the prepared baking sheet, with the seam underneath. Cut into 12 thick slices and arrange, cut side down, on the baking sheet, about ¾ inch apart.

5. Cover and let rise in a warm place until doubled in size and springy to the touch. Brush with egg and sprinkle with sea salt flakes, if using. Bake in the preheated oven for 20–25 minutes, until golden brown and firm. Transfer to a wire rack and let cool.

BROCCOLI

Of all the vegetables in the Brassica, or cabbage, family, broccoli has shown the highest levels of protection against prostate cancer.

MAJOR NUTRIENTS PER 1½ CUP BROCCOLI

34 cal	0.4g	6.6g	2.6g	2.8g	89 mg	361 mcg	47 mg	1403 mcg	2.5 mcg
CALORIES	TOTAL FAT	CARBS	FIBER	PROTEIN	VITAMIN C	BETA-CAROTENE	CALCIUM	LUTEIN/ZEAXANTHIN	SELENIUM

Broccoli comes in several varieties but the darker the color, the more beneficial nutrients the vegetable contains. It contains sulforaphane and indoles, which have strong anticancer effects, particularly against breast and colon cancer. Broccoli is also high in flavonoids, which have been linked with a significant reduction in ovarian cancer. The chemicals in broccoli protect against stomach ulcers, stomach and lung cancers, and possibly skin cancer. They also act as a detoxifier, helping lower "bad" blood cholesterol, boosting the immune system, and protecting against cataracts.

- Rich in a variety of nutrients that protect against some cancers.
- Contains chemicals that help to lower "bad" cholesterol and protect against heart disease.
- Lutein and zeaxanthin help prevent macular degeneration.
- Helps eradicate the *Helicobacter pylori* bacteria.
- High calcium content helps build and protect bones.
- Excellent source of the antioxidants vitamin C and selenium.
- Consuming 3–5 servings a week offers protection against cancer.

DID YOU KNOW?

You can eat the leaves of the broccoli as well as the stalks and florets. They contain as much goodness and taste great, too!

PRACTICAL TIPS

Look for heads rich with color and avoid any broccoli with pale yellow or brown patches on the florets. Store in the refrigerator and use within a few days of purchase. Frozen broccoli contains all the nutrients of fresh broccoli. Cook by lightly steaming or stir-frying.

ROASTED BROCCOLI WITH PINE NUTS & PARMESAN

This is a good side dish to serve with any roasted meat or fish, but it would also make a nutritious lunch or light supper dish served with crusty white bread.

SERVES 4 • PREP TIME: 20 MINS • COOK TIME: 25 MINS

PER SERVING:
 340 cal — CALORIES
 28.9g — FAT
 4.2g — SAT FAT
 17.2g — CARBS
 4.1g — SUGAR
 6.2g — FIBER
 8.8g — PROTEIN
760mg — SODIUM

INGREDIENTS

1½ heads of broccoli
⅓ tablespoon olive oil
1 teaspoon sea salt
¼ teaspoon pepper
¼ cup toasted pine nuts
grated zest of ½ lemon
1 ounce Parmesan cheese shavings
4 lemon wedges, to garnish

1. Preheat the oven to 450°F. Cut off the broccoli crowns where they meet the stems. Remove the outer peel from the stems. Slice the stems crosswise into 3¼-inch pieces, then quarter each slice lengthwise. Cut the crown into 1½-inch-wide wedges.

2. Put the broccoli wedges and stems into a bowl. Sprinkle with the oil, salt, and pepper, gently tossing to coat. Spread out in a large roasting pan. Cover tightly with aluminum foil and roast on the bottom rack of the preheated oven for 10 minutes.

3. Remove the foil, then roast for an additional 5–8 minutes, until just starting to brown. Turn the stems and wedges over, and roast for an additional 3–5 minutes, until tender.

4. Transfer to a shallow, warm serving dish, together with any cooking juices. Sprinkle with the pine nuts and lemon zest, tossing to mix. Sprinkle the cheese shavings over the top.

5. Garnish with lemon wedges and serve hot, warm, or at room temperature.

ASPARAGUS

The distinctive asparagus is an anti-inflammatory and contains
a type of fiber that keeps the digestive system healthy.

MAJOR NUTRIENTS PER 10 ASPARAGUS SPEARS

24 cal	TRACE	4.7g	2.5g	2.6g	6.7 mg	1.36 mg	29 mg	62 mcg	2.6 mg	17 mg	242 mg
CALORIES	TOTAL FAT	CARBS	FIBER	PROTEIN	VITAMIN C	VITAMIN E	CALCIUM	FOLATE	IRON	MAGNESIUM	POTASSIUM

The plant chemical glutathione contained in asparagus has been found
to be anti-inflammatory and may help rheumatoid arthritis symptoms.
The vegetable is also rich in the soluble fiber oligosaccharide, which acts
as a prebiotic in the digestive tract by stimulating the growth of "friendly"
bacteria. It is also a valuable source of vitamin C, folate, magnesium,
potassium, and iron. Unusually for a vegetable, it is a good source of vitamin
E, an antioxidant that helps keep the heart and immune system healthy.

- Glutathione content is anti-inflammatory.
- Fiber content acts as a prebiotic for digestive health.
- Good source of a wide range of important vitamins, including
  vitamin E.
- Rich in iron, promotes energy and healing, and helps
  fight infection.

DID YOU KNOW?

*Asparagus contains purines,
compounds that encourage the
production of uric acid in the
body, which can trigger an attack
of gout. People with gout should
avoid asparagus, or only consume
it in moderation.*

PRACTICAL TIPS

Asparagus doesn't store well and should be eaten as soon as possible
after picking. If necessary, store in a plastic bag in the refrigerator for
one to two days. If possible, cook the spears upright so that the delicate
tips don't overcook before the stems are tender. Large spears can also be
brushed with oil and broiled for 2–3 minutes on each side, until tender.
Small, thin asparagus spears can be used in quiches, soups, and risottos.

BROWN RICE RISOTTO PRIMAVERA

Loaded with fresh spring vegetables for vitality, this brown rice
risotto provides a delicious and balanced meat-free meal.

SERVES 4 • PREP TIME: 20–25 MINS • COOK TIME: 45–50 MINS

PER SERVING:

433 cal	16.8g	8.1g	59.6g	5.4g	5g	13.6g	1,480 mg
CALORIES	FAT	SAT FAT	CARBS	SUGAR	FIBER	PROTEIN	SODIUM

INGREDIENTS

5 cups vegetable broth
1 tablespoon olive oil
*1 large leek, thinly sliced, white
and green parts kept separate*
2 garlic cloves, finely chopped
1⅓ cups short-grain brown rice
*15 baby carrots, tops trimmed,
halved lengthwise*
*6 asparagus spears,
woody stems removed*
1 zucchini, cut into cubes
2 tablespoons butter
*¾ cup finely grated
Parmesan cheese*
*2¼ cups mixed baby spinach,
watercress, and arugula*

1. Bring the broth to a boil in a saucepan.

2. Meanwhile, heat the oil in a large skillet over medium heat.
Add the white leek slices and garlic and cook for 3–4 minutes,
or until soft but not brown.

3. Stir the rice into the pan and cook for 1 minute. Pour in half
of the hot broth, bring back to a boil, then cover and simmer
for 15 minutes.

4. Add the carrots and half of the remaining broth and stir
again. Cover and cook for 15 minutes.

5. Add the green leek slices, asparagus, and zucchini to the
rice, then add a little extra broth. Replace the lid and cook for
5–6 minutes, or until the vegetables and rice are just tender.

6. Remove from the heat, stir in the butter and two-thirds of
the cheese, then add a little more broth, if needed. Top with
the mixed greens, cover with the lid, and warm through for
1–2 minutes, or until the greens are just beginning to wilt.

7. Spoon the risotto into shallow bowls, sprinkle with the
remaining cheese, and serve immediately.

LEEKS

As a member of the onion family, leeks have many similar benefits, including an ability to reduce "bad" blood cholesterol and protect against heart disease.

MAJOR NUTRIENTS PER AVERAGE-SIZE LEEK

61 cal	0.3g	14g	1.8g	1.5g	12 mg	0.9 mg
CALORIES	TOTAL FAT	CARBS	FIBER	PROTEIN	VITAMIN C	VITAMIN E

1,000 mcg	59 mg	64 mcg	2.1 mg	1,900 mcg	28 mg	180 mg
BETA-CAROTENE	CALCIUM	FOLATE	IRON	LUTEIN/ZEAXANTHIN	MAGNESIUM	POTASSIUM

Leeks have a distinct, slightly sweet onion flavor but are milder than most onions. The long thick stems have a lower white area and dark green tops, which are edible but usually removed because they can be tough and strong-tasting. Leeks have been shown to reduce total "bad" blood cholesterol while raising "good" cholesterol, so they can help prevent heart and arterial disease. Regular consumption is also linked with a reduction in the risk of prostate, ovarian, and colon cancers. It is the allylic sulfides in the plants that appear to confer the benefits. They are also rich in vitamin C, fiber, vitamin E, folate, and several important minerals.

- Lower total "bad" blood cholesterol and raise "good" cholesterol.
- Anticancer action.
- Mildly diuretic to help prevent fluid retention.
- High in carotenes, including lutein and zeaxanthin, for eye health.

DID YOU KNOW?

In ancient Greece, leeks were prized for their beneficial effects on the throat. The leek is now the national emblem of Wales.

PRACTICAL TIPS

Wash leeks thoroughly before using—they may contain soil between the tight leaves. The more of the green section of the leek that you use, the more of the beneficial nutrients you will retain. Steam, bake, or stir-fry leeks instead of boil, to retain their vitamins. The darker green parts take a little longer to cook than the white part so, if chopped, first add the green parts to the pan.

ROASTED LEEKS WITH PARSLEY

Leeks are given the Mediterranean treatment in this quickly prepared dish. Roasted until slightly charred, they make a tasty accompaniment to fish or roasted lamb.

SERVES 4 • PREP TIME: 10 MINS • COOK TIME: 15–20 MINS

PER SERVING: 181 cal CALORIES | 10.6g FAT | 1.4g SAT FAT | 21.3g CARBS | 5.8g SUGAR | 2.7g FIBER | 2.3g PROTEIN | 40mg SODIUM

INGREDIENTS

4 large leeks, trimmed and halved lengthwise
3 tablespoons extra virgin olive oil
1 tablespoon chopped fresh flat-leaf parsley
sea salt flakes and pepper (optional)

1. Preheat the oven to 475°F. Pack the leeks in a single layer in a shallow casserole dish into which they fit tightly.

2. Brush with the oil, being careful that it goes into the crevices. Sprinkle with the parsley and salt and pepper, if using, turning to coat.

3. Roast in the preheated oven for 15–20 minutes, turning once, until the leeks begin to blacken at the edges.

CARROTS

The richest in carotenes of all plant foods, carrots offer protection from cancers and cardiovascular disease, and they help keep eyes and lungs healthy.

MAJOR NUTRIENTS PER 2 SMALL CARROTS

41 cal	TRACE	9.6g	2.8g	0.9g	6mg	0.7 mg	8,285 mcg	33 mg	256 mcg	320 mg
CALORIES	TOTAL FAT	CARBS	FIBER	PROTEIN	VITAMIN C	VITAMIN E	BETA-CAROTENE	CALCIUM	LUTEIN/ZEAXANTHIN	POTASSIUM

Carrots are one of the most nutritious root vegetables. They are an excellent source of antioxidant compounds and the richest vegetable source of carotenes, which give them their bright orange color. These compounds help protect against cardiovascular disease and cancer. Carotenes may reduce the incidence of heart disease by about 45 percent, promote good vision, and help maintain healthy lungs. They are also rich in fiber, antioxidant vitamins C and E, calcium, and potassium. A chemical in carrots, falcarinol, has been shown to suppress tumors in animals by one-third.

- High carotene content protects against high blood cholesterol and heart disease.
- May offer protection against some cancers and emphysema.
- People who eat at least five carrots a week are nearly two-thirds less likely to have a stroke than those who don't.
- Carrots help to protect sight and night vision.
- Carrots contain a good range of vitamins, minerals, and fiber.

DID YOU KNOW?

A high intake of carrots can cause the skin to appear orange. Called carotanemia, it is a harmless condition.

PRACTICAL TIPS

The darker orange the carrot, the more carotenes it will contain. Remove any green on the stem end of the carrot before cooking, because it can be mildly toxic. The nutrients in carrots are more available to the body when a carrot is cooked instead of raw, and adding a little oil during cooking helps the carotenes to be absorbed.

CARROT CAKE MUFFINS

These delicious carrot, raisin, and walnut muffins are surprisingly low in sugar
and fat, and are packed with fiber and vitamin A-rich carrots.

MAKES 10 • PREP TIME: 20–25 MINS • COOK TIME: 25 MINS

PER MUFFIN:

 318 cal CALORIES
 12.5g FAT
 4.2g SAT FAT
 47g CARBS
 9g SUGAR
 7.9g FIBER
 9g PROTEIN
40mg SODIUM

INGREDIENTS

3¾ cups whole-wheat flour
1 teaspoon baking soda
1 teaspoon baking powder
½ teaspoon salt
1 teaspoon ground cinnamon
¼ teaspoon ground ginger
2 tablespoons canola oil
1 egg
2 egg whites
3 tablespoons stevia granules
2 teaspoon vanilla extract
½ cup unsweetened applesauce
⅓ cup unsweetened almond milk
7–8 carrots (1 pound)
½ cup raisins
½ cup chopped walnuts
¾ cup dry unsweetened coconut

1. Preheat the oven to 350°F. Line ten cups in a 12-cup muffin pan with paper liners.

2. Sift together the flour, baking soda, baking powder, salt, cinnamon, and ginger into a bowl, adding in any bran left in the sifter.

3. Beat together the oil, egg, egg whites, stevia granules, and vanilla extract in a bowl until creamy, then stir in the applesauce and almond milk.

4. Peel and shred the carrots, then add to the liquid ingredients with the raisins, walnuts, and half the coconut. Add the flour mixture, stirring until just combined.

5. Divide the batter among the paper liners. Bake in the preheated oven for 25 minutes, or until a toothpick inserted into the center of a muffin comes out clean.

6. Let cool in the pan until cool enough to handle, then transfer to a wire rack and let cool completely. Decorate with the remaining coconut or wrap in plastic bags and freeze for up to 1 month.

BEAN SPROUTS

Bean sprouts are a low-calorie source of many nutrients,
including vitamin C, protein, calcium, and folate.

MAJOR NUTRIENTS PER 1 CUP RAW BEAN SPROUTS

30 cal	TRACE	6g	1.8g	3g	13 mg	13 mg	61 mcg	0.9 mg	21 mg	149 mg
CALORIES	TOTAL FAT	CARBS	FIBER	PROTEIN	VITAMIN C	CALCIUM	FOLATE	IRON	MAGNESIUM	POTASSIUM

While you can sprout many types of bean, many of the seed sprouts available in the stores are from the mung bean. Other sprouts you may find include alfalfa, azuki, lentil, and pea. Bean sprouts are a low-calorie source of nutrients and, thus, are useful for dieters. Dried beans contain no vitamin C, but once they are sprouted using water, they contain good levels of the vitamin. Bean sprouts are also a good source of protein and calcium, and are rich in folate, the vitamin important for healthy blood and essential for a healthy fetus in pregnant women.

- Low in calories and a rich source of low-fat protein.
- Good source of vitamin C.
- Especially good source of folate.
- Good source of several minerals, including iron, magnesium, calcium, and potassium.

DID YOU KNOW?

Raw sprouts, especially alfalfa sprouts and mung bean sprouts, have a higher than average risk of being contaminated with E. coli or salmonella bacteria, which can cause food poisoning. Be sure to wash all sprouts thoroughly before consuming.

PRACTICAL TIPS

Most beans can be easily sprouted by putting a layer on damp paper towels in a dark place for several days and watering daily. You can also purchase dedicated sprouters. Bean sprouts quickly lose their vitamin C after sprouting, so eat them as soon as possible. They can be used raw in salads and spring rolls, stir-fried or lightly steamed, or used as a garnish.

CHICKEN CHOW MEIN

Bean sprouts add delicious crunch and valuable nutrients to many standard Chinese dishes. They lend themselves especially well to quick cooking, as in stir-fries such this one.

SERVES 4 • PREP TIME: 20 MINS • COOK TIME: 15 MINS

PER SERVING:

485 cal	15.8g	2.6g	52.3g	4.8g	4.4g	33.4g	720mg
CALORIES	FAT	SAT FAT	CARBS	SUGAR	FIBER	PROTEIN	SODIUM

INGREDIENTS

9 ounces dried medium Chinese egg noodles
2 tablespoons sunflower oil
2 cups shredded, cooked chicken breasts
1 garlic clove, finely chopped
1 red bell pepper, thinly sliced
½ ounce shiitake mushrooms, sliced
6 scallions, sliced
1 cup bean sprouts
3 tablespoons soy sauce
1 tablespoon sesame oil

1. Put the noodles into a large bowl or dish and break them up slightly. Pour over enough boiling water to cover and set aside while preparing the other ingredients.

2. Heat the sunflower oil in a preheated wok or skillet over medium heat. Add the chicken, garlic, red bell pepper, mushrooms, scallions, and bean sprouts and stir-fry for about 5 minutes.

3. Drain the noodles thoroughly, then add them to the wok, toss well, and stir-fry for an additional 5 minutes. Drizzle with the soy sauce and sesame oil and toss until thoroughly combined. Transfer to warm serving bowls and serve immediately.

PEAS

Either freshly picked or bought frozen, peas are a rich source of vitamin C, fiber, and protein, with a high proportion of lutein for eye health.

MAJOR NUTRIENTS PER ⅔ CUP SHELLED PEAS

81 cal	0.4g	14.5g	5.1g	5.4g	40 mg	2.1 mg
CALORIES	TOTAL FAT	CARBS	FIBER	PROTEIN	VITAMIN C	VITAMIN B3

56 mg	65 mcg	1.5 mg	2,477 mcg	33 mg	244 mg	1.2 mg
CALCIUM	FOLATE	IRON	LUTEIN/ ZEAXANTHIN	MAGNESIUM	POTASSIUM	ZINC

Peas are rich in a wide range of useful vitamins and minerals. They are particularly high in antioxidant vitamin C, folate, and vitamin B3, and their high lutein and zeaxanthin content means that they help protect the eyes from macular degeneration. The B vitamins they contain may also help protect the bones from osteoporosis, and they help to decrease the risk of strokes by keeping levels of the amino acid homocysteine low in the blood. Peas, high in protein, are especially useful for vegetarians. In addition, their high fiber content partly comprises pectin, a gelatin-like substance that helps to lower "bad" blood cholesterol and may also help prevent heart and arterial disease.

- Contain several heart-friendly nutrients and chemicals.
- Rich in carotenes to protect eyes and reduce risk of cancers.
- High in total and soluble fiber to lower cholesterol.
- Rich in vitamin C.

DID YOU KNOW?

Frozen peas—usually frozen within hours of harvesting—can often contain more vitamin C and other nutrients than fresh peas in their pods, which may be several days old.

PRACTICAL TIPS

When buying peas in the pod, choose those that aren't packed in too tightly. Older peas become almost square, lose their flavor, and become mealy, because the sugars have been converted to starches. Young pods can be eaten with the peas inside and young peas can be eaten raw. To cook, steam lightly or boil in minimal water, because the vitamin C content diminishes in water.

PESTO SALMON WITH SPRING VEG

Spring vegetables are so tasty they don't need much doing to them, just gentle steaming and a little lemon dressing. The dressing cuts through the richness of the pesto salmon perfectly.

SERVES 4 • PREP TIME: 15 MINS • COOK TIME: 10–12 MINS

PER SERVING:

 646 cal CALORIES
 42.9g FAT
 7.6g SAT FAT
 21.9g CARBS
 7.7g SUGAR
 9.7g FIBER
 42g PROTEIN
280mg SODIUM

INGREDIENTS

1⅓ cups fresh or frozen peas
1⅓ cups fresh fava beans
12 asparagus spears, woody stems discarded
20 baby carrots, scrubbed
4 skinless salmon fillets, each weighing about 5½ ounces
¼ cup prepared pesto
3 tablespoons extra virgin olive oil
grated zest and juice of 1 lemon
2 tablespoons sunflower seeds, toasted
2 tablespoons pumpkin seeds, toasted
2 tablespoons shredded fresh basil

1. Put all the vegetables into a steamer and steam them for 10–12 minutes, until tender.

2. Meanwhile, preheat the broiler to hot and line a baking sheet with aluminum foil. Put the salmon onto the prepared baking sheet and spoon the pesto over them. Cook under the broiler for 3–4 minutes on each side.

3. Mix the oil with the lemon zest and juice and toss with the cooked vegetables.

4. Divide the vegetables among four warm shallow bowls and top each one with a salmon fillet.

5. Sprinkle with the sunflower seeds, pumpkin seeds, and shredded basil and serve.

HINT

Use really young fava beans. You won't have to skin them, which will save you a lot of time, and they taste delicious.

SPINACH

Contrary to popular belief, spinach doesn't contain as much iron as originally thought but, nevertheless, it has many excellent health benefits.

MAJOR NUTRIENTS PER 3½ CUPS SPINACH

23 cal	0.4g	3.6g	2.2g	2.9g	28 mg	194 mcg	2 mg
CALORIES	TOTAL FAT	CARBS	FIBER	PROTEIN	VITAMIN C	FOLATE	VITAMIN E

482 mcg	5,626 mcg	99 mg	2.7 mg	12,198 mcg	79 mg	558 mg
VITAMIN K	BETA-CAROTENE	CALCIUM	IRON	LUTEIN/ZEAXANTHIN	MAGNESIUM	POTASSIUM

Researchers have found many flavonoid compounds in spinach act as antioxidants and fight against stomach, skin, breast, prostate, and other cancers. Spinach is also extremely high in carotenes, which protect eyesight. It is also particularly rich in vitamin K, which helps to boost bone strength and may help to prevent osteoporosis. In addition, spinach contains peptides, which are aspects of protein that have been shown to lower blood pressure, and its relatively high vitamin E content may help protect the brain from cognitive decline as we age.

- Flavonoid and carotene content protects against many cancers.
- Vitamin C, folate, and carotene content helps maintain artery health and prevent atherosclerosis.
- Helps keep eyes healthy.
- Vitamin K content boosts bone density.

DID YOU KNOW?

Like cheese, chocolate, and wine, spinach contains the chemical tyramine, which increases the release of stimulating brain chemicals. If you don't sleep well, avoid these foods close to bedtime.

PRACTICAL TIPS

Avoid buying spinach with any yellowing leaves. The carotenes in spinach are better absorbed when the leaves are cooked instead of eaten raw, and also if eaten with a little oil. Steaming or stir-frying retains the most antioxidants. To cook, simply wash the leaves and cook in only the water still clinging to the leaves, stirring, if necessary.

SHRIMP WITH SPINACH

The quick cooking of this lightly spiced dish helps retain the important nutrients provided by the spinach. Make sure the spinach leaves are as dry as possible before adding them.

SERVES 4 • PREP TIME: 15 MINS • COOK TIME: 20 MINS

PER SERVING:	410 cal	39.3g	6.6g	6.1g	1.6g	2.7g	10.7g	1,000 mg
	CALORIES	FAT	SAT FAT	CARBS	SUGAR	FIBER	PROTEIN	SODIUM

INGREDIENTS

⅔ cup vegetable oil
½ teaspoon mustard seeds
½ teaspoon onion seeds
2 tomatoes, sliced
6⅓ cups coarsely chopped fresh spinach
1 teaspoon finely chopped fresh ginger
1 garlic clove, crushed
1 teaspoon chili powder
1 teaspoon salt
8 ounces frozen shrimp, thawed and drained

1. Heat the oil in a large skillet. Add the mustard and onion seeds to the pan.

2. Reduce the heat and add the tomatoes, spinach, ginger, garlic, chili powder, and salt and stir-fry for 5–7 minutes.

3. Add the shrimp, stir until well combined, then cover and simmer over low heat for 7–10 minutes.

4. Spoon the mixture into a warm serving dish and serve hot.

LETTUCE

Mildly sedative, lettuce can help promote sleep. It is also a useful low-calorie, high-fiber food for dieters.

MAJOR NUTRIENTS PER 1½ CUPS LETTUCE

14 cal	0.2g	2.6g	1.7g	1g	19 mg	2,787 mcg	26 mg	109 mcg	0.8 mg	1,850 mcg	198 mg
CALORIES	TOTAL FAT	CARBS	FIBER	PROTEIN	VITAMIN C	BETA-CAROTENE	CALCIUM	FOLATE	IRON	LUTEIN/ ZEAXANTHIN	POTASSIUM

There are dozens of different types of lettuce available both in the grocery stores and to buy as seeds for growing your own, but, when choosing them for health reasons, select varieties that are either mid- or deep green or with red tinges. These contain more carotenes and vitamin C than paler lettuce. Romaine lettuce, for example, contains five times as much vitamin C and more beta-carotene than iceberg lettuce. These more colorful heads will contain good amounts of folate, potassium, and iron. Lettuce is high in fiber, low in calories, and low on the glycemic index.

- Nutritious low-calorie food for dieters.
- High in antioxidant vitamin C and carotenes for disease prevention.
- Mildly sedative.
- High in folate for heart and arterial health.

DID YOU KNOW?

In most countries, lettuce is usually eaten raw, but in France it is cooked with peas. In China, it is often used in stir-fries and other cooked dishes.

PRACTICAL TIPS

Using a clean dish towel or a salad spinner, wash nonorganic lettuce well before use, because sometimes it contains high levels of pesticide residues and bacteria. If a whole lettuce is too much for one meal, pick leaves from the outside instead of cutting it in half, because the cut side will turn brown. Eating lettuce with oil increases absorption of carotenes, but add dressing just before serving so that the leaves do not deteriorate.

LETTUCE ELIXIR JUICE

Lettuce, celery, and apple all have a high water content, so they are useful in helping the body to flush out toxins. This cleansing drink also tastes delicious.

SERVES 1 • PREP TIME: 10–15 MINS • COOK TIME: NONE

PER SERVING:

157 cal	1.2g	0.1g	35.8g	23.6g	2.7g	5g	200mg
CALORIES	FAT	SAT FAT	CARBS	SUGAR	FIBER	PROTEIN	SODIUM

INGREDIENTS

2 cups coarsely chopped romaine lettuce
4 celery stalks, coarsely chopped
1 green apple, halved
⅔ cup fresh flat-leaf parsley
1 teaspoon spirulina powder
crushed ice, to serve
1 romaine lettuce leaf, to garnish

1. Feed the lettuce, celery, and apple through a juicer with the parsley.

2. Stir through the spirulina powder until combined.

3. Pour the drink over crushed ice and serve immediately, garnished with the lettuce leaf.

BRUSSELS SPROUTS

Containing many health-giving nutrients, Brussels sprouts
offer high levels of protection against cancers.

MAJOR NUTRIENTS PER 5 BRUSSELS SPROUTS

43 cal	0.3g	9g	3.8g	3.4g	85 mg	450 mcg	42 mg	61 mcg	1,590 mcg	23 mg	1.6 mcg	0.4 mg
CALORIES	TOTAL FAT	CARBS	FIBER	PROTEIN	VITAMIN C	BETA-CAROTENE	CALCIUM	FOLATE	LUTEIN/ZEAXANTHIN	MAGNESIUM	SELENIUM	ZINC

Brussels sprouts are an important winter vegetable, providing high levels of vitamin C and many other immune-boosting nutrients. They are rich in the sulforaphane compound, which is a detoxifier and has been shown to help the body clear itself of potential carcinogens. Brussels sprouts have also been shown to help prevent DNA damage when eaten regularly and may help minimize the spread of breast cancer. They even contain small amounts of beneficial omega-3 fats, zinc, and selenium, a mineral many adults do not eat in the recommended daily amount. People who eat large quantities of Brussels sprouts and other Brassicas (members of the cabbage family), have a lower risk of prostate, colorectal, and lung cancers.

- Rich in indoles and other compounds to protect against cancer; may reduce the spread of cancer.
- Extremely rich in immune-boosting vitamin C.
- Indole content can help lower "bad" blood cholesterol.
- High in fiber for colon health.

DID YOU KNOW?

Brussels sprouts are thought to come from a region in Belgium near Brussels. They were not widely used until the early twentieth century.

PRACTICAL TIPS

Select bright green sprouts with tight heads and no sign of yellow leaves. Lightly steaming or quickly boiling Brussels sprouts is the best way to cook them and preserve their nutrients. Don't overcook, because much of the vitamin C content will be destroyed. Overcooking also alters their flavor and gives them an unwelcome odor.

SPROUT TONIC SMOOTHIE

Brussels sprouts are associated with the cold days of winter, when they are ready for picking, but if available in other seasons, you they make a wonderful green smoothie.

SERVES 1 • PREP TIME: 10–15 MINS • COOK TIME: NO COOK

PER SERVING:	162 cal	2.7g	0g	31.8g	15.2g	5g	4.2g	0.5g
	CALORIES	FAT	SAT FAT	CARBS	SUGAR	FIBER	PROTEIN	SALT

INGREDIENTS
4 Brussels sprouts
¾ cup beet greens
½ cup Swiss chard
1 cup unsweetened rice milk

1. Put the Brussels sprouts, beet greens, and Swiss chard into a blender.

2. Pour the rice milk over the greens and blend until smooth and creamy. Pour into a glass and serve immediately.

HINT
Boost this juice's nutritional power and get your skin glowing by adding 2 teaspoons of acai powder.

GREEN BEANS

Green beans, peas, and dried beans are all legumes, with a high protein content
that is essential for the revitalization of the skin, bones, and muscles.

MAJOR NUTRIENTS PER 1 CUP GREEN BEANS

31 cal	0.1g	7.1g	3.6g	1.8g	16 mg	0.6 mg	0.8 mg	21 mcg	151 mg	0.7 mg	25 mg
CALORIES	TOTAL FAT	CARBS	FIBER	PROTEIN	VITAMIN C	VITAMIN B2	VITAMIN B3	VITAMIN B5	VITAMIN B6	CHOLINE	FOLATE

Plant protein is an important part of any diet, whether you eat animal products or not. We need protein for all structures in the body to do the continual work of rebuilding skin, bone, teeth, hair, and nails. The effects of too little protein are a dull complexion, lank hair, and brittle nails. Whereas animal protein forms acid in the body, protein derived from plants, such as beans, is more alkaline, the optimal state when it comes to detoxification, repair, and regulation of the metabolism. Plant sources also come with good levels of fiber that help clear harmful waste from the body, promote good digestion, and aid full absorption of the wide range of nutrients we need to stay young.

- Vitamin B6 and folate reduce blood levels of homocysteine, a substance that can create the risk of heart disease.
- B vitamins unlock energy from all the food we eat so that it can be used as fuel for all cell repair. Deficiency symptoms include dull skin and hair, poor nail health, cracked lips and acne, as well as fatigue, anxiety, insomnia, and depression.
- Contains choline, which helps move fatty deposits out of the liver and protects us from the harmful and aging effects of alcohol.

DID YOU KNOW?

Green beans are the unripe fruit of any bean plant. There are three main types: snap beans, wax beans, and scarlet runner beans.

PRACTICAL TIPS

Buy beans loose where possible so that you can select those with a smooth feel, bright green color, and a pleasing snap when broken in half.

BEAN SALAD WITH FETA

A little soft feta goes a long way in this salad, adding salty seasoning
to the crunchy beans and radishes and the sweet tomatoes.

SERVES 4 • PREP TIME: 15 MINS • COOK TIME: 10 MINS

PER SERVING:	249 cal	21.2g	5.2g	11.9g	6.3g	3.6g	5.2g	160mg
	CALORIES	FAT	SAT FAT	CARBS	SUGAR	FIBER	PROTEIN	SODIUM

INGREDIENTS

3½ cups green beans
1 red onion, finely chopped
3 tablespoons finely chopped fresh cilantro
2 radishes, thinly sliced
½ crumbled feta cheese
1 teaspoon finely chopped fresh oregano
2 tablespoons red wine vinegar
⅓ cup extra virgin olive oil
2 tomatoes, cut into wedges
pepper (optional)

1. Bring a saucepan of water to a boil. Add the beans, bring back to a boil, then simmer for 5 minutes, or until tender. Drain, rinse with cold water, then drain again. Cut them in half and transfer to a salad bowl. Add the onion, cilantro, radishes, and cheese.

2. Sprinkle the oregano over the salad, then season with pepper, if using.

3. To make the dressing, put the vinegar and oil into a bowl and whisk to combine. Drizzle the dressing over the salad, add the tomatoes, toss gently together, and serve.

PUMPKIN

Pumpkins contain the orange nutrients alpha- and beta-carotene and lutein, powerful anti-aging nutrients that protect you against skin damage from sunlight.

MAJOR NUTRIENTS PER 1 CUP PUMPKIN

| 13 cal CALORIES | 0.1g TOTAL FAT | 6.5g CARBS | 0.5g FIBER | 1g PROTEIN | 9mg VITAMIN C | 1.06 mg VITAMIN E | 0.11 mg VITAMIN B2 | 0.06 mg VITAMIN B6 | 3,100 mcg BETA-CAROTENE | 16 mcg FOLATE |  1,500 mcg LUTEIN/ ZEAXANTHIN | 12 mg PHYTOSTEROLS |

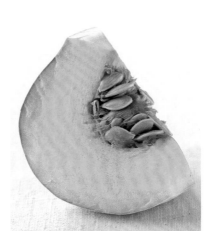

The fat-soluble carotenoids found in pumpkin are needed to protect fatty areas in, for example, the skin, heart, eyes, brain, and liver. As a winter vegetable, pumpkin is well placed to protect us when we need it most. We eat more fat in the winter and lay down more fat stores for insulation and to use as energy during the cold months. The seeds of the pumpkin are especially nutrient-rich, while the flesh contains malic acid—also found in apples and plums—which is needed by every cell in the body for renewal and to make repairs. In combination with the protective carotenoids, it helps keep skin firm, bones strong, and organs youthful.

- Contains phytosterols, needed for immune function and cholesterol regulation.
- Contains vitamin B2 to activate folate, and vitamin B6 to process fats and proteins from food to repair and rejuvenate body tissues and mucous membranes.
- Vitamin E supports fertility and young-looking skin.

DID YOU KNOW?

The name "pumpkin" originally comes from the Greek peponi, meaning "large melon." The French then called it pompon, and the British opted for pumpion, before finally taking the American name.

PRACTICAL TIPS

Like most squash, pumpkin can be boiled, steamed, baked, or roasted, and it can be used to make both sweet and savory dishes. Pumpkin is sometimes oversweetened, especially in some traditional pumpkin pie recipes, which masks its delicate flavor. Experiment with less sugar if using in sweet recipes.

PUMPKIN, FETA & ADZUKI BEAN PACKAGES

Served crisp, golden, and freshly baked from the oven, these fantastic feta, bean, and pumpkin-packed phyllo packages provide a wholesome, meat-free lunch or supper for all the family to enjoy.

MAKES 6 • PREP TIME: 40 MINS • COOK TIME: 45–50 MINS

PER PACKAGE:

 213 cal CALORIES

 13.4g FAT

 7.3g SAT FAT

 18.4g CARBS

 2.6g SUGAR

 1.9g FIBER

 6g PROTEIN

280mg SODIUM

INGREDIENTS

4 cups (¾-inch) pumpkin cubes
4 shallots, quartered
1 teaspoon smoked paprika
1 tablespoon olive oil
1¼ cups drained and rinsed canned adzuki beans
2 tablespoons coarsely chopped fresh parsley
zest of 1 lemon
⅔ cup crumbled feta cheese
3 sheets phyllo pastry, each measuring 16 x 12 inches
3½ tablespoons butter, melted
pepper (optional)
1 tablespoon chopped watercress, to garnish

1. Preheat the oven to 400°F. Put the pumpkin and shallots into a shallow roasting pan in an even layer and sprinkle with the paprika. Drizzle the oil over the vegetables and mix well. Roast in the preheated oven for 20–25 minutes, or until the pumpkin is slightly golden and soft. Do not turn off the oven.

2. Transfer the pumpkin mixture into a large bowl. Using a potato masher, mash until the cubes have broken up. Stir in the beans, parsley, lemon zest, and cheese. Mix until all the ingredients are well combined. Season with pepper, if using.

3. Cut a phyllo sheet in half to create two long lengths of pastry (about 16 x 6 inch) and brush one pastry length all over with melted butter. Keep the remaining pastry covered with a damp dish towel to prevent it from drying out.

4. Spoon one-sixth of the pumpkin mixture onto one end of the pastry length. Fold this edge up to meet one side to start the shape of a triangle. Fold the bottom point of the pastry up, sealing in the filling, then complete the triangle by folding again in the opposite direction. Keep folding until you reach the top and lightly brush with a little more melted butter. Repeat with the other sheets of phyllo until you have six triangles.

5. Place the packages on a baking sheet and cook for 25 minutes, or until golden. Garnish with watercress and serve immediately.

BEETS

This colorful sweet root may not be the richest vegetable in terms of nutrients, but it certainly should not be overlooked and is invaluable during the winter season.

36 cal	TRACE	7.6g	1.9g	1.7g	5mg	20 mg	150 mcg	1.0 mg	23 mg	380 mg
CALORIES	TOTAL FAT	CARBS	FIBER	PROTEIN	VITAMIN C	CALCIUM	FOLATE	IRON	MAGNESIUM	POTASSIUM

Beets come in white and gold varieties as well as the classic purple-red, which is the best source of nutrients. Betaine, which gives it its deep color, is even more potent an antioxidant than polyphenols in its effect on lowering blood pressure. A scientific study also found that the high levels of nitrates in beet juice work like aspirin to prevent blood clots and help to protect the lining of the blood vessels. Red beet is also rich in anthocyanins, which may help to prevent colon and other cancers.

- Contain betaine to lower blood pressure and may be anti-inflammatory.
- Contain nitrates to help prevent blood clots.
- Anthocyanins can help prevent cancers.
- A good source of iron, magnesium, and folate.

DID YOU KNOW?

Beets were originally cultivated for their nutritious leaves, which can still be eaten when young, cooked in the same way as spinach.

PRACTICAL TIPS

Cooked beets will keep in an airtight container for a few days in the refrigerator, or you can puree cooked beets and freeze them. To cook, cut off the leaves, leaving about 2 inches of stem and the root intact. This will prevent the beet from bleeding as it cooks. Beets can be boiled whole for about 50 minutes, or brushed with a little oil and baked in aluminum foil at 400°F for 1 hour. The skins can then be easily rubbed off. Beets can also be used raw, peeled and finely grated into salads or salsa, or juiced.

BEET
BROWNIE BITES

The addition of beets to these brownies not only adds depth of color and
texture, but reduces the guilt associated with a luscious sweet treat.

MAKES 36 PIECES • PREP TIME: 25 MINS • COOK TIME: 30–35 MINS

PER BITE:	75 cal	4g	1.5g	10g	7g	0.5g	1.5g	TRACE
	CALORIES	FAT	SAT FAT	CARBS	SUGAR	FIBER	PROTEIN	SODIUM

INGREDIENTS

1 tablespoon sunflower oil, for oiling
5½ ounces semisweet chocolate,
broken into small pieces
2 eggs
1 teaspoon vanilla extract
⅔ cup firmly packed dark brown sugar
⅓ cup sunflower oil
4½ cooked beets, grated
¾ cup all-purpose flour
¾ teaspoon baking powder
3 tablespoons unsweetened cocoa powder

1. Preheat the oven to 350°F. Lightly oil an 8-inch square baking
pan and line with parchment paper.

2. Place the chocolate in a heatproof bowl set over a saucepan
of gently simmering water and heat until just melted. Remove
from the heat.

3. Put the eggs, vanilla extract, and sugar into a bowl and whisk
at high speed for 3–4 minutes, or until pale and frothy. Beat in
the oil. Stir in the beets, then sift in the flour, baking powder,
and cocoa and fold in. Add the melted chocolate and stir evenly.

4. Spoon the batter into the prepared pan and bake in the
preheated oven for 25–30 minutes, or until just firm to the touch.
Let cool in the pan, then turn out onto a wire rack and let cool
completely.

5. Cut into about 36 bite-size squares and serve.

HINT
*This makes 36 bite-size squares, but you can, of course, cut them
into slightly larger squares and serve with ice cream for dessert.*

FENNEL

Fennel bulbs are rich in a variety of antioxidants,
which can reduce inflammation and help prevent cancer.

MAJOR NUTRIENTS PER HALF FENNEL BULB

12 cal	TRACE	1.8g	2.4g	0.9g	5mg	140 mg	24 mg	42 mcg	440 mg	0.7 mcg
CALORIES	TOTAL FAT	CARBS	FIBER	PROTEIN	VITAMIN C	BETA-CAROTENE	CALCIUM	FOLATE	POTASSIUM	SELENIUM

Fennel is grown for its thick, crunchy bulbous base. It is refreshing, slightly sweet, and has a strong licorice flavor. Fennel contains a potent combination of plant chemicals, which give it strong antioxidant activity. One of the most interesting compounds in fennel is anethole. In animal studies, the anethole in fennel has been shown to reduce inflammation and help prevent the occurrence of cancer. It is also a good source of fiber, folate, and potassium, and contains a wide range of other nutrients, including vitamin C, selenium, niacin (vitamin B3), and iron. The high potassium content means that fennel is a diuretic, helping to eliminate surplus fluid from the body.

- Diuretic, digestive aid, and antiflatulent.
- Low in calories, making it an ideal food for dieters.
- Anti-inflammatory.
- Rich in antioxidant compounds for disease prevention.

DID YOU KNOW?

Bulb fennel is closely related to the fennel herb, and the leafy tops of the bulb can be chopped and used in a similar way to the herb.

PRACTICAL TIPS

Choose bulbs that are firm and solid with a slight gloss and healthy looking leaf tops. Store in the refrigerator—fennel bulbs lose their flavor after a few days. Fennel is delicious thinly sliced raw in salads and goes particularly well with fish. Try baking small whole fish in aluminum foil on a bed of thinly sliced fennel. Fennel can also be quartered, browned in oil, then braised with a little vegetable broth. It loses a lot of its licorice flavor when cooked.

FENNEL & APPLE JUICE

This vibrant green juice is packed with fennel, mint, spinach, apple,
and lime. It's a healthy and delicious way to start the day.

SERVES 1 • PREP TIME: 10–15 MINS • COOK TIME: NONE

PER SERVING:

225 cal	1.5g	0.3g	55.9g	29.6g	4.3g	7.4g	200mg
CALORIES	FAT	SAT FAT	CARBS	SUGAR	FIBER	PROTEIN	SODIUM

INGREDIENTS

3½ cups spinach
½ cup fresh mint
1 large fennel bulb, coarsely chopped
1 green apple, halved
*1 lime, zest and pith removed, seeded,
and coarsely chopped*
crushed ice, to serve (optional)

1. Feed the spinach, mint, fennel, apple, and lime through a juicer.

2. Stir well and pour the drink over the crushed ice, if using. Serve immediately.

HINT

*For best results, wash vegetables in cold water to clean—don't
soak or you'll lose nutrients.*

BELL PEPPERS

The bright colors of bell peppers contain high levels of carotenes for heart health and cancer protection, and are also a rich source of vitamin C.

MAJOR NUTRIENTS PER AVERAGE-SIZE BELL PEPPER

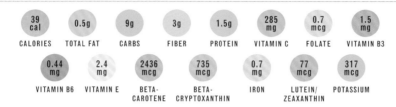

39 cal	0.5g	9g	3g	1.5g	285 mg	0.7 mcg	1.5 mg
CALORIES	TOTAL FAT	CARBS	FIBER	PROTEIN	VITAMIN C	FOLATE	VITAMIN B3

0.44 mg	2.4 mg	2436 mcg	735 mcg	0.7 mg	77 mcg	317 mcg
VITAMIN B6	VITAMIN E	BETA-CAROTENE	BETA-CRYPTOXANTHIN	IRON	LUTEIN/ZEAXANTHIN	POTASSIUM

Bell peppers come in a variety of colors, but red and orange bell peppers contain the highest levels of vitamin B_6 and carotenes. However, all of them are extremely rich in vitamin C, with an average serving providing more than a day's recommended intake. In general, the deeper the color of the bell pepper, the more beneficial plant compounds it contains. These include bioflavonoids to protect against cancer, and phenols, which help block the action of cancer-causing chemicals in the body. Bell peppers also contain plant sterols, which may have an anticancer effect.

- Rich source of a range of vitamins, minerals, and plant chemicals.
- Extremely rich in antioxidant vitamin C and excellent source of antioxidant vitamin E.
- Several components are strongly anticancer.
- High lutein levels protect from macular degeneration.
- Good source of vitamin B_6 for reducing blood homocysteine levels; high levels of this have been linked to increased risk of heart disease, stroke, Alzheimer's disease, and osteoporosis.

DID YOU KNOW?

Bell peppers are native to South America and date back about 5,000 years. They were introduced to Europe in the Middle Ages by Spanish and Portuguese explorers.

PRACTICAL TIPS

The carotenes in bell peppers are made more available to the body if the bell peppers are cooked and eaten with a little oil. Try stir-frying thinly sliced bell peppers or seed and halve the bell peppers, brush with oil, and roast. If using raw in a salad, drizzle with some olive oil to help absorption. Fresh bell peppers can be seeded, sliced, and frozen in plastic bags.

STUFFED BELL PEPPERS WITH CHICKPEAS & BULGUR WHEAT

These tasty low-fat bell peppers, stuffed with fiber-rich chickpeas and bulgur wheat, are simple to cook yet good enough to cook for a special occasion.

SERVES 4 • PREP TIME: 10 MINS, PLUS SOAKING • COOK TIME: 35 MINS

PER SERVING:

291 cal	9.5g	2.9g	41.2g	13.7g	8.2g	11g	640mg
CALORIES	FAT	SAT FAT	CARBS	SUGAR	FIBER	PROTEIN	SODIUM

INGREDIENTS

12 sprays cooking oil spray
2 large red bell peppers
2 large yellow bell peppers
1 vegetable bouillon cube
¾ cup boiling water
⅔ cup bulgur wheat
¾ cup drained and rinsed, canned chickpeas
⅓ cup slivered almonds, toasted
¼ cup raisins
4 large sun-dried tomatoes, chopped
4 scallions, finely chopped
½ teaspoon smoked paprika
3 tablespoons chopped fresh basil
⅓ cup finely crumbled feta cheese

1. Preheat the oven to 375°F. Spray a baking sheet with 4 sprays of the cooking oil spray. Halve the red bell peppers and yellow bell peppers from stem to the bottom, discarding the cores and seeds but leaving the stems in place. Place, cut side down, on the prepared sheet and roast in the preheated oven for 20 minutes.

2. Meanwhile, prepare the bulgur wheat. Dissolve the broth cube in a boiling water in a heatproof bowl and stir in the bulgur wheat. Set aside for 15 minutes, then fluff up with a fork.

3. Add the chickpeas, almonds, raisins, tomatoes, scallions, paprika, and basil to the bulgur wheat and stir well to combine.

4. Remove the bell peppers from the oven and stuff with the bulgur wheat mixture. Sprinkle a little cheese over the top of each stuffed bell pepper and spray with the remaining cooking oil spray. Roast for an additional 15 minutes, or until the tops are light golden and the bell peppers are tender when pierced with a sharp knife. Serve immediately.

HINT

These make a great appetizer or can be served as a side for any kind of broiled meat or fish.

SEAWEED

Rich in iodine for healthy thyroid action, zinc for fertility, and calcium for healthy bones, seaweed is highly nutritious.

MAJOR NUTRIENTS PER 1¾ OUNCES KELP

22 cal	0.3g	4.8g	0.7g	0.8g	84 mg	90 mcg	1,037 mcg	1.4 mg	61 mg	45 mg	0.06 mg
CALORIES	TOTAL FAT	CARBS	FIBER	PROTEIN	CALCIUM	FOLATE	IODINE	IRON	MAGNESIUM	POTASSIUM	ZINC

While there are thousands of different varieties of seaweed, only a few are widely available or commonly used as a vegetable. Often found dried, the best known are flat, dark green kelp (also known as kombu), dark red dulse, green or purple nori, and dark green or brown wakame. The nutritional value of the types varies, but they are usually rich in iron, calcium, zinc, magnesium, and iodine, a mineral that can help to boost the action of the thyroid gland, regulate the body's metabolism, and aid hearing. Seaweed is also rich in folate and low in calories.

- Rich in easily absorbed minerals and ideal for vegetarians.
- Good food for dieters, because seaweed is low in calories and has a gel-like substance called agar, which helps you feel full for longer.
- May be antiviral and anticancer.
- Excellent source of iodine to help the body's metabolism.

DID YOU KNOW?

Most types of seaweed are high in sodium (the sea is salty) and are, therefore, not suitable for anyone on a low-sodium diet.

PRACTICAL TIPS

Fresh seaweed for consumption should be sourced from unpolluted waters. It can be chopped and used in soups or stir-fried as a garnish. Laver, a type of seaweed, is used in parts of the United Kingdom to make a flat bread that is pan-fried. Dried seaweed can be reconstituted according to the package directions and used in a similar way. Large sheets of nori are used to wrap sushi.

SUSHI ROLL BOWL

Sushi is healthy: The omega-3 fats in the fish are linked to heart protection and improved circulation; rice provides energy; and wasabi aids cancer prevention.

SERVES 4 • PREP TIME: 15 MINS, PLUS COOLING • COOK TIME: 10 MINS

PER SERVING: **572 cal** CALORIES **17.7g** FAT **3.1g** SAT FAT **70.1g** CARBS **2.2g** SUGAR **7.6g** FIBER **32g** PROTEIN **960mg** SODIUM

INGREDIENTS

1⅔ cup glutinous rice
2 tablespoons rice vinegar
1 teaspoon sugar
1 large avocado, peeled, pitted, and sliced
7 ounces raw tuna, sliced
7 ounces raw salmon, sliced
juice of ½ lemon
4 sheets nori seaweed, shredded
¼ cucumber, cut into matchsticks
2 tablespoons snipped fresh chives
1 tablespoon black sesame seeds
¼ cup soy sauce, to serve

1. Cook the rice according to the package directions. When all the water has been absorbed and the rice is cooked, stir through the vinegar and sugar, then cover and let cool.

2. Divide the rice among four bowls.

3. Top each bowl with slices of avocado, tuna, and salmon.

4. Squeeze the lemon juice over the top, then add the nori, cucumber, chives, and sesame seeds.

5. Serve with the soy sauce.

CUCUMBER

Cucumber is related to squash and has long been used for its cooling effects, inside and outside the body, reducing inflammation and speeding repair for young-looking skin.

MAJOR NUTRIENTS PER ⅓ CUCUMBER, WITH PEEL

16 cal	0.11g	3.63g	0.5g	0.65g	2.8 mg	0.26 mg	13 mg	TRACE	147 mg	TRACE
CALORIES	TOTAL FAT	CARBS	FIBER	PROTEIN	VITAMIN C	VITAMIN B5	MAGNESIUM	MOLYBDENUM	POTASSIUM	SILICA

As well as drinking fluids directly, we need to receive water from the plant foods we eat. The high water content of cucumber makes it a hydrating food that prevents dryness and wrinkling of the skin, as well as helping to remove the toxins that can age us. Cucumber is a recommended food in the DASH (Dietary Approaches to Stop Hypertension) diet, because it is rich in potassium, magnesium, and fiber, so it works naturally to reduce high blood pressure by balancing the fluid in the body. The vitamin C and caffeic acid in cucumbers also help rid the body of excess fluid, because they both help prevent water retention.

- Source of silica, a trace mineral needed for a healthy complexion.
- Cucumber juice is known to alleviate the symptoms of rheumatic conditions and keep joints healthy and young.
- Contains the trace mineral molybdenum, which is needed to keep bones and teeth strong and healthy.

DID YOU KNOW?

The saying "cool as a cucumber" comes from the fact that the inside of a cucumber can be 20°F cooler than the outside air.

PRACTICAL TIPS

Cucumber combines well with other vegetables and fruits. Include its skin in juices and salads for maximum nutrition. The juice can be applied directly to cuts, burns, and skin conditions to bring immediate cooling relief, or you can puree the whole vegetable in a blender for use as a rejuvenating poultice or face mask, along with avocado, if you have some. Cucumber slices placed on the eyes will reduce puffiness and signs of tiredness.

CUCUMBER SOOTHER JUICE

This light, fresh-tasting juice made with the addition of soothing aloe vera gel can help to reduce digestive problems, such as heartburn.

SERVES 1 • PREP TIME: 10 MINS • COOK TIME: NONE

PER SERVING:

259 cal	0.8g	TRACE	67.9g	43.1g	3.2g	2.2g	TRACE
CALORIES	FAT	SAT FAT	CARBS	SUGAR	FIBER	PROTEIN	SODIUM

INGREDIENTS

1 large pear, halved
⅓ cup coarsely chopped cucumber
1 green apple, halved
¼ cup fresh mint
1 tablespoon aloe vera gel
crushed ice, to serve (optional)
1 cucumber slice, to garnish
1 fresh mint sprig, to garnish

1. Feed the pear, cucumber, apple, and mint through a juicer.

2. Stir through the aloe vera gel until combined. Pour the crushed ice, if using, into a glass, then pour in the juice.

3. Serve immediately, garnished with a cucumber slice and a sprig of mint.

BOK CHOY

This is a cruciferous vegetable in the same Brassica (cabbage) family as cabbage, broccoli, kale, and Brussels sprouts, and it offers the same protective and rejuvenating properties.

MAJOR NUTRIENTS PER 1½ CUPS BOK CHOY

13 cal CALORIES	0.2g TOTAL FAT	2.2g CARBS	1g FIBER	1.5g PROTEIN	4,468 IU VITAMIN A	45 mg VITAMIN C	2,681 mcg BETA-CAROTENE	105 mg CALCIUM	66 mcg FOLATE	19 mg MAGNESIUM

The anticancer properties of cruciferous vegetables are well documented. Research in Singapore found that these vegetables, including bok choy, reduce the risk of lung cancer in nonsmokers by 30 percent and in smokers by an astonishing 69 percent. Bok choy also enhances and balances all aspects of liver detoxification, a remedy against the ravaging effects of stress, pollution, and the aging factors in our modern environment. Bok choy contains a higher amount of vitamin A than other cabbages and so particularly protects the liver from aging damage from sugar, alcohol, and medications, because it is stored in high amounts in this organ.

- High calcium content keeps bones, teeth, and joints healthy and prevents osteoporosis; also supports heart health and optimum brain function.
- Contains beta-carotene that can be converted to vitamin A and used to fight toxins that cause premature aging.
- Vitamin C enables all other antioxidants to work effectively and so protect and repair the skin, bones, brain, and heart to keep you looking and feeling young.

DID YOU KNOW?

Bok choy literally means "white vegetable" in Chinese. The variety that is used today is similar to one cultivated in the fourteenth century.

PRACTICAL TIPS

Typically used in stir-fries and soups, such as miso, bok choy is quicker to cook and lighter than other cabbages, and it tastes particularly good when it retains its crunchiness. Darker varieties may need longer to cook than the smaller, light ones.

BOK CHOY WITH RED ONIONS & CASHEW NUTS

Bok choy is an ideal vegetable for stir-frying, which retains its characteristic crunchiness.
Given further crunch with roasted cashew nuts, this colorful dish is a delicious treat.

SERVES 4 • PREP TIME: 20 MINS • COOK TIME: 20 MINS

PER SERVING:

263 cal	18.6g	3.5g	21.8g	9.6g	3.2g	6g	80mg
CALORIES	FAT	SAT FAT	CARBS	SUGAR	FIBER	PROTEIN	SODIUM

INGREDIENTS

2 tablespoons peanut oil
2 red onions, cut into thin wedges
2 cups thinly shredded red cabbage
¼ head of bok choy, separated into leaves
2 tablespoons plum sauce
¾ cup roasted cashew nuts, to garnish

1. Heat the oil in a large preheated wok or skillet until hot. Add the onion wedges to the wok and stir-fry for about 5 minutes, or until the onions are just beginning to brown.

2. Add the cabbage and stir-fry for an additional 5 minutes.

3. Add the bok choy leaves and stir-fry for 2–3 minutes, or until the leaves have just wilted. Drizzle the plum sauce over the vegetables, toss together until well mixed, and heat until the liquid is simmering.

4. Garnish with the roasted cashew nuts and transfer to warm serving bowls. Serve immediately.

SAUERKRAUT

Sauerkraut is finely shredded cabbage that has been fermented by health-giving bacteria.
It has a long history as a highly nutritious, anti-aging food.

MAJOR NUTRIENTS PER ½ CUP SAUERKRAUT (INCLUDING LIQUID)

19 cal	0.14g	4.3g	2.9g	0.9g	15 mg	0.13 mg	1.5 mg
CALORIES	TOTAL FAT	CARBS	FIBER	PROTEIN	VITAMIN C	VITAMIN B6	IRON

Sauerkraut is among many traditional fermented foods associated with a youthful digestive system. This is due to the support these foods give to the 2¼–3¼ pounds of probiotic bacteria covering the lining of our digestive tract and other mucous membranes, such as in the throat. These are our first line of immune defense against bacteria, yeasts, and viruses. They effectively regulate the intestinal environment, taking care of any diarrhea or constipation problems, and can prevent inflammatory conditions and intolerances by ensuring the immune response reacts only to genuine threats and does not overreact to harmless agents such as food.

- Contains a high amount of glutamine, the amino acid found in muscle that is crucial for youthful movement and strength.
- Includes all the health benefits of the cruciferous cabbage it is made from. Like broccoli and Brussels sprouts, it contains revitalizing and detoxifying sulfur chemicals.
- Sauerkraut juice helps respiration. A good intake of oxygen to replenish body cells is a crucial factor in staying young.

DID YOU KNOW?

Before the Royal Navy made the change to limes, Captain James Cook took sauerkraut on his sea voyages as a vitamin C-rich preventative to scurvy. The lactic acid bacteria in sauerkraut gives it its distinctive taste.

PRACTICAL TIPS

The lactic acid in sauerkraut can be mildly upsetting for people who are not used to it, but starting with small amounts and building up can help address the bacterial digestive imbalance that is the reason for this. Its sourness is then a welcome complement to meat, cheese, and salads.

LAYERED PORK & SPICED SAUERKRAUT SOUP

This delicious soup is a great way to introduce valuable probiotics to your diet, helping to boost your immune system, keep your digestive tract healthy, and contribute to a feeling of good well-being.

SERVES 4 • PREP TIME: 20 MINS • COOK TIME: 1 HOUR

PER SERVING:

207 cal	6.6g	1.7g	20.6g	10.1g	5.8g	18.9g	1,160 mg
CALORIES	FAT	SAT FAT	CARBS	SUGAR	FIBER	PROTEIN	SODIUM

INGREDIENTS

1 tablespoon olive oil
12 ounces pork tenderloin, thinly sliced
1 onion, chopped
2 garlic cloves, finely chopped
3¾ cups chicken broth
1 teaspoon fennel seeds
1 teaspoon English mustard
10 Brussels sprouts, thinly sliced
1 teaspoon caraway seeds
2 carrots, shredded
1 sweet, crisp apple, cored and coarsely grated
¾ cup drained sauerkraut
½ cup drained and diced pickles
2 tablespoons chopped fresh dill
salt and pepper (optional)

1. Heat the oil in a saucepan, add the pork, and cook, stirring, for 5 minutes, until brown all over. Add the onion and sauté for 5 minutes, until lightly browned.

2. Mix in the garlic and broth, then add the fennel seeds and mustard. Bring to a boil, cover, and simmer for 30 minutes.

3. When the pork is almost cooked, mix the Brussel sprouts with the caraway seeds and steam for 5 minutes, until just tender.

4. Divide half the pork mixture among four large, heatproof glasses, arranging it on the bottom. Mix the carrot and apple and spoon into the glasses, then top with the sprouts, followed by the remaining pork. Mix the sauerkraut with the pickles and the chopped dill, then spoon the mixture into the glasses.

5. Season the hot broth with salt and pepper, if using, then pour it into the glasses until all the vegetables are just covered. Serve immediately.

HINT

Choose a chicken broth that is low in sodium and not too highly flavored or it will dominate the other flavors in the soup.

PURPLE BABY BROCCOLI

Purple baby broccoli (also known as broccolini or sprouting broccoli), has the same health benefits as its stockier cousin, but has the added bonus of antioxidant proanthocyanidins.

MAJOR NUTRIENTS PER 8 PURPLE BABY BROCCOLI STALKS

3 cal	0.37g	6.64g	2.6g	2.82g	89.2 mg	0.57 mg	361 mcg	47 mg	1121 mcg
CALORIES	TOTAL FAT	CARBS	FIBER	PROTEIN	VITAMIN C	VITAMIN B5	BETA-CAROTENE	CALCIUM	LUTEIN/ ZEAXANTHIN

The proanthocyanidins, which give purple baby broccoli its color, are the same protective polyphenols found in dark red and purple berries, which promote circulation and glowing skin as well as protect veins and arteries to support heart and brain health. The characteristic taste of cruciferous vegetables comes from sulfurous compounds called isothiocyanates, which have been shown to have a strongly protective effect in people showing a genetic predisposition for lung cancer. Another sulfur compound, sulforaphane, triggers our natural detoxification enzymes.

- Contains the rare vegetable fiber calcium pectate, which holds cholesterol in the liver, limiting its release into the bloodstream.
- Source of the trace mineral chromium, which enables the hormone insulin to move sugar from the bloodstream to cells, so helping to prevent adult-onset diabetes.
- Vitamin C and the carotenoids beta-carotene and lutein provide further antioxidant protection for youthful-looking skin.
- Contains vitamin B5, needed to release energy from the plant foods we eat, encouraging age-defying vigor.

DID YOU KNOW?

Although it has only come back into fashion in the last 30 years, purple baby broccoli is the most ancient of broccoli, and was cultivated by the Romans.

PRACTICAL TIPS

Cook broccoli only lightly, preferably by steaming, to make sure that it remains slightly crunchy. The baby broccoli variety has a finer stalk than the fatter vegetable so can be eaten whole. Broccoli works well in stir-fries or served cold in salads.

PURPLE BABY BROCCOLI SALAD

Salads are a great way of making sure that you are eating enough greens. Here, lightly steamed purple baby broccoli is combined with cabbage, beets, and cranberries.

SERVES 4 • PREP TIME: 10–15 MINS • COOK TIME: 15–20 MINS

PER SERVING:	229 cal	10.9g	1.4g	29.5g	13g	5.9g	6.1g	120mg
	CALORIES	FAT	SAT FAT	CARBS	SUGAR	FIBER	PROTEIN	SODIUM

INGREDIENTS

2¼ cups purple baby broccoli (about 16 stalks)
3 cups shredded red cabbage
2 cooked beets in natural juices, cut into matchsticks
2 tablespoons dried cranberries
3 tablespoons balsamic vinegar

CROUTONS

2 tablespoons olive oil
3 slices country-style whole-grain bread, torn into small pieces
1 tablespoon sunflower seeds
1 tablespoon flaxseed

1. Put the baby broccoli into the top of a steamer, cover, and set over a saucepan of simmering water. Steam for 3–5 minutes, or until tender. Cool under cold running water, then cut the stems in half and the lower stems in half again lengthwise, and transfer to a salad bowl.

2. Add the red cabbage, beets, and cranberries to the bowl.

3. To make the croutons, heat the oil in a skillet over medium heat, add the bread, and fry for 3–4 minutes, stirring, until just beginning to brown. Add the sunflower seeds and flaxseed and cook for an additional 2–3 minutes, until lightly toasted.

4. Drizzle the balsamic vinegar over the salad and toss gently together. Sprinkle with the croutons and seeds and serve.

HINT

Steaming is the method of cooking vegetables that preserves the most nutrients. Try cooking all your vegetables in this way.

SQUASH

Orange-fleshed squash offers protection against lung cancer,
and it is particularly rich in vitamins C and E.

MAJOR NUTRIENTS PER QUARTER SMALL BUTTERNUT SQUASH

68 cal	TRACE	17.5g	3g	1.5g	1.8 mg	31 mg	2.2 mg
CALORIES	TOTAL FAT	CARBS	FIBER	PROTEIN	VITAMIN B3	VITAMIN C	VITAMIN E

6,339 mcg	5,207 mcg	72 mg	41 mcg	1mg	51 mg	528 mg
BETA-CAROTENE	BETA-CRYPTOXANTHIN	CALCIUM	FOLATE	IRON	MAGNESIUM	POTASSIUM

Squashes are related to pumpkin, cucumber, and melon, and they have a slightly nutty flavor that is ideal in both sweet and savory cooking. The orange-fleshed varieties, such as butternut, tend to contain the highest levels of beneficial nutrients. Butternut squash is one of our richest sources of beta-cryptoxanthin, a carotene that is linked with protection from lung cancer. The other carotenes it contains reduce the risk of colon cancer and prostate problems in men. They may also help reduce the inflammation associated with conditions such as asthma and arthritis. The vegetable is also a good source of several vitamins and minerals, including antioxidant vitamins C and E, calcium, iron, and magnesium.

- Contains protective chemicals against lung and colon cancers.
- Anti-inflammatory.
- Rich in a range of vitamins and minerals.
- High-fiber source of complex carbohydrates.

DID YOU KNOW?

Don't throw away nutritious squash seeds—they can be dried in a low oven and eaten in the same way as pumpkin seeds.

PRACTICAL TIPS

All winter squashes can be stored for up to six months in a cool, dry, dark, airy, frost-free place. To prepare, cut in half with a sharp knife and scoop out the seeds. Squashes can be stuffed and baked, or skinned, sliced, and roasted as an alternative to potatoes. Roasted squash makes an excellent soup. The carotenes in squash are better absorbed if eaten with a little oil.

SQUASH, KALE & FARRO STEW

You'll feel warmer just looking at this colorful and health-boosting vegetable stew. Farro is ideal for adding to soups and stews—use it for bulking out instead of barley or rice.

SERVES 6 • PREP TIME: 30 MINS • COOK TIME: 55 MINS

PER SERVING:

246 cal	7.2g	1.5g	38.4g	9.4g	6.4g	9.2g	440mg
CALORIES	FAT	SAT FAT	CARBS	SUGAR	FIBER	PROTEIN	SODIUM

INGREDIENTS

1 winter squash, such as kabocha or butternut, weighing about 2¾ pounds
2 tablespoons vegetable oil
1 onion, finely chopped
2 teaspoons dried oregano
2 garlic cloves, finely sliced
1⅔ cups canned diced tomatoes
3 cups vegetable broth
¾ cup quick-cooking farro, rinsed
3¾ cups sliced kale (cut into ribbons)
2½ cups drained and rinsed, canned chickpeas
⅓ cup chopped fresh cilantro
juice of 1 lime
salt and pepper (optional)

1. Cut the squash into quarters, peel, and seed. Cut the flesh into large cubes (you will need about 5½ cups).

2. Heat the oil in a flameproof casserole dish or heavy saucepan. Add the onion and sauté over medium heat for 5 minutes, until translucent. Add the oregano and garlic and sauté for 2 minutes.

3. Add the squash and cook, covered, for 10 minutes.

4. Add the tomatoes, broth, and farro, cover, and bring to a boil. Reduce the heat to a gentle simmer and cook for 20 minutes, stirring occasionally.

5. Add the kale and chickpeas. Cook for an additional 15 minutes, or until the kale is just tender.

6. Season with salt and pepper, if using. Stir in the cilantro and lime juice just before serving.

HINT
For best results, chop the squash into cubes of the same size to be sure of even cooking.

WATERCRESS

Peppery watercress leaves are rich in vitamin C and also contain chemicals to help protect against lung cancer.

MAJOR NUTRIENTS PER 12 WATERCRESS SPRIGS

3 cal	TRACE	0.3g	TRACE	0.6g	11mg	62 mcg	705 mcg	30 mg	1,442 mcg	83 mg
CALORIES	TOTAL FAT	CARBS	FIBER	PROTEIN	VITAMIN C	VITAMIN K	BETA-CAROTENE	CALCIUM	LUTEIN/ZEAXANTHIN	POTASSIUM

Watercress leaves are a powerhouse of nutrients—even if eaten in small quantities—and provide good amounts of vitamins C and K, potassium, and calcium. They are also a great source of carotenes and lutein for eye health. Watercress is rich in a variety of plant chemicals that can help prevent or minimize cancers, including phenylethyl isothiocynate, which can help to block the action of cells that are linked with lung cancer. Watercress is also said to detoxify the liver and cleanse the blood, and the benzyl oils it contains are powerful antibiotics. It can also help improve night blindness and the sun-sensitive condition called porphyria.

- Helps prevent lung and other cancers.
- Detoxifying and blood cleansing.
- Can improve eye health and night blindness.
- High in vitamin K for bone health and healthy blood.

DID YOU KNOW?

It is best to buy commercially produced watercress instead of searching for wild watercress, because it mainly grows in polluted waters and may carry bacteria.

PRACTICAL TIPS

Buy watercress that has no yellowing or wilting leaves, and store in a plastic bag in the refrigerator or, if bunched, put the bunch in a mug of water up to leaf height. Wash watercress before use and shake to remove excess water. Increase your intake of watercress by using it in a soup with onion and potato. Watercress also goes well with fresh orange sections in a salad.

FIG, GOAT CHEESE & WATERCRESS SALAD

This light salad makes an elegant appetizer, light lunch, or delicious summer supper.
It also works well served as a side dish for spicy lamb dishes.

SERVES 4 • PREP TIME: 10 MINS • COOK TIME: NONE

PER SERVING:	205 cal	12g	3.1g	21.4g	17.1g	3.5g	6.1g	240mg
	CALORIES	FAT	SAT FAT	CARBS	SUGAR	FIBER	PROTEIN	SODIUM

INGREDIENTS

6 figs, halved lengthwise
¾ bunch of watercress (4 cups packed)
2¼ ounces soft goat cheese
¼ cup blanched almonds, toasted

DRESSING

2 tablespoons finely chopped fresh mint
juice of ½ lemon
1 tablespoon honey
1 tablespoon extra virgin olive oil
pinch of sea salt
pinch of pepper

1. To make the dressing, whisk together the mint, lemon juice, honey, and oil in a small bowl and season with salt and pepper.

2. Put the figs in a small bowl, drizzle with a tablespoon of the dressing, and mix gently.

3. Pile the watercress onto a large serving plate. Drizzle the remaining dressing over the salad and toss. Sprinkle the figs, cheese, and almonds over the watercress. Serve immediately.

RADICCHIO

The red pigments of radicchio provide anticancer compounds to protect the heart and compounds to help prevent blood clots.

MAJOR NUTRIENTS PER ½ SMALL HEAD RADICCHIO

12 cal	TRACE	2.2g	0.5g	0.7g	4mg	10 mg	30 mcg	4,416 mcg	151 mg	0.5 mg
CALORIES	TOTAL FAT	CARBS	FIBER	PROTEIN	VITAMIN C	CALCIUM	FOLATE	LUTEIN/ ZEAXANTHIN	POTASSIUM	SELENIUM

Tightly packed heads of radicchio, sometimes known as Italian chicory, have a strong, slightly bitter flavor that can lift a mixed leaf salad and provide contrasting color. The astringent taste awakens the palate and promotes the secretion of hydrochloric acid, which aids digestion. Radicchio is rich in phenolic compounds, such as quercetin glycosides, which help prevent precancerous substances from causing damage in the body, and anthocyanins, which help protect against both cancer and heart disease. The total phenolic content in red forms of radicchio is four to five times higher than in green varieties. Radicchio also contains good levels of vitamin C, potassium, and folate.

- Acts as a digestive aid.
- Contains high levels of cancer-blocking compounds.
- Protection against heart disease.
- Rich in lutein and zeaxanthin for eye health.

DID YOU KNOW?

Two common types of red radicchio are Verona, with a small, loose head, burgundy leaves, and white ribs, and Treviso, which has a tighter, more tapered head and leaves that are narrower and more pointed.

PRACTICAL TIPS

Look for firm heads with crisp, colorful leaves and no signs of wilting or browning. Store in a plastic bag in the refrigerator for up to five days. Although usually served raw in salads, radicchio heads can be quartered, basted with olive oil, lemon juice, and seasoning, and lightly broiled or baked. Radicchio can also be sautéed in oil and drizzled with balsamic vinegar.

RADICCHIO CAESAR SALAD

The traditional Caesar salad is made with romaine lettuce, but here ruby-red radicchio is used instead. Its bittersweet flavor goes well with Parmesan and pancetta and the mustard dressing.

SERVES 2 • PREP TIME: 20 MINS • COOK TIME: 5 MINS

PER SERVING:

453 cal	34.8g	8g	21.9g	1.7g	1.8g	14g	880mg
CALORIES	FAT	SAT FAT	CARBS	SUGAR	FIBER	PROTEIN	SODIUM

INGREDIENTS

4 thin slices of pancetta
½ head of radicchio, tough outer leaves discarded and coarse stems removed
2 cups prepared croutons
4 anchovies in oil, drained
⅓ cup freshly grated Parmesan cheese

DRESSING

2 teaspoons lemon juice
1 teaspoon Dijon mustard
1 small garlic clove, crushed
dash of Worcestershire sauce
3 tablespoons extra virgin olive oil
salt and pepper (optional)

1. To make the dressing, combine the lemon juice, mustard, garlic, and Worcestershire sauce in a small bowl. Add salt and pepper, if using, then gradually whisk in the oil until thick.

2. Add the pancetta to a dry skillet and cook for 2–3 minutes, until crisp. Drain on paper towels. Break into bite-size pieces and set aside.

3. Tear the radicchio leaves into bite-size pieces. Put into a salad bowl with the croutons, anchovies, and cheese. Whisk the dressing, pour it over the greens, and toss to coat.

4. Top the salad with the pancetta and serve immediately.

VARIATION

If you don't have anchovies, you can replace them with a teaspoon of capers in liquid.

CELERY

High in potassium and calcium, celery helps to reduce fluid retention and prevent high blood pressure.

MAJOR NUTRIENTS PER 2½ CELERY STALKS

14 cal	TRACE	3g	1.6g	0.7g	3mg	35 mcg	40 mg	36 mcg	11 mg	260 mg
CALORIES	TOTAL FAT	CARBS	FIBER	PROTEIN	VITAMIN C	VITAMIN K	CALCIUM	FOLATE	MAGNESIUM	POTASSIUM

Celery has long been regarded as an ideal food for dieters, because of its high water content and, therefore, its low calorie load. In fact, celery is a useful and healthy vegetable for many other reasons. It is a good source of potassium and is also surprisingly high in calcium, vital for healthy bones, healthy blood pressure levels, and nerve function. The darker green stalks and the leaves of celery contain carotenes and more of the minerals and vitamin C than the paler leaves, so don't discard them. Celery also contains the compounds polyacetalenes and phthalides, which may protect from inflammation and high blood pressure.

- Low in calories and fat and high in fiber.
- Good source of potassium.
- Calcium content protects bones and may help regulate blood pressure.
- May offer protection from inflammation.

DID YOU KNOW?

Celery can contain high levels of nitrates, which have been linked with an increased risk of cancer. However, research has found that vegetables high in nitrates also usually contain high levels of nitrate-neutralizing chemicals.

PRACTICAL TIPS

Choose celery heads with leaves that look bright green and fresh. Store in a plastic bag or wrap in plastic wrap to prevent the stalks from turning limp. Celery is ideal for adding flavor and bulk to soups and stews and quartered heads can be braised in vegetable broth for an excellent accompaniment to fish, poultry, or game. The leaves can be added to salads and stir-fries or used as a garnish.

GREEN ENVY SMOOTHIE

This smoothie packs a real nutritional punch, and your friends will be green with
envy when they see you glowing with health and full of energy.

SERVES 1 • PREP TIME: 10 MINS • COOK TIME: NONE

PER SERVING:	163 cal	1.2g	0.2g	38g	21.4g	10.5g	6g	240mg
	CALORIES	FAT	SAT FAT	CARBS	SUGAR	FIBER	PROTEIN	SODIUM

INGREDIENTS

1 green apple
4 celery stalks
½ cucumber
3½ cups spinach
½ cup fresh mint
1 teaspoon chlorophyll powder
ice cubes, to serve
celery stalks, to garnish (optional)

1. Coarsely chop the apple, celery stalks, and cucumber.

2. Put the spinach, mint, apple, celery, and cucumber through
a juicer.

3. Stir through the chlorophyll powder until combined. Fill
a glass with ice, pour in the juice, and serve immediately,
garnished with a trimmed celery stalk, if using.

RADISHES

Radishes are among the most nutritious of plant roots, and they have traditionally been used to help maintain a youthful appearance and control weight.

2 cal	0g	0.30g	0.2g	0.06g	1.4 mg	2 mg	2 mcg	20 mg
CALORIES	TOTAL FAT	CARBS	FIBER	PROTEIN	VITAMIN C	CALCIUM	FOLATE	POTASSIUM

Radishes have long been used to treat thyroid conditions. This is because they contain a chemical called raphanin, which, according to researchers, regulates the thyroid gland by tempering its tendency to produce too little or too much thyroid hormone. Low function or hypothyroidism is more common, especially as we age, when the thyroid can slow down and result in weight gain, cold hands, and fatigue. Radishes also have good levels of the trace mineral molybdenum, which helps balance blood sugar levels, again supporting the thyroid in its job of managing body weight and energy use.

- The chemical xylogen in radishes reduces infection and inflammation, thereby strengthening the immune system to help prevent disease and premature aging.
- The slightly bitter taste encourages bile flow, helping with the digestion of fats and the regulation of cholesterol to maintain a trim figure and healthy weight.
- Potassium regulates blood pressure to keep the heart healthy and able to pump revitalizing nutrients around the body.

DID YOU KNOW?

Radishes are used in traditional Chinese medicine to provide kidney, digestive, and liver support and to reduce mucus, sinusitis, and throat problems.

PRACTICAL TIPS

As well as being a colorful, crisp, and sharp salad vegetable, radishes taste refreshing in juices. To combat nasal congestion, try processing together six radishes, one cucumber, and one apple. Daikon radish is a long, white radish used in Asian cooking that can be eaten raw in salads.

PAN-COOKED TUNA WITH RADISH RELISH

Borrowing from the Japanese tradition of pickling vegetables, the radishes and cucumber are marinated in a delicious mixture of sweet and sour, which goes well with the tuna.

SERVES 4 • PREP TIME: 15 MINS, PLUS MARINATING • COOK TIME: 10 MINS

PER SERVING:	279 cal	12.1g	1.5g	2.2g	1g	0.7g	38.3g	520mg
	CALORIES	FAT	SAT FAT	CARBS	SUGAR	FIBER	PROTEIN	SODIUM

INGREDIENTS

4 tuna steaks, each weighing 5½ ounces
1 tablespoon sesame seeds
cooked rice, to serve (optional)

MARINADE

2 tablespoons dark soy sauce
2 tablespoons sunflower oil
1 tablespoon sesame oil
1 tablespoon rice vinegar
1 teaspoon grated fresh ginger

RELISH

½ cucumber, peeled
1 bunch red radishes, trimmed

1. Put the tuna steaks into a dish and sprinkle with the sesame seeds, pressing them in with the back of a spoon so they stick to the fish.

2. To make the marinade, whisk together all the ingredients. Transfer 3 tablespoons of the marinade to a medium bowl. Pour the remaining marinade over the fish, turning each steak to coat lightly. Cover and marinate in the refrigerator for 1 hour.

3. Slice the cucumber and radishes thinly and add to the marinade in the bowl. Toss the vegetables to coat, then cover and chill.

4. Heat a large, heavy skillet over high heat. Add the steaks and cook for 3–4 minutes on each side, depending on the thickness of the fish. Serve immediately with the radish relish and rice, if using.

VARIATION
You could use any firm-fleshed fish steaks or fillets for this dish, although tuna is a typically Asian ingredient.

SAVOY CABBAGE

The green leaves of the savoy contain a range of nutrients and plant chemicals to help fight cancer, and they are also rich in minerals and vitamin C.

MAJOR NUTRIENTS PER 1½ CUPS SAVOY CABBAGE

27 cal	TRACE	6g	3g	2g	31 mg	600 mcg	35 mg	3 mcg	28 mg	230 mg	0.9 mcg
CALORIES	TOTAL FAT	CARBS	FIBER	PROTEIN	VITAMIN C	BETA-CAROTENE	CALCIUM	FOLATE	MAGNESIUM	POTASSIUM	SELENIUM

Savoy, along with other dark green cabbages, are rich in plant chemicals, which may inhibit the growth of cancerous tumors, and which seem to have particular benefit in offering protection from colon, lung, and hormone-base cancers, such as breast cancer, probably by increasing the metabolism of estrogen. Cabbage is also rich in vitamin C, folate, fiber, and minerals, and is a source of the B vitamins, vitamin K, iron, and beta-carotene. Its other benefits are that its juice is a traditional remedy for peptic ulcers and its indoles can help lower "bad" cholesterol.

- High in several nutrients, including vitamin C and calcium.
- Proven anticancer and anti-inflammatory effect.
- Helps protect against high "bad" cholesterol and heart disease.
- Can treat peptic ulcers.

DID YOU KNOW?

This popular crinkle-leaf cabbage was originally grown in the Savoie, an Alpine region bordering Italy and France, and it is from here that it got its name.

PRACTICAL TIPS

Store the cabbage in the refrigerator in a plastic bag to retain its vitamin C and freshness. To retain most of its nutrients, cook lightly by steaming or stir-frying for a few minutes. To avoid that distinctive cabbage odor, don't overcook—cooking with a dash of vinegar also helps.

GRAPE & CABBAGE BOOSTER

Naturally sweet pears and grapes can disguise the taste of vegetables, such as cabbage, in a juice. The pumpkin seeds are finely ground, so no one will know they are there.

SERVES 1 • PREP TIME: 15 MINS • COOK TIME: NONE

PER SERVING:	416 cal	5.7g	0.9g	94.5g	62.6g	6.3g	9.3g	40mg
	CALORIES	FAT	SAT FAT	CARBS	SUGAR	FIBER	PROTEIN	SODIUM

INGREDIENTS

2 pears, halved
¼ small head of savoy cabbage,
coarsely chopped
1 tablespoon pumpkin seeds
1 cup seedless green grapes
small handful of crushed ice (optional)

1. Feed the pears and cabbage through a juicer.

2. Put the pumpkin seeds into a blender and process until finely ground, then add the grapes and crushed ice, if using, and blend. Pour in the pear juice mix and blend until smooth.

3. Pour into a glass and serve immediately.

POTATOES

Potatoes are rich in minerals that you need for the effective functioning of your brain and muscles to keep you thinking and moving youthfully.

MAJOR NUTRIENTS PER 1 POTATO

77 cal	0.1g	19g	2.2g	2g	0.25 mg	20 mg	421 mg
CALORIES	TOTAL FAT	CARBS	FIBER	PROTEIN	VITAMIN B6	VITAMIN C	POTASSIUM

The high starchy carbohydrate content of potatoes makes them number one on the satiety index, which scores foods according to how much they satisfy our hunger right after eating them. Healthy boiled potatoes are actually three times as satisfying as fried potatoes and can be helpful in curbing cravings for sweet, unhealthy foods that lead to aging weight gain. Potatoes also provide dense fuel for people who exercise and can help regulate energy and weight.

- Source of kukoamines, also found in goji berries, which, along with the high potassium content, help lower blood pressure.
- Contains vitamin B6, needed to produce the neurotransmitter GABA that helps us cope with stress, a major factor in staying young.
- Vitamin C protects sensitive brain and nerve cells from toxins, helping to keep our brains sharp and our muscles responsive.

DID YOU KNOW?

Potatoes are the most grown and eaten vegetable in the world, but their high starch content excludes them from the recommended daily amounts of vegetables.

PRACTICAL TIPS

Most nutrients in potatoes are found just under the skins, and removing these also cuts out the rich fiber there. The older and larger potatoes have a higher score on the glycemic index, meaning that their sugars hit the bloodstream quicker, upsetting blood sugar balance. New potatoes with their skins intact are the healthiest option.

NEW POTATOES WITH GARLIC & SPICY BUTTER

Nothing beats the flavor of those first potatoes of the season, although we can now get new potatoes all year round. Garlic, chile, and fresh cilantro add the perfect touch.

SERVES 4 • PREP TIME: 10 MINS • COOK TIME: 20 MINS

PER SERVING: | 198 cal CALORIES | 8.3g FAT | 5.2g SAT FAT | 28.8g CARBS | 2.6g SUGAR | 4.4g FIBER | 3.3g PROTEIN | 40mg SODIUM

INGREDIENTS

1–2 teaspoons salt
1 pound 9 ounces baby new potatoes
3 tablespoons butter
1 garlic clove, finely chopped
1 red chile, seeded and finely chopped
salt and pepper (optional)
1 tablespoon chopped fresh cilantro leaves, to garnish

1. Add the salt to a large saucepan of water and bring to a boil. Add the potatoes, bring back to a boil, and cook for 15 minutes, or until tender. Drain well.

2. Melt the butter in a separate large saucepan, add the garlic and chile, and gently stir-fry for 30 seconds, without browning.

3. Add the potatoes and stir to coat in the butter, then season with salt and pepper, if using. Sprinkle with the cilantro and serve hot.

ARUGULA

This deep green, peppery green contains carotenes,
which have several cancer-preventing qualities.

MAJOR NUTRIENTS PER ¾ CUP ARUGULA

4 cal	TRACE	0.5g	0.2g	0.4g	2.3 mg	214 mcg	24 mg	15 mcg	533 mcg	55 mg
CALORIES	TOTAL FAT	CARBS	FIBER	PROTEIN	VITAMIN C	BETA-CAROTENE	CALCIUM	FOLATE	LUTEIN/ZEAXANTHIN	POTASSIUM

Arugula, a member of the Brassica (or cabbage) family that grows wild across much of Europe, is closely related to the mustard plant. It is a small plant with elongated, serrated leaves. Today, much of the arugula we buy is cultivated, but wild arugula leaves contain more of the protective plant chemicals than cultivated hybrids. The leaves are rich in carotenes and are an excellent source of lutein and zeaxanthin for eye health, including cataracts. The indoles contained in arugula and other cabbages are linked with protection from colon cancer. The leaves also supply good amounts of folate—which is especially important in pregnancy, because it helps protect the fetus—and calcium for healthy bones and heart.

- Contains carotenes to protect against cancers.
- Lutein content helps protect eye health, especially in the elderly.
- Contains indoles, linked with a reduction in the risk of colon cancer.
- Good source of calcium for bone protection.

DID YOU KNOW?
Arugula grows quickly from seed and is ideal for window boxes or flowerpots.

PRACTICAL TIPS

When buying arugula, the deeper the color of the leaves, the more carotenes they contain. Arugula can be used in salads or as a garnish. Alternatively, it can be stirred into pasta instead of spinach, added to soup, made into a pesto, or added to the top of a pizza. It doesn't keep fresh for long, so use within one to two days.

ARUGULA FUEL SOUP

The spice from the arugula and mustard leaves is softened by the mild avocado
and coconut milk, creating a creamy but healthy soup.

SERVES 1 • PREP TIME: 10 MINS • COOK TIME: NONE

PER SERVING:	379 cal	37.9g	25.2g	11.9g	4.4g	6.1g	5.4g	TRACE
	CALORIES	FAT	SAT FAT	CARBS	SUGAR	FIBER	PROTEIN	SODIUM

INGREDIENTS

1½ cups arugula
⅓ cup mustard greens
1 cup chilled water
½ avocado, pitted and flesh scooped from skin
½ cup coconut milk
½ cup arugula leaves, to garnish

1. Put the arugula, mustard greens, and water into a blender and blend until smooth.

2. Add the avocado to the blender with the coconut milk and blend until smooth and creamy.

3. Serve immediately or chill in the refrigerator. Stir well just before serving, garnished with a few arugula leaves.

MEAT, FISH, DAIRY & EGGS

TURKEY

A low-fat protein source, turkey helps promote a positive
outlook as well as high levels of energy and vitality.

MAJOR NUTRIENTS PER 3½ OUNCES SKINLESS TURKEY

111 cal	0.65g	0.21g	0.11g	0mg	0mg	24.6g	6.23 mg	0.72 mg	0.58 mg	1.17 mg	 4.02g	1.24 mg
CALORIES	TOTAL FAT	SATURATED FAT	MONO UN-SATURATED FAT	CARBS	FIBER	PROTEIN	VITAMIN B3	VITAMIN B5	VITAMIN B6	IRON	GLUTAMIC ACID	ZINC

Turkey is known for its high tryptophan content, a protein constituent from which the body makes the mood-, sleep-, and appetite-regulating brain chemical serotonin. This is believed to be one of the reasons that we fall asleep after a heavy Christmas meal: the serotonin encourages us to rest, which is a crucial component of staying young. Turkey's high protein content also helps control appetite by balancing blood sugar levels, so curbing sugar cravings and energy fluctuations. The white meat of turkey is considered healthier than the brown meat due to its lower fat content, but the difference is small. In fact, the brown meat can actually help raise your metabolism more, making you more efficient at burning fuel, more likely to lose weight, and less susceptible to overeating.

- Iron supports energy levels by producing the cells that your body uses for fuel and helping muscles store rejuvenating oxygen.
- Glutamic acid helps balance blood sugar and combat the aging effects of stress.
- Contains the zinc that is needed to make serotonin, which makes you feel good. It is also vital in the process of repair to the body and helps you maintain a youthful appearance.

DID YOU KNOW?

The Aztecs domesticated the turkey and used its feathers decoratively. It was associated with Tezcatlipoca, their god of tricks.

PRACTICAL TIPS

Turkey can be a lower-fat alternative to chicken, with many similar health benefits. A cage-free bird that has had a healthy diet itself and lived more naturally, will be leaner, taste better, and lose less water when cooked than a caged bird. Cook a whole turkey by roasting.

RED CABBAGE, TURKEY & QUINOA PILAF

Red cabbage comes into its own here, adding rich color to this magnificent dish. Cranberries and Brazil nuts add flavor and crunch, while quinoa provides a moist and fluffy base.

SERVES 4 • PREP TIME: 30 MINS • COOK TIME: 55 MINS

PER SERVING:

 697 cal CALORIES
 34.8g FAT
 7.3g SAT FAT
 64.6g CARBS
 22.9g SUGAR
 10.3g FIBER
 37.2g PROTEIN
680mg SODIUM

INGREDIENTS

½ cup white quinoa
½ cup red quinoa
½ teaspoon salt
¼ cup vegetable oil
1 large red onion, halved and sliced
1 teaspoon cumin seeds, crushed
4-inch cinnamon stick, broken
½ head of red cabbage, core removed, leaves sliced into ribbons
1–1¼ cups chicken broth
¼ teaspoon pepper
2½ cups coarsely chopped cooked turkey
2 carrots, shaved into ribbons
⅔ cup dried cranberries
⅔ cup Brazil nuts, coarsely chopped
handful of fresh flat-leaf parsley leaves, to garnish

1. Combine the white quinoa and red quinoa, then put into a strainer and rinse under cold running water. Put into a saucepan with the salt and enough water to cover by ⅝ inch. Bring to a boil, cover, and simmer over low heat for 15 minutes. Remove from the heat but keep the pan covered for 5 minutes to let the grains swell. Fluff up the grains with a fork and set aside.

2. Heat the oil in a large skillet over medium–high heat. Add the onion with the cumin seeds and cinnamon and sauté for 5 minutes, until the onion is soft but not browned.

3. Add the cabbage, 1 cup of the broth, and the pepper. Cover and cook over medium heat for 15–20 minutes, until the cabbage is just tender. Add the turkey, carrots, cranberries, and Brazil nuts. Cook, uncovered, for 5 minutes, until the turkey is heated through.

4. Gently stir in the cooked quinoa. Add the remaining broth if the mixture seems dry. Cook for 2 minutes to heat through. Garnish with parsley and serve immediately.

CHICKEN

Grandma was right—scientists have confirmed that chicken soup
boosts the immune system and helps fight colds and flu.

MAJOR NUTRIENTS PER 5½ OUNCES SKINLESS CHICKEN

166 cal	4g	30.5g	11.8g	1.5g	0.6 mg	0.5 mcg	15mg	1.5mg	34mg	356 mg	25 mcg	1.8mg
CALORIES	TOTAL FAT	PROTEIN	VITAMIN B3	VITAMIN B5	VITAMIN B6	VITAMIN B12	CALCIUM	IRON	MAGNESIUM	POTASSIUM	SELENIUM	ZINC

Scientists believe that chicken soup relieves the symptoms of colds and flu by stimulating the production of infection-fighting cells. Using chicken bones in the soup greatly boosts the effect. A portion of lean chicken meat contains nearly half of the daily recommended intake of protein for an adult woman, a whole day's intake of niacin (vitamin B3), and makes a large contribution to our intake of minerals, such as iron, the antioxidant zinc, and potassium. Chicken is rich in selenium, one of the minerals that is often lacking in our diets and that has strong anticancer action. Studies also show that organic cage-free chicken contains higher levels of omega-3 fats, vitamin E, and other nutrients than nonorganic meat.

- Helps boost immune system and protect against cancer.
- Niacin content helps protect against Alzheimer's disease and cognitive decline.
- Vitamin B content helps release energy from our food.
- Vitamin B6 content helps protect arteries from damage from homocysteine, a risk factor for heart disease.

DID YOU KNOW?

*Chicken fat is in its skin.
For it to be a low-fat food,
you need to remove all the skin
before cooking or eating it.*

PRACTICAL TIPS

Fresh chicken should be kept covered in a refrigerator for no more than three days—longer storage increases bacteria count. Do not wash before cooking, because this can spread bacteria. Use a separate cutting board for preparing raw chicken and wash hands and utensils carefully.

CHICKEN & KIMCHI SOUP

Kimchi is a fermented vegetable pickle that can help promote the growth of healthy bacteria in the digestive tract, which can be suppressed by a diet high in sugar and processed foods.

SERVES 4 • PREP TIME: 20 MINS • COOK TIME: 45–50 MINS

PER SERVING:	179 cal CALORIES	6.6g FAT	1.8g SAT FAT	12.8g CARBS	6.6g SUGAR	2.8g FIBER	16.7g PROTEIN	1,160 mg SODIUM

INGREDIENTS

2 teaspoons rice bran oil

4 boneless, skinless chicken thighs, 10½ ounces total weight

4 scallions, thinly sliced

2 carrots, thinly sliced

1 red bell pepper, cored, seeded and diced

3¾ cups chicken broth

1 tablespoon brown rice miso

2 tablespoons mirin

¾ cup sliced kimchi from a jar, with the sauce clinging to the pickle

1. Heat the oil in a saucepan, then add the chicken and cook for 5 minutes, until lightly browned on both sides. Add the scallions, carrots, and red bell pepper. Stir in the broth, miso, and mirin.

2. Bring to a boil, then cover and simmer for 30 minutes, until the chicken is cooked through and there are no pink juices when the thickest part of the meat is pierced with a knife. Lift the chicken out with a slotted spoon, then shred into strips using two forks.

3. Return the chicken to the soup and add the kimchi, then heat through, ladle into warm bowls, and serve immediately.

LAMB

Lamb is an energy-rich, high-quality meat that contains important nutrients for immunity and the slowing down of aging.

MAJOR NUTRIENTS PER 3½ OUNCES LAMB

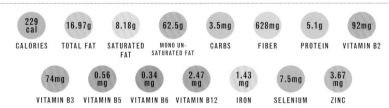

229 cal	16.97g	8.18g	62.5g	3.5mg	628mg	5.1g	92mg
CALORIES	TOTAL FAT	SATURATED FAT	MONO UN-SATURATED FAT	CARBS	FIBER	PROTEIN	VITAMIN B2

74mg	0.56 mg	0.34 mg	2.47 mg	1.43 mg	7.5mg	3.67 mg
VITAMIN B3	VITAMIN B5	VITAMIN B6	VITAMIN B12	IRON	SELENIUM	ZINC

Animal, as well as plant sources of food, supply antioxidants that support immunity. Lamb is rich in the antioxidant trace minerals zinc and selenium. These produce liver enzymes that are our most powerful defense against free radicals, the harmful molecules that damage and age all parts of the body, from the skin to the internal organs. Another antioxidant that is present in lamb, coenzyme Q-10, works to protect the heart and to provide energy for the body as a whole. Coenzyme Q-10 has also been shown to reduce the incidence of congestive heart failure, Alzheimer's disease, Parkinson's disease, chronic fatigue, breast cancer, and gum disease.

- Quality source of protein, for repairing and rebuilding worn-out cells. A single serving provides about 60 percent of your daily requirements.
- Contains the B vitamins that support vitality in every cell of the body to keep you looking and feeling young.
- Although high in saturated fat, it also contains beneficial levels of heart-healthy monounsaturated fats.

DID YOU KNOW?

Lamb is the meat of a sheep that is under a year old. If the meat is from an adult animal, it is referred to as mutton. Most people prefer lamb to mutton, because the older meat has a much stronger flavor and is also much tougher.

PRACTICAL TIPS

As a red meat, lamb is generally higher in saturated fat than white. You don't need to eat it often to enjoy its benefits. It's best to be picky about the cuts you choose—chops are the healthiest option. Lamb also makes a delicious burger alternative to beef, and works well with apricots and prunes, as in Middle Eastern stews.

PISTACHIO-CRUSTED LAMB CHOPS

This is a delicious method of cooking lamb chops, with pistachios and dried cherries. Red stone fruits, such as cherries or plums, have a great depth of flavor that goes particularly well with lamb.

SERVES 4 • PREP TIME: 20 MINS • COOK TIME: 40 MINS

PER SERVING:

| 859 cal CALORIES | 47.1g FAT | 16.2g SAT FAT | 50g CARBS | 29.4g SUGAR | 11.7g FIBER | 43.4g PROTEIN | 1,400 mg SODIUM |

INGREDIENTS

2 tablespoons olive oil
½ onion, thinly sliced
1 cup ruby port
1 cup dried sweet cherries, coarsely chopped
1 cup chicken broth
1 tablespoon honey
1¾ teaspoons salt
3 garlic cloves
¾ cup roasted, unsalted pistachio nuts
8 lamb chops
½ teaspoon pepper
1 tablespoon Dijon mustard mixed
with 1 tablespoon water

1. Preheat the oven to 425°F.

2. Heat the oil in a heavy skillet over medium–high heat. Add the onion and cook for about 5 minutes, stirring occasionally, until soft. Add the port, cherries, broth, honey, and ¾ teaspoon of the salt and bring just to a boil. Reduce the heat to medium–low and simmer for about 20 minutes, until the sauce is thick and syrupy.

3. Meanwhile, put the garlic into a processor and pulse until finely chopped. Add the nuts and pulse until finely chopped. Transfer to a plate.

4. Season the lamb chops on all sides with the remaining salt and the pepper, then brush with the mustard mixture. Press each lamb chop into the nut mixture to coat well all over.

5. Transfer the chops to a baking sheet and bake in the preheated oven for 6 minutes. Turn over and cook for an additional 6 minutes for medium rare, or 7–8 minutes for well done. Remove from the oven and loosely tent with aluminum foil. Let rest for 5 minutes before serving.

6. Serve hot, with the sauce spooned over the top.

BEEF

Beef provides fats that help with weight loss and promote youthful skin, bones, and heart. For the healthiest beef, look for cuts from grass-fed cattle that were allowed to roam freely.

MAJOR NUTRIENTS PER 3½ OUNCES BEEF

192 cal	12.73g	5.34g	4.8g	0mg	19.42g	4.82 mg
CALORIES	TOTAL FAT	SATURATED FAT	MONO UN-SATURATED FAT	FIBER	PROTEIN	VITAMIN B3

0.58 mg	0.36 mg	1.97 mg	930 mcg	1.99mg	14.2 mcg	4.55 mg
VITAMIN B5	VITAMIN B6	VITAMIN B12	VITAMIN E	IRON	SELENIUM	ZINC

Grass-fed cattle generally get more exercise, making their meat leaner. For every 3-ounce serving, there is about ⅛ ounce less fat in grass-fed beef than in its grain-fed counterpart. This is good news for calorie counters but, more important, the quality of fat contained in grass-fed beef is better. Grass-fed beef contains high levels of omega-3 oils, which keep the heart, joints, brain, and skin appearing youthful. Another fat, CLA (conjugated linolenic acid), comes direct from the grass, and it enables stored fat to be burned as energy, raising the metabolism and helping maintain a trim figure. Low levels of CLA in our diet have been partly linked to the rise of obesity.

- Contains four times more vitamin E than grain-fed beef, which can hold back wrinkles and prevent age spots.
- Good selenium levels lessen anxiety, depression, and fatigue. Low levels are associated with heart and bone degeneration.
- Contains the highest level of zinc in any meat, promoting clear skin and strong nails.
- Coenzyme Q-10 increases energy in all cells, especially the heart, so supporting overall vigor.

DID YOU KNOW?

Cattle naturally roam and feed on pasture. Cows were only fed grain when humans moved on from their role as hunter-gatherers to become farmers, around 10,000 BC.

PRACTICAL TIPS

Ask your butcher for the best source or find a farm store attached to its own pasture. Sirloin and tenderloin steak are the healthiest, leanest cuts. This is a nutrient-dense food, so you only need to eat it two to four times a month to get the benefits.

BEEF STIR-FRY

A quick and healthy meal that comes together in less than half an hour—perfect for a delicious midweek meal for four.

SERVES 4 • PREP TIME: 10 MINS • COOK TIME: 10–12 MINS

PER SERVING:

167 cal	3.4g	1.1g	9.3g	5.4g	2.5g	25.8g	80mg
CALORIES	FAT	SAT FAT	CARBS	SUGAR	FIBER	PROTEIN	SODIUM

INGREDIENTS

2-3 sprays olive oil
14 ounces bottom round or rump roast,
cut into thin strips (fat removed)
1 orange bell pepper, seeded and cut
into thin strips
4 scallions, chopped
1-2 fresh jalapeño peppers, seeded and chopped
2-3 garlic cloves, chopped
1½ cups diagonally halved snow peas
4 ounces large portobello mushrooms, sliced
1-2 teaspoons hoisin sauce, or to taste
1 tablespoon orange juice
4 cups arugula or watercress

1. Preheat a wok, then spray in the oil and heat for 30 seconds. Add the beef and stir-fry for 1 minute or until browned. Using a slotted spoon, remove and reserve.

2. Add the orange bell pepper, scallions, jalapeño peppers, and garlic and stir-fry for 2 minutes. Add the snow peas and mushrooms and stir-fry for an additional 2 minutes.

3. Return the beef to the wok and add the hoisin sauce and orange juice. Stir-fry for 2–3 minutes, or until the beef is tender and the vegetables are tender but still firm to the bite. Stir in the arugula and stir-fry until it starts to wilt. Serve immediately.

VARIATION
This delicious stir-fry goes well with brown rice or whole-wheat noodles to boost fiber.

PORK

Pork has an unfair reputation as a high calorie choice. In fact, if you choose the right cut, it is a good lean source of protein and contains an impressive number of nutrients.

MAJOR NUTRIENTS PER 3½ OUNCES LEAN PORK TENDERLOIN

109 cal	21g	2.2g	6.7 mg	0.8 mg	0.5 mg	0.2 mcg	80 mg	1mg	27 mg	399 mg	31 mcg	1.9mg
CALORIES	PROTEIN	TOTAL FAT	VITAMIN B3	VITAMIN B6	VITAMIN B12	VITAMIN D	CHOLINE	IRON	MAGNESIUM	POTASSIUM	SELENIUM	ZINC

Lean, high-protein pork, such as cutlets or steaks from the leg, contains vitamin D, which is hard to find in the diet and is vital to help make and maintain our bone density throughout life. Pork is higher than most other meats in healthy monounsaturated fats and is also rich in choline and the B vitamins, all of which can protect the arteries from cholesterol damage and, therefore, help prevent cardiovascular disease. The meat is high in potassium to balance sodium in our bodies and act as a natural diuretic, reducing fluid retention and helping control high blood pressure. Eating pork is an excellent way to get your zinc, as well. This antioxidant mineral can help support optimal immune system function, fight infection, and heal wounds quickly. There's iron, too, half of which is heme iron—the type that is most easily absorbed by our bodies.

- Good source of lean high-quality protein.
- Source of bone-building vitamin D.
- Contains several heart-protective nutrients.
- Rich in zinc for immune function, and heme iron for healthy blood.

DID YOU KNOW?

Cured pork products, such as bacon, ham, and sausages, are high in salt, may be high in fat, and may contain nitrites, which are linked with an increased risk of cancers. The smoking process some cured meats undergo also produces carcinogens. Stick to fresh pork.

PRACTICAL TIPS

Pork tenderloin or leg can be cubed and used for kabobs, with a yogurt, garlic, and cucumber sauce. Or try cooking in a similar way to steak cuts from beef. Thinly sliced, pork makes a good addition to vegetable stir-fries. Lean pork freezes well and will keep for a year. For the best health, aim to eat no more than 2½ ounces red meat a day, because high meat intake is linked with increased risk of bowel cancer.

PORK-STUFFED CABBAGE LEAVES

This is a great way to use the leaves of the cabbage to make
a healthy wrap for the tasty pork and rice filling.

SERVES 4 • PREP TIME: 45 MINS • COOK TIME: 1 HOUR

PER SERVING:

 364 cal — CALORIES
 24.8g — FAT
 9.1g — SAT FAT
 18.8g — CARBS
 6.9g — SUGAR
 3.1g — FIBER
17.5g — PROTEIN
920g — SODIUM

INGREDIENTS

1 tablespoon olive oil
1 tablespoon butter
1⅔ cups canned diced tomatoes
2 cups chicken broth
1 onion, grated
8 large cabbage leaves, thick stems removed
10½ ounces fresh ground pork
⅔ cup cooked white rice
finely grated zest of 1 lemon
2 teaspoons paprika
½ teaspoon dill seeds
1 egg, lightly beaten
¾ teaspoon salt
¼ teaspoon pepper
salt and pepper (optional)
1 teaspoon chopped fresh dill, to garnish

1. Heat the oil and butter in a large skillet. Add the tomatoes, broth, and all but 2 tablespoons of the grated onion. Season with salt and pepper, if using. Bring to a boil, then reduce the heat and simmer gently while you prepare the cabbage leaves.

2. Bring a large saucepan of water to a boil. Add the cabbage leaves and blanch for 2 minutes. Drain and rinse under cold running water, then pat dry.

3. Combine the pork, rice, lemon zest, paprika, dill seeds, egg, and the remaining onion. Add ¾ teaspoon of salt and ¼ teaspoon of pepper and mix well. Divide the stuffing among the cabbage leaves. Fold over the bottom and sides of each leaf, then roll up to make a package.

4. Place the packages, seam side down, in the sauce. Cover and simmer over low heat for 45 minutes, until cooked through.

5. Sprinkle with fresh dill and serve immediately.

HINT

*Ask your butcher to ground a lean cut of pork for this dish—
fat is easily camouflaged in ground pork due to its pale color.*

SALMON

Salmon is an excellent source of omega-3 fats, cancer-fighting selenium, and vitamin B12, which helps protect against heart disease and a form of anaemia.

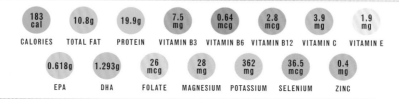

183 cal	10.8g	19.9g	7.5 mg	0.64 mcg	2.8 mcg	3.9 mg	1.9 mg
CALORIES	TOTAL FAT	PROTEIN	VITAMIN B3	VITAMIN B6	VITAMIN B12	VITAMIN C	VITAMIN E

0.618g	1.293g	26 mcg	28 mg	362 mg	36.5 mcg	0.4 mg
EPA	DHA	FOLATE	MAGNESIUM	POTASSIUM	SELENIUM	ZINC

Much of the salmon that we eat today is farmed instead of being wild. Although wild salmon tends to contain less fat and a little more of some of the nutrients, the two kinds are broadly comparable. Salmon is our major source of fish oils, which provide protection against heart disease, blood clots, stroke, high blood pressure, high blood cholesterol, Alzheimer's disease, depression, and certain skin conditions. Salmon is also an excellent source of selenium—which protects against cancer—protein, niacin, vitamin B12, magnesium, and vitamin B6.

- Protection against cardiovascular diseases and stroke.
- Helps keep the brain healthy and improve insulin resistance.
- May help children's concentration and brainpower and protects against childhood asthma.
- Helps keep skin smooth, minimizes sunburn, can help beat eczema, and helps prevent dry eyes.
- Helps minimize joint pain and may protect against cancers.

DID YOU KNOW?

Farmed salmon has been found to contain up to twice the fat of wild salmon—the wild fish is leaner.

PRACTICAL TIPS

For optimum omega-3 content, cook salmon lightly and poach or broil rather than pan-fry. Overcooking can oxidize the essential fats and this means that they are no longer beneficial. Frozen salmon retains the beneficial oils, vitamins, and minerals, while canned salmon loses a proportion of these valuable nutrients.

BROILED SALMON WITH CITRUS SALSA

The salsa really makes this dish—citrus fruits and fish have long been recognized as good companions, and this zesty accompaniment really proves the case.

SERVES 4 • PREP TIME: 10 MINS • COOK TIME: 10 MINS

PER SERVING:

 387 cal CALORIES
 27.1g FAT
 5.2g SAT FAT
 9.6g CARBS
 6.1g SUGAR
 2g FIBER
26.7g PROTEIN
200mg SODIUM

INGREDIENTS
4 salmon fillets
1 tablespoon olive oil
1 tablespoon light soy sauce
pepper (optional)

CITRUS SALSA
1 large orange
1 lime
2 tomatoes, peeled and diced
2 tablespoons extra virgin olive oil
2 tablespoons chopped fresh cilantro
¼ teaspoon sugar
salt and pepper (optional)

1. Preheat the broiler to high. To make the salsa, cut all the peel and white pith from the orange and lime and remove the sections, discarding the membranes and reserving the juices.

2. Chop the orange sections and mix with the reserved juice, the tomatoes, oil, and cilantro. Add the sugar and season with salt and pepper, if using.

3. Put the salmon fillets onto the broiler rack. Mix the oil and soy sauce together, brush over the salmon, and season with pepper, if using. Place under the preheated broiler and cook, turning once, for 8–10 minutes, until the fish is firm and flakes easily.

4. Serve with a spoonful of the citrus salsa on the side.

VARIATION
This citrus salsa would also work well with broiled trout or tuna.

MACKEREL

Relatively inexpensive, mackerel is an excellent source of omega-3 fats and is also rich in minerals and vitamin E. It is also anti-inflammatory, which can help ease joint pain.

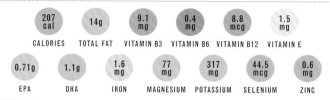

MAJOR NUTRIENTS PER 3½ OUNCES MACKEREL

207 cal	14g	9.1 mg	0.4 mg	8.8 mcg	1.5 mg
CALORIES	TOTAL FAT	VITAMIN B3	VITAMIN B6	VITAMIN B12	VITAMIN E

0.71g	1.1g	1.6 mg	77 mg	317 mg	44.5 mcg	0.6 mg
EPA	DHA	IRON	MAGNESIUM	POTASSIUM	SELENIUM	ZINC

Mackerel is a good choice for anyone seeking their weekly one to two portions of oily fish. It is one of the fish with the highest content of EPA and DHA—the two special omega-3 fats found in significant amounts almost exclusively in oily fish and fish livers. Multiple scientific papers provide the evidence that increased consumption confers many important, and even vital, health benefits. Numerous trials show that a regular intake of fish oils protects us against heart disease and stroke by reducing inflammation and blood pressure and improving the blood fat and cholesterol profile.

- Anti-inflammatory that can ease symptoms of Crohn's disease, joint pain, and arthritis.
- Can help prevent heart disease and stroke.
- Rich in selenium, magnesium, iron, potassium, and vitamins D and E.

PRACTICAL TIPS

Look for mackerel with firm, shiny bodies and bright eyes. Fresh mackerel won't droop if held horizontally by the head. Oily fish spoils faster than white fish and mackerel is best eaten within 24 hours of purchase. Baking, broiling, grilling, or pan-frying are excellent cooking methods and, because it has a rich taste, instead of using creamy sauces, it is best served with sharp or spicy flavors, such as a rhubarb sauce, mustard, or horseradish.

GRILLED MACKEREL
ON RYE BREAD

Fresh mackerel is packed with healthy fats and protein
and this hearty lunch is ideal for busy days.

SERVES 4 • PREP TIME: 10 MINS • COOK TIME: 10 MINS

PER SERVING:

 458 cal CALORIES
 26.3g FAT
 5.4g SAT FAT
 25.5g CARBS
 2.1g SUGAR
 3.4g FIBER
28.4g PROTEIN
600mg SODIUM

INGREDIENTS

4 mackerel fillets,
each weighing 4½ ounces
4 slices dark rye bread
1 tablespoon chopped fresh flat-leaf parsley,
to garnish

ANCHOVY RELISH

¼ cup chopped fresh flat-leaf parsley
2 tablespoons capers from a jar, drained
2 teaspoons Dijon mustard
6 anchovy fillets in oil, drained
juice of ½ lemon
1 teaspoon pepper
2 tablespoons extra virgin olive oil

1. To make the relish, put the parsley, capers, mustard, anchovy fillets, and lemon juice into a blender or food processor and process for a few seconds to blend. Alternatively, finely chop the parsley, capers, and anchovies and stir them together with the mustard and lemon juice in a small bowl. Stir the pepper and oil into the relish and set aside.

2. Put a ridged grill pan over high heat, then add the mackerel fillets and cook for 2–3 minutes on each side, or until bubbling and cooked through. Meanwhile, toast the rye bread.

3. Place the mackerel on the toasted bread and drizzle with the relish. Garnish with the parsley and serve immediately.

VARIATION

If you have run out of rye bread, whole-wheat bread or
whole-grain bread will work just as well with the mackerel.

TUNA

Fresh tuna is an important source of omega-3 fats and antioxidant minerals for arterial and heart health, and it is also rich in vitamin E for healthy skin.

MAJOR NUTRIENTS PER 3½ OUNCES TUNA

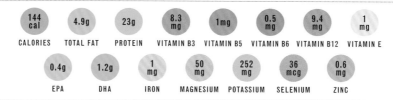

144 cal	4.9g	23g	8.3 mg	1mg	0.5 mg	9.4 mg	1 mg
CALORIES	TOTAL FAT	PROTEIN	VITAMIN B3	VITAMIN B5	VITAMIN B6	VITAMIN B12	VITAMIN E

0.4g	1.2g	1 mg	50 mg	252 mg	36 mcg	0.6 mg
EPA	DHA	IRON	MAGNESIUM	POTASSIUM	SELENIUM	ZINC

The firm, dense, and meaty flavorful flesh of fresh or frozen tuna makes it an ideal choice of fish for nonfish lovers. Quick to cook, it is an excellent source of protein and is especially rich in the B vitamins, selenium, and magnesium. A small portion will contain about 20 percent of your daily vitamin E needs. While most types of tuna contain fewer of the essential omega-3 fats than some other oily fishes, there is still a good content of EPA and DHA fats. DHA is particularly effective at keeping our hearts and brains healthy and in good working order. Just one portion of tuna per week can provide the recommended weekly intake of 1.4 g of these fats.

- A good source of omega-3 EPA and DHA fats, which offer protection against a range of diseases.
- High in protein.
- Rich in selenium and magnesium for heart health.
- Extremely rich in vitamin B12 for healthy blood.

DID YOU KNOW?

Research has found that when tuna is canned (whether in oil, water, a salt solution, or a sauce), it loses most of its beneficial omega-3 fats, so it shouldn't count toward your oily fish intake.

PRACTICAL TIPS

Fresh fish should be odorless and is best cooked and eaten on the day of purchase. To retain all the health benefits of the omega-3 fats, lightly sear tuna in a skillet on both sides and cook for as little time as possible. Tuna steaks can also be sliced and stir-fried for one minute with sliced vegetables—unlike many types of fish, it won't disintegrate.

TUNA WITH BOK CHOY & SOBA NOODLES

The addition of ginger and fresh chile brings out the flavor of the tuna in this fresh-tasting stir-fry. Don't overcook the bok choy or it will lose its characteristic crunchiness.

SERVES 2 • PREP TIME: 25 MINS • COOK TIME: 20 MINS

PER SERVING:

717 cal	27.2g	4.2g	53.2g	7.1g	7.4g	63.8g	720mg
CALORIES	FAT	SAT FAT	CARBS	SUGAR	FIBER	PROTEIN	SODIUM

INGREDIENTS

½ head of bok choy
1–2 teaspoon salt
4 ounces soba noodles
2 tuna steaks, each weighing about 6 ounces and ⅝ inch thick
1 tablespoon peanut oil, for brushing
2 tablespoons peanut oil
2 slices fresh ginger, cut into matchsticks
½–1 fresh red chile, seeded and thinly sliced
4 scallions, some green included, thicky sliced diagonally
1 cup frozen soybeans, thawed
2 tablespoons chicken broth
squeeze of lime juice
3 tablespoons chopped fresh cilantro
sea salt and pepper (optional)

1. Slice the bok choy stems into bite-size pieces. Slice the leaves into broad ribbons.

2. Add the salt to a large saucepan of water and bring to a boil. Add the noodles, bring back to a boil, and cook for 5–6 minutes, or according to package directions, until just tender. Drain, reserving the cooking water. Rinse well and set aside. Return the reserved water to the pan and keep warm over low heat.

3. Meanwhile, cut the tuna steaks into thirds. Brush with oil and season with sea salt and pepper, if using. Heat a ridged grill pan over high heat. Add the tuna and cook for 2–2½ minutes on each side. Transfer to a plate and set aside in a warm place.

4. Heat a wok over medium–high heat. Add the oil and sizzle the ginger, chile, and scallions for a few seconds.

5. Add the bok choy stems, soybeans, and broth and stir-fry for 3 minutes. Add the bok choy leaves and stir-fry for an additional minute. Add the lime juice and cilantro, then season with sea salt and pepper, if using.

6. Reheat the noodles in the cooking water, then drain. Divide the noodles between two plates, add the vegetables, and arrange the tuna on top. Serve immediately.

CLAMS

Low in fat and high in protein, clams are an ideal food for dieters and
they are rich in calcium for a healthy heart and bones.

MAJOR NUTRIENTS PER 3½ OUNCES SHUCKED CLAMS

74 cal	0.9g	12.8g	1.8g	49.4 mcg	46 mg	16 mcg	14 mg	9 mg	314 mg	24 mcg	1.4 mg
CALORIES	TOTAL FAT	PROTEIN	VITAMIN B3	VITAMIN B12	CALCIUM	FOLATE	IRON	MAGNESIUM	POTASSIUM	SELENIUM	ZINC

There are various types of clams, ranging in size and shape. All edible clams are highly nutritious, being low in fat and high in a wide range of minerals and the B vitamins. Clams have a particularly high iron content and just 3½ ounces shelled clams provide a whole day's intake. Iron carries oxygen from the lungs to all parts of the body and is vital for our immune system, helping to increase resistance to infection and aid the healing process. For women who experience anemia due to iron loss during menstruation, eating clams is a great way to replenish iron in the blood.

- High in iron for healthy blood.
- Provide high amounts of calcium for strong bones.
- High in selenium, the anticancer mineral.
- Good source of zinc to boost the immune system and fertility.

DID YOU KNOW?

Clams are usually found buried in sand or mud. Although native to both salt and fresh water, salt-water clams are considered to have a superior flavor.

PRACTICAL TIPS

Be careful when "shucking" clams (removing them from their shells). The clam should be held in a thick cloth and a proper shucking knife used to pry open the shell. Clams in their shells can be cooked like mussels—in a little liquid over high heat, covered. Any that don't open after 3 minutes should be discarded. Clams go well with spaghetti, or can be used in a seafood chowder soup. Garlic, parsley, and tomato are natural culinary companions.

CLAMS IN BLACK BEAN SAUCE

Clams cooked in black bean sauce are a popular partnership in Chinese cooking.
Traditionally inexpensive and widely available, clams provide many essential minerals.

SERVES 4 • PREP TIME: 18 MINS • COOK TIME: 10 MINS

PER SERVING:	75 cal	3.7g	0.6g	3.9g	0.1g	0.7g	5.7g	200mg
	CALORIES	FAT	SAT FAT	CARBS	SUGAR	FIBER	PROTEIN	SODIUM

INGREDIENTS

2 pounds small clams
1 tablespoon vegetable oil or peanut oil
1 teaspoon finely chopped fresh ginger
1 teaspoon finely chopped garlic
1 tablespoon rinsed and coarsely chopped
fermented black beans
2 teaspoons Chinese rice wine
1 tablespoon finely chopped scallion
salt (optional)

1. Discard any clams with broken shells and any that refuse to close when tapped. Thoroughly wash the remaining clams and let soak in clean water until ready to cook.

2. Heat a wok over medium–high heat and add the oil. Add the ginger and garlic and stir-fry until fragrant. Add the beans and cook for 1 minute.

3. Increase the heat to high, add the clams and rice wine, and stir-fry for 2 minutes to combine everything. Cover and cook for an additional 3 minutes or until the clam shells have opened. Discard any that remain closed. Add the scallion and season with salt, if using. Serve immediately.

ANCHOVIES

Anchovies are a delicious way to combine the benefits of omega-3 oils
with a healthy dose of rejuvenating high-quality protein.

131 cal	4.84g	0mg	0mg	20.35g	14.02 mg	0.65 mg	0.54g	0.91g	147 mg	36.5 mg
CALORIES	TOTAL FAT	CARBS	FIBER	PROTEIN	VITAMIN B3	VITAMIN B5	OMEGA-3 OILS: EPA	OMEGA-3 OILS: DHA	CALCIUM	SELENIUM

Anchovies contain high levels of essential omega-3 oils and protein, which help the body to repair and renew skin, bone, and muscle and hold back the ravages of time. The protein in anchovies also helps regulate energy levels by reducing sugar cravings, making it an important player in effective metabolism and weight management. Oily fish is high in omega oils and low in saturated fats, so it is the perfect alternative to red meat. Anchovies support heart health, and also have a high vitamin B profile. Two portions a week of anchovies, or any oily fish, has been shown to significantly reduce the risk of heart attack, which increases as we grow older.

- The small bones in anchovies provide calcium to keep bones strong and the heart pumping efficiently.
- Selenium helps detoxify heavy metals, such as mercury and cadmium, that have an aging effect.
- Vitamins B3 and B5 create energy in all cells to keep the body young.

DID YOU KNOW?

The strong flavor of anchovies makes them a common ingredient in many popular condiments, not just fish sauces but also Worcestershire sauce.

PRACTICAL TIPS

Fresh anchovies are hard to find but some anchovies are more healthily preserved than others. Anchovies in a jar are preserved in oil instead of salt, and marinated white anchovies (available in most delis and supermarkets) have a less intense flavor than canned ones.

STUFFED TOMATOES

These stuffed tomatoes make an excellent, quick-and-easy summer snack or appetizer.
Avocado, olives, and anchovies add essential nutrients.

MAKES 12 • PREP TIME: 20 MINS • COOK TIME: NONE

PER STUFFED TOMATO:	77 cal	6.5g	1g	4.1g	1.8g	1.9g	1.5g	120mg
	CALORIES	FAT	SAT FAT	CARBS	SUGAR	FIBER	PROTEIN	SODIUM

INGREDIENTS

12 small ripe tomatoes,
about 1¾ inches in diameter
1 large ripe avocado
1 tablespoon lemon juice
¼ cup mayonnaise
6 canned anchovy fillets in oil,
drained and finely chopped
8 pitted black olives, finely chopped
pepper (optional)
1 tablespoon snipped fresh chives, to garnish

1. Cut a thin slice from the bottom of each tomato and scoop out the seeds. Put, cut side down, onto several layers of paper towels and let drain.

2. Meanwhile, halve the avocado and remove the pit. Scoop the flesh into a bowl and mash with the lemon juice. Add the mayonnaise, anchovies, and olives. Mix well and season with pepper, if using.

3. Spoon the avocado mixture into the tomatoes. Arrange on a serving plate and sprinkle with the chives.

CRAB

This low-fat, high-protein shellfish contains l-tyrosine for brainpower
and high levels of selenium for protection from cancer.

MAJOR NUTRIENTS PER 3½ OUNCES CRABMEAT

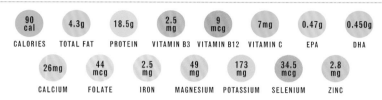

90 cal	4.3g	18.5g	2.5 mg	9 mcg	7mg	0.47g	0.450g
CALORIES	TOTAL FAT	PROTEIN	VITAMIN B3	VITAMIN B12	VITAMIN C	EPA	DHA

26mg	44 mcg	2.5 mg	49 mg	173 mg	34.5 mcg	2.8 mg
CALCIUM	FOLATE	IRON	MAGNESIUM	POTASSIUM	SELENIUM	ZINC

Like mussels, crabs are low in total fat and saturates and rich in minerals. Crabmeat is a good source of l-tyrosine, an amino acid that has been shown to help brainpower. It contains as much protein as a similar weight of lean beef and is, therefore, ideal for pescatarians. A 3½-ounce portion of crab provides over half the recommended daily intake of selenium, a powerful mineral with anticancer action, as well as one-quarter of a day's folate. This vitamin helps to protect against birth defects and is also linked to a reduction in levels of blood homocysteine, which is a contributing factor in heart disease.

- Excellent source of low saturated fat protein, which also contains omega-3 fats.
- Rich in several important minerals.
- Contributes a range of the B vitamins in good amounts.
- Good choice for people watching their weight.

DID YOU KNOW?

There are more than 8,000 species of fresh and saltwater crabs. Every year, more than one million tons are eaten.

PRACTICAL TIPS

You can buy live crabs and boil them at home, but many people prefer to buy prepared and dressed crabs, or packages of frozen cooked crabmeat. Unfortunately, canned crab is often high in sodium and has lost much of its omega-3 fats. The white meat is delicately flavored, while the brown meat is rich and has a strong taste—both are best served simply with lemon and black pepper.

LITTLE CURRIED CRAB CAKES WITH AVOCADO SALAD

Once you've done the preparation, these little crab cakes are easy to put together, and they are perfectly complemented by the tangy avocado salad.

SERVES 4 • PREP TIME: 20 MINS • COOK TIME: 10 MINS

PER SERVING:

362 cal	14g	2.3g	40g	3.9g	7.7g	23.7g	520mg
CALORIES	FAT	SAT FAT	CARBS	SUGAR	FIBER	PROTEIN	SODIUM

INGREDIENTS

10½ ounces white crabmeat
1 cup drained, canned corn kernels
1¼ cups whole-wheat panko bread crumbs
1 extra-large egg, beaten
1½ tablespoons light mayonnaise
1½ tablespoons fat-free Greek-style yogurt
2 tablespoons snipped fresh chives
2 teaspoons Dijon mustard
1 teaspoon curry powder and ¼ teaspoon pepper
10 sprays cooking spray, for oiling
1 large ripe avocado
1 tomato, finely chopped
juice of ½ lime
small bunch of fresh cilantro, leaves only
½ fresh red jalapeño chile, seeded and chopped
3 scallions, chopped

1. Mix together the crabmeat, corn, bread crumbs, egg, mayonnaise, yogurt, chives, mustard, curry powder, and pepper in a bowl.

2. Using your hands, shape the mixture into eight patties. Spray a nonstick skillet with cooking spray to coat, then heat to just below medium–high and add the patties to the pan. Cook the patties for 4 minutes, without turning or moving them.

3. Meanwhile, make the salad. Pit, peel, and slice the avocado, then lightly crush it in a bowl. Add the tomato, lime juice, cilantro leaves, chile, and scallions and stir to combine.

4. Spray the tops of the patties with more cooking spray, then use a metal spatula to turn each one over carefully. Cook for an additional 3 minutes, or until the crab cakes are golden and piping hot. Serve immediately with the avocado salad.

HINT
Try serving these mini crab cakes with some extra Greek-yogurt lightly drizzled over the top.

SARDINES

Sardines are one of the best sources of omega-3 fats and can protect us against heart disease and Alzheimer's disease. They can also help lower "bad" blood cholesterol.

MAJOR NUTRIENTS PER 5 OUNCES (ABOUT 3) SARDINES

280 cal	16g	33g	7mg	15 mcg	2.7mg
CALORIES	TOTAL FAT	PROTEIN	VITAMIN B3	VITAMIN B12	VITAMIN E

1.147g	1.550g	3.9 mg	53 mg	536 mg	71 mcg	1.8 mg
EPA	DHA	IRON	MAGNESIUM	POTASSIUM	SELENIUM	ZINC

Sardines are usually eaten canned. They retain most of the nutrients of fresh sardines, but fresh sardines are a healthy treat. They are one of the richest fish in omega-3 fats DHA and EPA. These fatty acids can help prevent or control diseases including arthritis, cardiovascular disease, and Alzheimer's disease, and an adequate intake can help improve depression and enhance cognitive powers. Sardines are one of the few foods rich in vitamin D, which helps form and protect our bones throughout life. They are also high in other vitamins and minerals, and one portion provides about one-third of an adult's daily requirement of iron, vitamin E, vitamin B12, and selenium.

- Excellent source of omega-3 fats for disease prevention.
- Ideal food for long-term brain health and cognitive powers.
- Help lower "bad" blood cholesterol and high blood pressure.
- Regular consumption can give up to 50 percent reduced risk of stroke.

DID YOU KNOW?

Weight for weight, sardines provide more protein than steak, more potassium than bananas, and more iron than cooked spinach.

PRACTICAL TIPS

Fresh sardines can be cleaned (ask your fish seller to do this) and then broiled and served with lemon juice and bread, or with broiled tomatoes on whole-wheat toast. Sardines can also be filleted for people who don't want to deal with the bones, although the bones are edible and are an excellent source of calcium. Filleted fish can be enhanced with a mustard sauce, which cuts through the oily richness.

BROILED SARDINES STUFFED WITH FETA & PINE NUTS

The delicately herby stuffing brings feta and pine nuts together with raisins and lemon in this Mediterranean-inspired dish. It complements the broiled sardines perfectly.

SERVES 4 • PREP TIME: 30 MINS • COOK TIME: 12 MINS

PER SERVING:

767 cal	47.7g	10.8g	22.3g	14.7g	2.3g	67.9g	720mg
CALORIES	FAT	SAT FAT	CARBS	SUGAR	FIBER	PROTEIN	SOIDUM

INGREDIENTS

12 sardines, gutted and heads removed
¾ cup pine nuts
½ cup raisins
⅔ cup crumbled feta cheese
grated zest of 2 unwaxed lemons
¾ cup finely chopped fresh flat-leaf parsley
pinch of sea salt
¼ teaspoon of pepper
3 tablespoons olive oil
1 lemon, cut into wedges,
to serve (optional)

1. Butterfly the sardines and remove the backbones.

2. Heat a skillet over low heat. Add the pine nuts and toast for 5–6 minutes, or until golden, tossing halfway through. Let cool, then grind half the nuts in a mortar and pestle. Transfer to a bowl, add the raisins, cheese, lemon zest, parsley, whole pine nuts, salt, and pepper, and mix well.

3. Spoon 2 teaspoons of the filling into the cavity of each butterflied sardine. Close each sardine like a book and secure using a couple of toothpicks or a piece of kitchen twine.

4. Preheat the broiler to high. Line a baking sheet with aluminum foil. Lay the filled sardines on the prepared sheet and drizzle with half the oil. Broil for 6 minutes, turning halfway through and drizzling with the remaining oil. Serve hot, with lemon wedges for squeezing over the fish, if using.

HINT
You will need 24 wooden toothpicks or some kitchen twine to prepare the sardines for cooking.

TROUT

Trout provides a package that safeguards the joints, eyes, and brain from damage and keeps them working like new. It also helps to increase energy levels.

MAJOR NUTRIENTS PER 3½ OUNCES FRESH TROUT

148 cal	6.61g	0mg	0mg	20.77g	0.35 mg	4.5 mg	7.79 mg	155IU	0.2g	0.53g
CALORIES	TOTAL FAT	CARBS	FIBER	PROTEIN	VITAMIN B1	VITAMIN B3	VITAMIN B12	VITAMIN D	OMEGA-3 OILS: EPA	OMEGA-3 OILS: DHA

Omega-3 oils are crucial players in mood and behavior regulation, because they affect how we use the stabilizing brain chemicals serotonin and dopamine. Eating oily fish one to three times a week has also been shown to improve brainpower and slow down the loss in concentration, memory, and mental acuity associated with aging and stress. Of all the oily fish, trout is one of the least contaminated by mercury toxicity. Mercury is common in larger oily fish, such as tuna and swordfish, which can spend years accumulating this dangerous and aging substance.

- Contains pink astaxanthin, which supports good eye health and keeps the brain firing on all cylinders.
- Vitamin D is needed for an agile brain; low levels are linked to depression and dementia.
- High levels of the B vitamins promote youthful vitality and increased energy levels.
- Omega-3 oils lubricate joints to ensure pain-free agility.

DID YOU KNOW?

Trout is a type of salmon that spends its life in freshwater streams and ponds.

PRACTICAL TIPS

Trout can be bought both fresh and smoked. The fresh fish are easy to stuff with herbs and lemon and bake, and the smoked variety makes a good alternative to salmon, if you don't like its stronger flavor. This is a great choice of oily fish for people who are put off by a strong fishy flavor.

GINGER & SESAME TROUT WITH BRAISED BOK CHOY

Recipes with Asian ingredients have a reputation for being high in salt, but here the sodium content has been reduced, while keeping all the delicious flavors.

SERVES 2 • PREP TIME: 10 MINS • COOK TIME: 10 MINS

PER SERVING:

376 cal	18.2g	3g	12.2g	5.6g	2.9g	36.5g	360mg
CALORIES	FAT	SAT FAT	CARBS	SUGAR	FIBER	PROTEIN	SODIUM

INGREDIENTS

2 heads of bok choy
½ tablespoons peanut oil
½ teaspoon Chinese five spice
2 tablespoons rice wine
1 small green chile, seeded and finely chopped
6 sprays cooking oil spray
4 rainbow trout fillets
1 tablespoon sesame oil
¾-inch piece fresh ginger, finely grated
1 tablespoon low-salt soy sauce
½ tablespoons rice vinegar
1 teaspoon sesame seeds
1 tablespoon ketjap manis (Indonesian soy sauce)
4 scallions, chopped, to garnish

1. Quarter each head of bok choy lengthwise, rinse under cold running water, and pat dry on paper towels. Put a large saucepan over medium–high heat and add the peanut oil. Add the bok choy and cook for 3 minutes, or until starting to brown. Stir in the five spice and rice wine and cook for an additional minute, then add 1 tablespoon of boiling water and sprinkle in the chile. Bring to a simmer, cover, reduce the heat to low, and cook for 2–3 minutes, or until the bok choy is just tender.

2. Meanwhile, put a large skillet over medium–high heat and spray with 3 sprays of cooking oil spray. Add the trout fillets and cook for 2–3 minutes, then turn over with a spatula. Spray the pan with 3 sprays of cooking spray and cook for an additional 2 minutes, or until the fillets are just cooked through. Remove from the pan and keep warm.

3. Reduce the heat to medium, add the sesame oil to the pan, and stir in the ginger. Cook for 1 minute, then add the soy sauce, vinegar, sesame seeds, and ketjap manis and stir to combine.

4. Serve the trout fillets with the sesame mixture spooned over the top. Garnish with the scallions and serve with the bok choy mixture on the side.

SCALLOPS

They may be a luxurious treat, but scallops can also help boost your vitamin B12 and magnesium intake to protect the arteries and bones.

MAJOR NUTRIENTS PER 3½ OUNCES SHUCKED SCALLOPS

88 cal	0.8g	16.8g	1.5g	24 mg	16 mcg	56 mg	314 mg	22 mcg	0.95 mg
CALORIES	TOTAL FAT	PROTEIN	VITAMIN B12	CALCIUM	FOLATE	MAGNESIUM	POTASSIUM	SELENIUM	ZINC

Scallops are an excellent source of vitamin B12, which is needed by the body to deactivate homocysteine, a chemical that can damage blood vessel walls. High homocysteine levels are also linked to osteoporosis. A recent study found that osteoporosis occurred more frequently among women whose vitamin B12 status was deficient. A high intake of vitamin B12 has also been shown to be protective against colon cancer. Scallops are also a good source of magnesium and a regular intake helps build bone, release energy, regulate nerves, and keep the heart healthy. Deficiency can cause abnormal heart rhythms.

- Low in calories and fat so ideal for dieters.
- Rich in magnesium, which has several roles to play in body maintenance.
- A good source of vitamin B12 for arterial and bone health. Regular intake may help to protect against colon cancer.

DID YOU KNOW?

Scallops are rich in tryptophan, an amino acid that may help cure insomnia and aids the production of mood-enhancing serotonin in our brains.

PRACTICAL TIPS

Fresh scallops should have flesh that is white and firm, have no evidence of browning, and be free of odor. Scallops should be cooked for only a few minutes, because exposure to too much heat will cause them to become tough. The sweet flavor of scallops goes well with chile, cilantro, garlic, and parsley.

SPICY ORANGE NOODLES WITH SEARED SCALLOPS

Delicate scallops are delicious when paired with a chile-orange dressing,
and the noodles help to make a healthy and satisfying meal.

SERVES 4 • PREP TIME: 10 MINS • COOK TIME: 10 MINS

PER SERVING:	563 cal	38g	4.9g	54.9g	15.1g	2.8g	13.2g	160mg
	CALORIES	FAT	SAT FAT	CARBS	SUGAR	FIBER	PROTEIN	SODIUM

INGREDIENTS

12 ounces fresh udon noodles
12–16 scallops, corals removed
1 tablespoon unsalted butter
1 tablespoon olive oil
salt and pepper (optional)
3 scallions, thinly sliced, to garnish

DRESSING

3 garlic cloves, finely chopped
1 tablespoon finely chopped fresh ginger
zest and juice of 1 orange
¼ cup soy sauce
⅓ cup sweet chili sauce
½ cup vegetable oil

1. Cook the noodles according to the package directions. Drain and set aside.

2. To make the dressing, combine the garlic, ginger, orange zest and juice, soy sauce, and sweet chili sauce in a bowl and whisk to combine. Add the oil and whisk until emulsified.

3. Rinse the scallops, pat them dry, and season with salt and pepper, if using. Heat the butter and oil in a large skillet over high heat until the butter is melted. Add the scallops and sear for about 1½ minutes on each side, until they have a golden brown crust but are still translucent in the center.

4. In a large bowl, toss the noodles with most of the dressing. Divide the noodles among four plates. Top each with 3–4 scallops. Drizzle a little more dressing over the scallops and serve immediately, garnished with scallions.

HINT

To get maximum nutrients from the scallops, be careful not to overcook them—a searing hot pan is the best cooking method.

MUSSELS

Inexpensive and delicious, mussels are a source of protein, the B vitamins for nerve health, and iodine for thyroid function.

MAJOR NUTRIENTS PER 3½ OUNCES SHUCKED MUSSELS

86 cal	2.2g	11.9g	0.41g	0.16g	8mg	1.6 mcg	12 mcg
CALORIES	TOTAL FAT	PROTEIN	EPA	DHA	VITAMIN C	VITAMIN B3	VITAMIN B12

0.55 mg	26 mg	42mg	3.9 mg	34 mg	320 mg	44.5 mcg	1.6 mg
VITAMIN E	CALCIUM	FOLATE	IRON	MAGNESIUM	POTASSIUM	SELENIUM	ZINC

Mussels are low in saturated fat and high in protein, while also containing some omega-3 essential fats, a wide range of vitamins, and many minerals in excellent amounts. They are also low in cholesterol. A portion of mussels will provide about one-third of the recommended daily intake of iron for an adult, and about three-quarters of a day's selenium requirement. Mussels are a good source of the B vitamins, providing more than 100 percent of daily vitamin B_{12} needs, one-quarter of necessary folate, and a useful amount of niacin. Like most shellfish, mussels are also a good source of fluoride for healthy teeth and iodine for healthy thyroid function.

- A low-calorie, low-fat source of good quality protein.
- Contain useful amounts of omega-3 essential fats.
- Rich in iron and selenium.
- Good source of the B vitamins.

DID YOU KNOW?
A mussel with orange flesh is female, while a whiter mussel is usually male. Both are equally tasty and rich in nutrients.

PRACTICAL TIPS
Fresh mussels should not smell fishy or of iodine. They should have a slight salty odor. Farmed mussels are considered safer to eat than wild mussels, which can harbor toxins from the sea. Discard any live mussels that don't close tight when tapped and, discard any that have failed to open during cooking. Mussels go well with garlic, parsley, and white wine and can be added to fish stews, soups, paella, and shellfish salads.

MIXED SEAFOOD CHOWDER

Chowder is a traditional East Coast main-meal soup that is normally made with clams, but this mixed seafood version is equally good and just as nutritious.

SERVES 4 • PREP TIME: 10 MINS • COOK TIME: 30–35 MINS

PER SERVING:

362 cal	15.5g	5g	22.7g	6.7g	2.3g	30.4g	1,080 mg
CALORIES	FAT	SAT FAT	CARBS	SUGAR	FIBER	PROTEIN	SODIUM

INGREDIENTS

1 tablespoon vegetable oil
1 large onion, chopped
2¾ ounces pancetta, cubed
1 tablespoon all-purpose flour
2½ cups fish broth,
made from 1 fish broth cube
8 ounces small new potatoes, halved
pinch of saffron threads
pinch of cayenne pepper
1¼ cups low-fat milk
7 ounces haddock, halibut, or other
white fish fillet, cubed
5½ ounces salmon fillet, cubed
7 ounces cooked shelled mussels
pepper (optional)

1. Heat the oil in a large saucepan over medium heat, then add the onion and pancetta. Cook for 8–10 minutes, until the onion is soft and the pancetta is cooked. Stir in the flour and cook for an additional 2 minutes.

2. Stir in the broth and bring to a gentle simmer. Add the potatoes, then cover and simmer for 10–12 minutes, until the potatoes are tender and cooked through.

3. Add the saffron, cayenne pepper, and pepper, if using, then stir in the milk. Transfer the fish to the pan and gently simmer for 4 minutes.

4. Add the mussels and cook for an additional 2 minutes to warm through. Serve immediately.

VARIATION

For a richer, creamier, and more luxurious chowder, replace half the milk with light cream.

OYSTERS

Prized for their nutritional qualities, oysters are rich in zinc, which boosts fertility and skin health, as well as wound-healing and immune-boosting properties.

MAJOR NUTRIENTS PER 6 OYSTERS

50 cal	1.3g	4.4g	13.6 mcg	37 mg	15 mcg	4.9 mcg	28 mg	53.5 mcg	31.8 mg
CALORIES	TOTAL FAT	PROTEIN	VITAMIN B12	CALCIUM	FOLATE	IRON	MAGNESIUM	SELENIUM	ZINC

Although there is little scientific evidence that oysters are an aphrodisiac, they are one of our best sources of zinc, and this mineral is strongly linked with fertility and virility. Zinc is also important for skin health, wound healing, and the immune system and is an antioxidant. Recent research has found that ceramide compounds in oysters inhibit the growth of breast cancer cells. Oysters also contain a reasonable amount of essential omega-3 fats, are rich in selenium for a healthy immune system, and contain easily absorbed iron for energy and healthy blood.

- Excellent source of zinc for fertility and virility.
- Contain compounds and minerals that can protect against cancers.
- High iron content for energy, resistance to infection and healthy blood.
- A good source of the B vitamins.

DID YOU KNOW?

Traditionally, an oyster is eaten all in one go from the shell, sliding down your throat without chewing. You can also cook oysters, but some of the beneficial compounds may be lost.

PRACTICAL TIPS

Oysters need to be fresh and, if eaten raw, they should be alive. It is safest to eat farmed oysters, because in recent years wild oysters have been found to contain toxic levels of contaminants. A healthy way to serve fresh oysters is to top them with chopped shallots, chile, lime juice, and arugula.

OYSTERS VALENTINO

If you prefer your oysters cooked instead of raw, this traditional recipe is probably the best ever created. The hot pepper sauce adds great depth of heat.

SERVES 2 • PREP TIME: 20 MINS • COOK TIME: 5 MINS

PER SERVING:

142 cal	4.6g	1.9g	11.4g	1g	0.8g	12.5g	200mg
CALORIES	FAT	SAT FAT	CARBS	SUGAR	FIBER	PROTEIN	SODIUM

INGREDIENTS

12 unopened fresh oysters
¼ cup fresh bread crumbs
2 tablespoons diced red bell pepper
1 tablespoon finely chopped scallion
1 tablespoon chopped fresh parsley
zest of 1 lime
hot pepper sauce (optional)
3 tablespoons freshly grated Parmesan cheese

1. To open the oysters, hold them flat side up above a strainer set over a bowl to catch the juices. Insert the point of an oyster knife into the hinge and work it around until you can pry off the top shell and discard. Loosen the oyster from the deep shell and strain off and reserve the juice.

2. Crumple a sheet of aluminum foil and place in a broiler pan. Arrange the shells in the pan. Preheat the broiler to hot.

3. In a small bowl, mix together the bread crumbs, red bell pepper, scallion, parsley, and lime zest. Add enough of the oyster juice to moisten and a few drops of hot pepper sauce, if using, then divide the mixture among the oysters.

4. Sprinkle each oyster with a little cheese and cook under the preheated broiler for 3–4 minutes, or until golden and bubbling. Serve immediately.

HINT
The foil will help the oysters stay level and make sure that they broil evenly.

CRAYFISH

Low in sodium and rich in vitamin E, crayfish are good for heart health and excellent skin, as well as offering protection against heart disease and some cancers.

MAJOR NUTRIENTS PER 3½ OUNCES CRAYFISH TAILS

77 cal	1g	16g	2.2 mg	2 mcg	2.8 mg	27 mg	0.8 mg	37 mcg	27 mg	302 mg	31.5 mcg	1.3 mg
CALORIES	TOTAL FAT	PROTEIN	VITAMIN B3	VITAMIN B12	VITAMIN E	CALCIUM	IRON	FOLATE	MAGNESIUM	POTASSIUM	SELENIUM	ZINC

Crayfish are freshwater crustaceans—you can find them in some fish markets or as prepared tails in the freezer or chiller cabinets. They have a bright pink appearance and a sweet flavor and make a good substitute for shrimp in recipes. They are much lower in sodium and cholesterol than shrimp and, like most other shellfish, crayfish contain an excellent range of minerals. They are a good source of the antioxidant vitamin E, which is linked with protection from arterial and heart disease and some cancers, and can reduce the pain of arthritis.

- Low in calories and saturated fat.
- Excellent source of vitamin E.
- Rich in a range of vital minerals.
- Reasonably low in sodium and cholesterol.

PRACTICAL TIPS

If you buy uncooked crayfish, they should be live. To cook, drop into boiling water for 8–15 minutes, depending on size. Cooked, chilled or frozen crayfish can be eaten at room temperature or added to stir-fries for the last minute of cooking to heat through. Don't overcook or they will be tough. Try serving cooked crayfish tails on whole-wheat toast sprinkled with lemon juice and black pepper, garnished with arugula. Crushed crayfish shells make a good base for a seafood broth or sauce.

DID YOU KNOW?

Crayfish are closely related to lobsters, and have a similar, sweet flavor and nutritional profile.

CRAYFISH CAKES WITH SPICY MASHED AVOCADO

These delicious crayfish cakes are a low-fat treat and are excellent served with the creamy mashed avocado, given a spicy kick with chile.

SERVES 2 • PREP TIME: 15 MINS • COOK TIME: 10 MINS

PER SERVING:							
313 cal	14g	2.1g	22.6g	4.3g	7.4g	23.6g	0.8g
CALORIES	FAT	SAT FAT	CARBS	SUGAR	FIBER	PROTEIN	SALT

INGREDIENTS

¾ cup fresh whole-wheat bread crumbs
½ teaspoon pepper
2 tablespoons finely chopped fresh flat-leaf parsley
7 ounces peeled and cooked crayfish tails
¼ cup drained and chopped, roasted red pepper from a jar
1 teaspoon medium-hot peri peri sauce
1 tablespoon extra-light mayonnaise
1 medium egg white, beaten
1 tablespoon flour, for dusting
1 ripe avocado, sliced
1 small fresh red chile, seeded and chopped
1 scallion, finely chopped
½ teaspoon smoked paprika
juice of ¼ lime
6 sprays cooking oil spray

1. Put the bread crumbs, pepper, and parsley into a bowl and stir well to combine.

2. Coarsely chop the crayfish tails. In a separate bowl, combine the crayfish tails, roasted red pepper, peri peri sauce, and mayonnaise. Stir the bread crumb mixture into the crayfish mixture.

3. Add the beaten egg and mix to a moderately firm mixture—the cakes will become firm once they are cooked. Form into four patties and sprinkle with flour. If you have time, chill for up to 1 hour.

4. To make the mashed avocado, put the avocado slices into a bowl and coarsely mash with a fork. Stir in the chile, scallion, paprika, and lime juice.

5. Spray a nonstick skillet with the cooking oil spray and place over medium–high heat. Add the crayfish cakes and cook for 2–3 minutes, or until the underside is crisp and golden. Turn and cook for an additional 2–3 minutes, or until cooked through. Serve the cakes immediately topped with the mashed avocado.

LOBSTER

Low-fat lobster flesh is an excellent source of minerals, including zinc, potassium, selenium, and calcium. Their health benefits mean they are a treat worth indulging in.

MAJOR NUTRIENTS PER 1 SMALL LOBSTER

135 cal	1.35g	28g	2mg	1.4 mcg	2.2 mg	72 mg	0.45 mg	41 mg	2.4 mg	413 mg	62 mcg	4.5g
CALORIES	TOTAL FAT	PROTEIN	VITAMIN B3	VITAMIN B12	VITAMIN E	CALCIUM	IRON	MAGNESIUM	PANTOTHENIC ACID	POTASSIUM	SELENIUM	ZINC

For most of us, lobster is probably an occasional indulgence instead of an everyday food but, despite its luxurious connection, it is a healthy treat. Lobsters, like crayfish and crabs, are rich in minerals, including zinc, potassium, and selenium. They are richer in calcium than many other shellfish and one portion provides about one-tenth of the recommended daily intake. Calcium can help prevent osteoporosis and is important for heart health and muscle function. Lobster is also a good source of vitamin E, which acts as an antioxidant and helps to keep arteries healthy.

- One lobster portion provides a whole day's selenium intake.
- Rich source of zinc, the antioxidant mineral that boosts immunity, protects the skin, and is vital for fertility.
- High in pantothenic acid, the B vitamin essential for the conversion of food to energy.

DID YOU KNOW?

Lobsters can live for more than 50 years in the wild and are dark blue in appearance. It is only when they are cooked that they become deep pink.

PRACTICAL TIPS

Fresh lobsters are usually sold live, because the meat deteriorates quickly after the lobster is killed. They should be frozen for 1 hour and then boiled for 15 minutes, depending on size. Prepared lobster tails can be bought from the freezer or chill cabinet of most supermarkets. A large lobster claw yields a lot of meat so don't discard it—simply crush to remove the meat. Cooked lobster tail can be eaten simply as a salad, with lemon juice.

BEET, LOBSTER & SPINACH RISOTTO

With beets and spinach as well as lobster, this unusual and attractive red risotto provides a powerful nutrient boost on a single plate.

SERVES 4 • PREP TIME: 15 MINS • COOK TIME: 30 MINS

PER SERVING:

 683 cal CALORIES
 30.9g FAT
 16.4g SAT FAT
 69.6g CARBS
 7.5g SUGAR
 3.8g FIBER
 26.1g PROTEIN
 1,520 mg SODIUM

INGREDIENTS

6¾ cups reduced-salt vegetable broth
2 tablespoons butter
2 tablespoons olive oil
1 small onion, diced
1½ cups Arborio rice
½ cup dry white wine
5 small raw beets, grated
1 teaspoon grated horseradish
juice of ½ lemon
6 cups baby leaf spinach
8 ounces ready-to-eat lobster meat
1¼ cups freshly grated Parmesan cheese
salt and pepper (optional)
⅔ cup crème fraîche, to serve

1. Bring the broth to a boil in a large saucepan, then simmer over low heat. Meanwhile, heat the butter and oil in a separate large saucepan over medium heat, add the onion, and sauté for 3 minutes. Add the rice and stir to coat with the butter and oil. Cook for an additional 2 minutes. Add the wine and simmer for 2 minutes, or until absorbed.

2. Add the beets and stir well. Add 2 ladles of hot broth to the pan, then cover and cook for 2 minutes, or until absorbed. Stir well and add another ladle of broth. Stir constantly until the broth is absorbed, then add another ladle. Continue adding the broth, one ladle at a time, until it has all been absorbed and the rice is almost cooked.

3. Stir in the horseradish and lemon juice, then add the spinach and season with salt and pepper, if using. Divide among warm bowls, top with the lobster and cheese, and serve immediately, accompanied by the crème fraîche.

VARIATION
If you don't have vegetable broth, or you just prefer the taste, you can use chicken broth instead.

GREEK YOGURT

Greek yogurt with live and active cultures contains bacterial cultures that boost the immune system and keep the digestive system young and robust.

MAJOR NUTRIENTS PER ½ CUP GREEK YOGURT

61 cal	3.25g	4.66g	3.47g	99IU	0.14 mg	 0.39 mg	0.37 mcg	121 mg	15.2 mg	155 mg
CALORIES	TOTAL FAT	CARBS	PROTEIN	VITAMIN A	VITAMIN B2	VITAMIN B5	VITAMIN B12	CALCIUM	CHOLINE	POTASSIUM

Greek yogurt contains less sugar and more protein than other yogurts, because it is strained to remove the carbohydrate-rich whey. Its thickness leaves you fuller than more watery versions and the lower level of lactose (milk sugar) it contains makes it easier to digest. Eating yogurt with live and active cultures regularly has been shown to enhance immune responses and our resistance to disease.

- All yogurt helps reduce "bad" cholesterol/LDL, but only yogurt with live and active cultures raises "good" cholesterol/HDL levels, making sure the arteries stay functioning youthfully.
- People who regularly eat yogurt increase their fat-burning capacity, which leads to weight loss—especially around the waist.
- An important B12 source for vegetarians that helps to prevent dry skin and premature aging, as well as Alzheimer's disease, heart disease, and diabetes.

DID YOU KNOW?

People have been making yogurt for around 5,000 years. However, yogurt wasn't commercially produced until 1919, in Barcelona, Spain.

PRACTICAL TIPS

Always choose yogurts with live and active cultures, because these contain the beneficial bacteria. If possible, buy from local farms via health food stores or farmers' markets: these products will have their own natural bacteria instead of bacteria that has been added in the production process. Avoid fruit-flavored yogurt, which contains added sugar, and instead sweeten your yogurt with fruit or cinnamon. The creamy, fresh taste of Greek yogurt makes it a good alternative to milk, cream, sour cream, or crème fraîche in savory dishes.

HEALTHY CAESAR DRESSING

Low-fat plain yogurt and reduced-fat mayo combine to provide the perfect
basis for this lighter, healthy alternative to Caesar dressing.

MAKES ABOUT ½ CUP • PREP TIME: 15 MINS • COOK TIME: NONE

PER ½ CUP	147 cal	5.3g	0.7g	10.6g	5g	1.2g	15g	600mg
	CALORIES	FAT	SAT FAT	CARBS	SUGAR	FIBER	PROTEIN	SODIUM

INGREDIENTS
½ cup low-fat Greek-style plain yogurt
3 anchovy fillets, coarsely chopped
2 garlic cloves, crushed
grated zest and juice of ½ lemon
⅔ cup coarsely chopped fresh flat-leaf parsley
1 tablespoon low-fat mayonnaise

1. Put all of the ingredients, except the mayonnaise, into a small bowl and blend with a handheld blender until the parsley and anchovies have disintegrated. As the parsley breaks down, the dressing will take on a beautiful green color and become easier to blend.

2. Stir in the mayonnaise. Serve immediately as an alternative to Caesar dressing. It will keep for three to four days in a covered container in the refrigerator.

MILK

Milk provides a complete source of easily digested protein and is one of our major sources of calcium for bone health.

MAJOR NUTRIENTS PER ⅓ CUP PLUS 1 TABLESPOON LOW-FAT (2% FAT) MILK

52 cal	2g	4.9g	3.4g	0.55 mcg	124 mg	144 mg	0.49 mg
CALORIES	TOTAL FAT	CARBS	PROTEIN	VITAMIN B12	CALCIUM	POTASSIUM	ZINC

This versatile food is particularly good for vegetarians, who have a limited number of sources of complete protein (which is a protein source containing all nine of the indispensible amino acids—the building blocks of protein) in their diet. Milk is also one of the best sources of the mineral calcium, adequate intake of which is needed to help us build and maintain bone volume and density, and is also vital for muscle, heart, and nerve function. Calcium absorption is also helped by essential fatty acids, which is why organic milk is preferable—it contains about 62 percent more essential omega-3 fats than standard milk. Milk is also a good source of vitamin B12, which can be lacking in a vegetarian diet.

- A complete protein source suitable for vegetarians.
- A good source of calcium vital for bone health.
- Organic milk is a source of omega-3 fats, which aid calcium absorption.

DID YOU KNOW?

If you do choose organic milk, you will also reduce your intake of hormones and antibiotics that are regularly added to the feed of cows on nonorganic farms. In order to reap the most benefit from the omega-3 fats in organic milk, choose whole or low-fat varieties. Skim milk will contain virtually none.

PRACTICAL TIPS

Coffee and strong tea can interfere with the absorption of calcium, so it is best to drink your milk on its own or as the basis for a smoothie. Or use it to make desserts, pour over breakfast cereal, and so on. Some people have an intolerance to lactose, a type of sugar found in milk, which can give them digestive problems. This should be diagnosed by a physician.

BEE POLLEN & NECTARINE SMOOTHIE

Nutritious bee pollen adds an intriguing touch to this nifty and nourishing
nectarine milk shake. The honey adds natural sweetness, too.

SERVES 2 • PREP TIME: 15 MINS • COOK TIME: NONE

PER SERVING: **163 cal** CALORIES | **3.2g** FAT | **1.8g** SAT FAT | **28.7g** CARBS | **22.8g** SUGAR | **2.6g** FIBER | **7.3g** PROTEIN | **40mg** SODIUM

INGREDIENTS

2 ripe nectarines, quartered
1 cup low-fat milk
2 tablespoons Greek-style plain yogurt
1 tablespoon bee pollen
1 teaspoon honey
handful of ice cubes
1 teaspoon bee pollen, to decorate
2 nectarine slices, to decorate

1. Put the nectarines, milk, yogurt, bee pollen, and honey into
a blender and process until smooth. Add the ice cubes and
process again until completely blended.

2. Pour the milk shake into chilled glasses and decorate with
the bee pollen and a slice of nectarine. Serve immediately.

GOAT CHEESE

Goat cheese is higher in calcium and lower in fat than cheese made from cow milk, making it better for bone strength and as a rejuvenating source of protein.

MAJOR NUTRIENTS PER 3½ OUNCES GOAT CHEESE

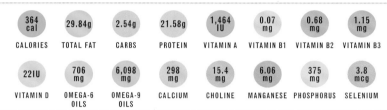

364 cal	29.84g	2.54g	21.58g	1,464 IU	0.07 mg	0.68 mg	1.15 mg
CALORIES	TOTAL FAT	CARBS	PROTEIN	VITAMIN A	VITAMIN B1	VITAMIN B2	VITAMIN B3

22IU	706 mg	6,098 mg	298 mg	15.4 mg	6.06 mg	375 mg	3.8 mcg
VITAMIN D	OMEGA-6 OILS	OMEGA-9 OILS	CALCIUM	CHOLINE	MANGANESE	PHOSPHORUS	SELENIUM

Cheese is especially valuable for vegetarians as an alternative to meat. Goat cheese tends to be more traditionally made than cow milk cheeses, so can contain fewer chemical additives and preservatives. Although it contains the same protein, casein, that is present in cow milk and may cause allergies, it takes a different form and is often more tolerated by people with digestive sensitivities. Goat cheese provides a type of saturated fat that is needed for nervous system communication and that is healthy when eaten in a diet that is also high in omega-3 and omega-6 oils, such as those found in oily fish, nuts, and seeds.

- Contains phosphorus, manganese, vitamin B3, and vitamin A, which all help to lock calcium into the bones, keeping them strong.
- The combination of protein with quality saturated fat can help prevent the sugar cravings that lead to premature aging of the skin, eyes, and organs.
- Goat milk is higher in vitamins B1 and B3 than cow milk. These B vitamins make energy to repair cells and boost vitality.

DID YOU KNOW?

The fat particles in goat milk are much smaller than those in cow milk, being closer in size to those in human milk. This is why goat milk is easier to digest and why there is no need for the homogenization process.

PRACTICAL TIPS

Choose soft cheeses for less saturated fat, and cheeses from farm stores or markets for optimum nutritional benefits. Check the labels of well-known cheeses, such as feta, because they are sometimes made with cow milk. Cheeses may also be made with sheep milk, which is similar to cheese made with goat milk.

COOL WATERMELON, GOAT CHEESE & ARUGULA SALAD

The creaminess of the goat cheese in this salad complements the citrus- and chile-dressed watermelon to make a quick summer salad.

SERVES 4 • PREP TIME: 10–15 MINS • COOK TIME: NONE

PER SERVING: 215 cal CALORIES 10.8g FAT 7.1g SAT FAT 21g CARBS 14.6g SUGAR 2.1g FIBER 11.1g PROTEIN 120mg SODIUM

INGREDIENTS

5¼ cups large watermelon cubes
grated zest and juice of 2 large limes
½–1 red chile, seeded and finely chopped
1¼ cups coarsely chopped fresh cilantro
3 cups arugula
4 ounces firm goat cheese, cut into cubes
salt and pepper (optional)
4 lime wedges, to serve

1. Put the watermelon into a large salad bowl. Sprinkle with the lime zest and juice and the chile, then season with a little salt and pepper, if using, and gently toss together.

2. Sprinkle with the cilantro, arugula, and cheese and gently toss together. Serve with lime wedges.

FREE-RANGE EGGS

Eggs are a perfect protein source, containing all of the amino acids
needed for the body to repair itself and stay young looking.

MAJOR NUTRIENTS PER LARGE EGG

65 cal	4.37g	1.68g	0.34g	5.53g	214IU	0.21 mg	0.63 mg	0.57 mcg
CALORIES	TOTAL FAT	MONO UN- SATURATED FAT	CARBS	PROTEIN	VITAMIN A	VITAMIN B2	VITAMIN B5	VITAMIN B12

22IU	0.1 mcg	32.6 mg	505 mg	1,582 mg	110.5 mg	0.81 mg	146 mcg	13.9 mcg	0.49 mg
VITAMIN D	VITAMIN K	OMEGA-3 OILS	OMEGA-6 OILS	OMEGA-9 OILS	CHOLINE	IRON	LUTEIN/ ZEAXANTHIN	SELENIUM	ZINC

Eggs are ideally packaged to support new life, so they contain all
the nutrients we need for growth: iron, zinc, vitamin A, vitamin D, the
B vitamins, and omega-3 fats. Many people avoid them because of their
high cholesterol content, but the body can regulate it if the diet is low in
sugar and saturated fat. Many studies show that egg consumption helps
prevent chronic age-related conditions, such as coronary heart disease,
loss of muscle mass, eye degeneration, hearing loss, and memory loss.

- Contain vitamin B12 to help combat fatigue, depression, and lethargy.
- Vitamin A and lutein ensure eye protection and continuing good sight.
- One of the few dietary sources of vitamins K and D, which work
  together to keep bones strong.
- Contain sulfur and lecithin, substances that help the liver with
  digestion and detoxification.

DID YOU KNOW?

*Organic eggs are laid by hens that
are raised organically, with organic
feed and without vaccines and
antibiotics, but the hens may still
be caged—look for organic eggs
from cage-free hens.*

PRACTICAL TIPS

Eggs are a truly useful standby food. They can be cooked in many different
ways, including poaching, scrambling, and boiling. Omelets or frittatas,
loaded with healthy vegetables, can also be eaten cold as a snack at any
time. Buy organic free-range eggs, because the chicken feed gives these
eggs a higher nutritional value, indicated by their deeper yellow yolk and
richer taste.

POACHED EGGS & KALE WITH WHOLE-WHEAT SOURDOUGH

Kale adds valuable nutrients and vivid green color to these
poached eggs, which are served on sensational sourdough toast.

SERVES 4 • PREP TIME: 20 MINS • COOK TIME: 15–17 MINS

PER SERVING:	324 cal	15.1g	3g	36.3g	2.6g	4.4g	12.6g	40mg
	CALORIES	FAT	SAT FAT	CARBS	SUGAR	FIBER	PROTEIN	SODIUM

INGREDIENTS

4 eggs
1½ cups chopped kale
4 large slices of whole-wheat sourdough bread
2 garlic cloves, halved
2 tablespoons olive oil
1 teaspoon crushed red pepper flakes
salt and pepper (optional)

1. Bring a shallow saucepan of water to a gentle simmer. Crack an egg into a small bowl or ramekin, then slide the egg into the water, lowering the bowl as close to the water as possible. Using a large spoon, gently fold any stray strands of white around the yolk. Repeat with the other eggs.

2. Cook for 2–3 minutes, or until set to your preference, then remove with a slotted spoon. Place the eggs in a small bowl of warm water and set aside until needed.

3. Bring a saucepan of water to a boil and add the kale. Simmer for 3–4 minutes, or until the kale is just cooked but still retains a little crunch. Drain, season with salt and pepper, if using, and set aside.

4. Meanwhile, toast the bread. Place the toast on four plates, then rub each slice with the garlic and drizzle with the oil. Top with some kale and a poached egg, sprinkle with the crushed red pepper flakes, and serve immediately.

HINT

For best results, try and use very fresh eggs for this recipe, because they make the best poached eggs.

QUAIL EGGS

Weight for weight, quail eggs contain even more nutrients and accessible protein than hen eggs, helping to repair and renew skin, bones, and muscles.

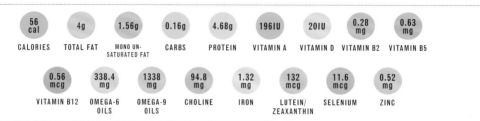

MAJOR NUTRIENTS PER 4 QUAIL EGGS

56 cal	4g	1.56g	0.16g	4.68g	196IU	20IU	0.28 mg	0.63 mg
CALORIES	TOTAL FAT	MONO UN-SATURATED FAT	CARBS	PROTEIN	VITAMIN A	VITAMIN D	VITAMIN B2	VITAMIN B5

0.56 mcg	338.4 mg	1338 mg	94.8 mg	1.32 mg	132 mcg	11.6 mcg	0.52 mg
VITAMIN B12	OMEGA-6 OILS	OMEGA-9 OILS	CHOLINE	IRON	LUTEIN/ZEAXANTHIN	SELENIUM	ZINC

Quail eggs have a higher yolk-to-white ratio than hen eggs. This means that for their size you get a good dose of the yellow carotenoid lutein, which helps prevent damage to fats in your body. The brain, heart, skin, eyes, and liver are just a few of these fatty areas and they are susceptible to damage, so protecting them from the aging effects of toxins is crucial to staying young. Quail eggs have been used for hundreds of years in traditional Chinese medicine to help combat immune-compromising allergies, such as hay fever and asthma, and skin conditions, such as acne, psoriasis, and eczema.

- Vitamin D helps revitalize bone and brain, so a dietary source is especially important when we can't get it from sunlight in the winter.
- Choline helps brain function, keeping memory and concentration performing youthfully.
- High selenium, zinc, and vitamin A content provides antioxidant protection, preventing aging and supporting new skin growth.

DID YOU KNOW?

In Romania, quail eggs are traditionally eaten to treat minor ailments as part of a "120-egg cure" (over 25 days). For more serious problems, there is the "240-egg cure," (over 45 days).

PRACTICAL TIPS

Quail eggs can replace hen eggs in any dish, but their beauty lies in their miniature yolk and white, so simply boiling and slicing into a salad is the best option. They fall apart less easily than hen eggs and have a slightly richer, gamier flavor.

TUNA & ASPARAGUS SALAD WITH QUAIL EGGS

This quick and delicious salad combines healthy quinoa with quail eggs for a protein-packed lunch or light supper.

SERVES 4 • PREP TIME: 10 MINS • COOK TIME: 20 MINS

PER SERVING:	392 cal	12.5g	1.9g	34.1g	3.3g	5.7g	35.4g	360mg
	CALORIES	FAT	SAT FAT	CARBS	SUGAR	FIBER	PROTEIN	SODIUM

INGREDIENTS

1 cup quinoa, rinsed
8 quail eggs
6 sprays cooking oil spray
24 asparagus spears, woody stems discarded
4 tuna steaks, each weighing 3½ ounces
2 tablespoons olive oil
½ tablespoons white wine vinegar
½ teaspoon Dijon mustard
½ teaspoon sugar
½ teaspoon salt
½ teaspoon pepper
12 cherry tomatoes
4 small scallions, finely chopped, to garnish

1. Bring a saucepan of water to a boil and add the quinoa. Cook for 15–18 minutes, or until just tender. Drain and set aside.

2. Meanwhile, bring a separate saucepan of water to a boil and add the eggs. Cook for 3 minutes, then drain and rinse in cold water to cool. Peel the shells from the eggs.

3. Place a ridged grill pan over high heat and spray with 2 sprays of cooking spray. Add the asparagus spears and cook, turning once, for 4 minutes, until slightly charred and just tender.

4. Spray the tuna steaks with the remaining cooking oil spray and cook in the pan for 1½ minutes. Turn and cook for an additional minute, or until cooked to your preference. Transfer to a plate and let rest for 2 minutes.

5. Beat together the olive oil, vinegar, mustard, sugar, salt, and pepper in a small bowl. Stir two-thirds of this oil mixture into the cooked quinoa.

6. Cut each tuna steak into three pieces. Divide the quinoa among four serving plates and top evenly with the tuna pieces, asparagus, eggs, and tomatoes. Drizzle the remaining dressing over the top and garnish with the scallions.

GRAINS, LEGUMES, NUTS & SEEDS

QUINOA

The best source of complete protein in the plant kingdom, quinoa provides all the necessary building blocks for age-defying skin, and bone and brain regeneration.

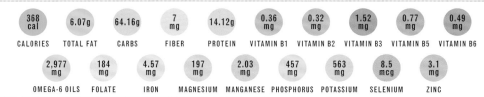

MAJOR NUTRIENTS PER ½ CUP PLUS 1 TABLESPOON UNCOOKED QUINOA

368 cal	6.07g	64.16g	7 mg	14.12g	0.36 mg	0.32 mg	1.52 mg	0.77 mg	0.49 mg
CALORIES	TOTAL FAT	CARBS	FIBER	PROTEIN	VITAMIN B1	VITAMIN B2	VITAMIN B3	VITAMIN B5	VITAMIN B6

2,977 mg	184 mg	4.57 mg	197 mg	2.03 mg	457 mg	563 mg	8.5 mcg	3.1 mg
OMEGA-6 OILS	FOLATE	IRON	MAGNESIUM	MANGANESE	PHOSPHORUS	POTASSIUM	SELENIUM	ZINC

Most plant foods are lacking in one or more essential amino acid, meaning that vegetarians and vegans need to consider carefully what range of foods they eat in order to get the right spread for youthful health. Quinoa is an easy one-food solution, containing all the essential amino acids, and it also provides a good range of minerals and the B vitamins. These enable the protein content of quinoa to be used effectively, so that it can provide the vast amount of energy needed for the constant renewal of skin, hair, nails, teeth, bone, and organs. Quinoa is actually a seed, not a grain. As such, it is high in anti-inflammatory omega-6 oils and is ideal for those people who cannot tolerate wheat or gluten.

- Contains phosphorus to make phospholipids in the brain and nervous system, which enable you to move and think youthfully.
- Potassium balances out the sodium in your diet, reducing bloating, puffiness, and high blood pressure.
- Zinc and selenium offer potent antioxidant protection from aging elements in your life, such as pollution, sunlight, and chemicals.

DID YOU KNOW?

Quinoa is a seed from South America that the Incas called the mother grain. It was traditionally offered to the sun god Inti, and the first crop of the season was dug up with a golden shovel.

PRACTICAL TIPS

Quinoa cooks in a similar way to rice. It has a pleasant, nutty flavor, and it is delicious in Mexican and Indian meals. You can also make a great quinoa porridge, either from flakes or from the grain itself. Quinoa is versatile enough to be cooked in both sweet and savory dishes.

SMASHED AVOCADO & QUINOA WRAP

Filled with nourishing, natural goodness, fresh avocado and spinach combine with colorful, crunchy raw red cabbage to create these appealing quinoa-topped wraps.

SERVES 4 • PREP TIME: 20 MINS • COOK TIME: 15–18 MINS

PER SERVING:

386 cal	13.2g	2.8g	56.8g	3.6g	10.4g	11.8g	560mg
CALORIES	FAT	SAT FAT	CARBS	SUGAR	FIBER	PROTEIN	SODIUM

INGREDIENTS

1 cup quinoa
1¾ cups vegetable broth
1 large ripe avocado, pitted and peeled
½ teaspoon smoked paprika
2 garlic cloves, crushed
finely grated zest and juice of 1 lemon
4 whole-wheat tortillas
1¾ cups baby spinach
1½ cups finely sliced red cabbage
salt and pepper (optional)

1. Put the quinoa and broth into a small saucepan and bring to a simmer. Simmer, covered, for 15–18 minutes, or until the broth has been completely absorbed. Set aside to cool.

2. Meanwhile, gently mash the avocado with the paprika, garlic, lemon zest, and just enough lemon juice to achieve a thick consistency.

3. Spread the mashed avocado down the center of each wrap and then top with the warm quinoa, spinach, and red cabbage. Season with salt and pepper, if using. Tuck in the ends and tightly fold or roll into a wrap and serve immediately.

RYE

Rye has many health benefits that make it an excellent food to incorporate into your diet—most notably the good levels of protein and fiber.

MAJOR NUTRIENTS PER 1 CUP RYE FLOUR

MAJOR NUTRIENTS PER 1 CUP RYE FLOUR

325 cal	2.22g	15.91g	23.8 mg	15.91 mg	0.32 mg	0.25 mg	4.27 mg	1.46 mg
CALORIES	TOTAL FAT	CARBS	FIBER	PROTEIN	VITAMIN B1	VITAMIN B2	VITAMIN B3	VITAMIN B5

0.44 mg	958 mg	4.97 mg	210 mcg	160 mg	6.06 mg	18 mcg	5.04 mg
VITAMIN B6	OMEGA-6 OILS	IRON	LUTEIN/ ZEAXANTHIN	MAGNESIUM	MANGANESE	SELENIUM	ZINC

Rye contains generous amounts of minerals and fiber, both of which help the body to clear out damaging toxins and harmful cholesterol. It also provides approximately 20 percent of its calories from protein and a good mix of the amino acids necessary to rebuild and repair all our body structures, from skin to teeth. The levels of protein and fiber in rye ensure that it has low glycemic index score of 26, meaning it releases its sugars slowly into the bloodstream, which gives us energy over a long period without wanting to eat more. Good levels of magnesium, vitamin B6, and zinc support this action by helping the body to produce the hormone insulin and use sugars efficiently.

- Lutein and zeaxanthin offer carotenoid antioxidant protection from damage to our brains, hearts, liver, and skin.
- High magnesium content helps us to make the body proteins we need, and so build skin and bone like new.
- Vitamin B5 holds back the aging effects of stress.

DID YOU KNOW?

In many countries, including Poland, Finland, and Russia, rye is a more popular bread flour than wheat. It is often sold with the addition of flavorings, such as fennel, coriander, molasses, or cardamom.

PRACTICAL TIPS

Dark rye is denser and more nutritious than medium and light types. The average supermarket loaf uses medium rye, which is often mixed with wheat to make the bread fluffier, so check labels. Pumpernickel is a dark rye flour and is used to make the pure rye bread of the same name.

CREPES WITH CREAMY CITRUS FILLING

This breakfast or dessert has a great balance of protein, carbohydrates, and fat.
The rye and spelt flours give these extra-thin pancakes a nutty, slightly sweet taste.

SERVES 4 • PREP TIME: 20 MINS • COOK TIME: 10 MINS

PER SERVING:

 316 cal CALORIES **10.7g** FAT **4.3g** SAT FAT **35.8g** CARBS **9.1g** SUGAR **3.4g** FIBER **19.7g** PROTEIN **640mg** SODIUM

INGREDIENTS

¾ cup ricotta cheese
¾ cup fat-free Greek-style yogurt
1 tablespoon grated orange zest
2 tablespoons orange juice
1–2 teaspoons stevia granules
⅓ cup rye flour
⅓ cup spelt flour
⅓ cup all-purpose flour
1 teaspoon salt
2 medium eggs
1 tablespoon peanut oil
⅔ cup skim milk
½ cup water
8 sprays cooking spray, for oiling
1 orange, peeled, sectioned and chopped
2 teaspoons confectioners' sugar, for dusting

1. In a bowl, combine the ricotta cheese, yogurt, orange zest, orange juice, and stevia granules. Set aside in the refrigerator until ready to serve.

2. In a mixing bowl, stir together the rye flour, spelt flour, all-purpose flour, and salt, then whisk in the eggs, oil, milk, and water until completely smooth.

3. Heat a small, nonstick skillet over medium–high heat and coat with cooking spray.

4. When the pan is hot, pour in one-quarter of the batter and swirl it around to coat the pan. Cook for 1 minute, or until the underside is golden, then flip the pancake over with a spatula and cook for 1 minute on the other side. Transfer the cooked pancake to a warm plate while you cook the remaining batter.

5. Repeat to make another three pancakes, spraying the pan between each addition. (You could make eight mini pancakes, if you prefer.)

6. Place the pancakes on serving plates, then fill with the ricotta mixture and a little of the chopped orange and fold over. Decorate with the remaining chopped orange and dust with the confectioners' sugar.

POT BARLEY

This extremely nutritious starchy grain contains soluble fiber that helps to lower "bad" blood cholesterol and protect us from hormonal cancers and heart disease.

MAJOR NUTRIENTS PER ⅓ CUP RAW POT BARLEY

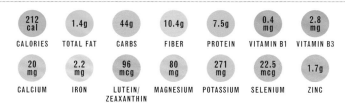

212 cal	1.4g	44g	10.4g	7.5g	0.4 mg	2.8 mg
CALORIES	TOTAL FAT	CARBS	FIBER	PROTEIN	VITAMIN B1	VITAMIN B3

20 mg	2.2 mg	96 mcg	80 mg	271 mg	22.5 mcg	1.7g
CALCIUM	IRON	LUTEIN/ ZEAXANTHIN	MAGNESIUM	POTASSIUM	SELENIUM	ZINC

Pot barley is a grain with a rich, slightly nutty flavor and a chewy texture. Most barley that is sold is pearl barley, which has had almost all of the nutrients and fiber removed by processing, whereas pot, or hulled, barley, has had minimal processing and is, therefore, a good source of nutrients. These include a high level of fiber, including soluble fiber and a fiberlike compound called lignan, which may protect against breast and other hormone-dependent cancers, as well as heart disease. Unusually for a grain, barley contains luteiṅ and zeaxanthin, which help to protect eyesight and eye health.

- Whole grain that protects against cancers and heart disease.
- A good source of minerals and the B vitamins.
- High in fiber to keep the colon healthy and soluble fiber to lower blood cholesterol.
- Helps to keep eyes healthy.

DID YOU KNOW?

Barley water, made by steeping the grains in water, has long been considered a health drink for its diuretic and kidney-supporting effect.

PRACTICAL TIPS

Pot barley needs up to two hours' simmering in water, but presoaking it for several hours will shorten the cooking time. Add it to soups and casseroles for extra nutrition and fiber. The fats in barley can make it turn rancid after a short time, especially if kept in warm, light conditions, so store in a cool, dry, dark place in an airtight container and use within two to three months.

HEARTY BARLEY VEGETABLE SOUP

This is a warming winter soup full of delicious vegetables. The addition of barley gives it good body, as well as loads of fiber and essential minerals and vitamins.

SERVES 6 • PREP TIME: 20-25 MINS • COOK TIME: 1 HOUR 20 MINS–1 HOUR 50 MINS

PER SERVING:

							1,000 mg
153 cal	6.7g	4g	22.2g	6.4g	5.7g	4.5g	
CALORIES	FAT	SAT FAT	CARBS	SUGAR	FIBER	PROTEIN	SODIUM

INGREDIENTS

2 tablespoons sunflower oil
1 onion, finely chopped
1 celery stalk, finely chopped
1 garlic clove, crushed
6⅓ cups vegetable broth or water
½ cup pot barley, rinsed
1 bouquet garni, made with 1 bay leaf, fresh thyme sprigs, and fresh parsley sprigs
2 carrots, diced
1⅔ cups canned diced tomatoes
pinch of sugar
½ head of savoy cabbage, cored and shredded
salt and pepper (optional)
fresh crusty bread, to serve (optional)

1. Heat the oil in a large saucepan. Add the onion, celery, and garlic and cook over medium heat for 5–7 minutes, until soft.

2. Pour in the broth and bring to a boil, skimming off any foam that rises to the surface with a slotted spoon. Add the barley and bouquet garni, reduce the heat to low, cover, and simmer for 30 minutes–1 hour, until the grains are just beginning to soften.

3. Add the carrots, tomatoes with their can juices, and the sugar to the pan. Bring the liquid back to a boil, then reduce the heat to low, cover, and simmer for an additional 30 minutes, or until the barley and carrots are tender.

4. Just before serving, remove the bouquet garni, stir in the cabbage, and season with salt and pepper to taste, if using.

5. Continue simmering until the cabbage wilts, then ladle into warm soup bowls and serve with the bread, if using.

VARIATION
Try serving this soup with some freshly grated Parmesan cheese over the top.

BROWN RICE

The fiber in brown rice can help to lower blood cholesterol levels
and keep blood sugar levels even.

MAJOR NUTRIENTS PER ⅓ CUP RAW BROWN RICE

222 cal	1.8g	46g	3.6g	5g	0.2 mg	3mg	0.3 mg	20 mg	0.8 mg	86 mg	19.6 mcg	1.3g
CALORIES	TOTAL FAT	CARBS	FIBER	PROTEIN	VITAMIN B1	VITAMIN B3	VITAMIN B6	CALCIUM	IRON	MAGNESIUM	SELENIUM	ZINC

While white rice contains few nutrients other than starch, brown rice has several nutritional benefits. Regular consumption of brown rice and other whole grains has been shown to help prevent heart disease, diabetes, and some cancers. It is a good source of fiber, which can help reduce cholesterol levels in the blood and keep blood sugar levels even. Brown rice also contains some protein, and is a good source of several of the B vitamins and minerals, particularly selenium and magnesium.

- One of the least allergenic foods.
- A reasonably low glycemic index food that can help control blood sugar levels and may be helpful for diabetics.
- Useful B-vitamin content to help convert food into energy and keep the nervous system healthy.
- High selenium content may help protect against cancers; high magnesium content for a healthy heart.

DID YOU KNOW?

About 90 percent of all rice is still grown and consumed in Asia, where it has been eaten for more than 6,000 years.

PRACTICAL TIPS

Store rice in a cool, dark cabinet and use within a few months. Brown rice tends not to keep as well as white rice, because it contains small amounts of fat, which can turn rancid over time. The longer you store raw rice, the longer it may take to cook. Leftover cooked rice can be kept for a day or two in the refrigerator if you cool it quickly, but it must be reheated until piping hot before serving.

PROTEIN RICE BOWL

Brown rice adds important fiber and fresh chile supplies some heat to this protein-rich vegetarian lunch for two.

SERVES 2 • PREP TIME: 25 MINS • COOK TIME: 30 MINS

PER SERVING:

 653 cal CALORIES   **33.9g** FAT   **5.9g** SAT FAT   **71.1g** CARBS   **4g** SUGAR   **8.7g** FIBER   **19.1g** PROTEIN   **120mg** SODIUM

INGREDIENTS

¾ cup brown rice
2 extra-large eggs
2½ cups spinach
4 scallions, finely chopped
1 red chile, seeded and finely sliced
½ ripe avocado, sliced
2 tablespoons roasted peanuts

VINAIGRETTE

2 tablespoons olive oil
1 teaspoon Dijon mustard
1 tablespoon apple cider vinegar
juice of ½ lemon

1. Put the rice into a large saucepan and cover with twice the volume of water. Bring to a boil, then reduce the heat and simmer for 25 minutes, until the rice is tender and the liquid has nearly all disappeared. Continue to simmer for an additional few minutes if any liquid remains. Alternatively, prepare according to package directions.

2. Meanwhile, bring a small saucepan of water to a boil. Carefully add the eggs to the pan and boil for 7 minutes—the whites will be cooked and the yolks should still be slightly soft. Drain the eggs and pour cold water over them to stop them from cooking. When cool enough to handle, tap them on the work surface to crack the shells and peel them. Cut the eggs into quarters.

3. Stir the spinach, half of the scallions, and a little of the chile into the cooked rice.

4. To make the vinaigrette, whisk together the oil, mustard, vinegar, and lemon juice. Pour the dressing over the warm rice and mix to combine.

5. Divide the rice between two bowls and top each with the remaining scallions, the avocado, the remaining red chile, the peanuts, and egg quarters.

OATS

Economical oats are high in soluble fiber and a source of healthy fats. They can keep hunger at bay, lower "bad" cholesterol, and keep blood sugar levels even.

MAJOR NUTRIENTS PER ⅔ CUP OATS

233 cal	4g	40g	6.4g	10g	0.5 mg	0.6 mg
CALORIES	TOTAL FAT	CARBS	FIBER	PROTEIN	VITAMIN B1	VITAMIN B3

1.5 mg	32 mg	34 mcg	2.8 mg	106 mg	257 mg	2.4g
VITAMIN E	CALCIUM	FOLATE	IRON	MAGNESIUM	POTASSIUM	ZINC

Oats have several health-giving properties. They are rich in the soluble fiber beta-glucan and have been proven to help lower "bad" cholesterol, boost "good" cholesterol, maintain a healthy circulatory system, and help prevent heart attacks. Oats also contain a range of antioxidants and plant chemicals to help keep heart and arteries healthy, such as avenanthramides (a phytoalexin plant chemical with antibiotic properties), saponins, and vitamin E. They also contain polyphenols, plant compounds that can suppress tumor growth. They are also relatively low on the glycemic index, which means they are particularly suitable for dieters, people with insulin resistance, and diabetics.

- One of the best grains to keep the heart and arteries healthy.
- Contain plant chemicals to help reduce the risk of cancers.
- Lower on the glycemic index than many cereals.
- A good source of a wide range of vitamins and minerals, including the B vitamins, vitamin E, magnesium, calcium, and iron.

DID YOU KNOW?

Although oats do contain small amounts of gluten, people with gluten intolerance (celiac disease) often find they can tolerate oats in their diet, especially if limited to no more than 1¼ cups a day. People with celiac disease should check with their physician before eating oats.

PRACTICAL TIPS

The fat content of oats means that they don't store well for long, so keep them in an airtight container in a cool, dry, dark place and use within 2–3 weeks. Use oat flakes to make your own homemade muesli. Oat flakes can be used for making cookies and crumble toppings, and oat flour can replace wheat flour.

CREAMY OATMEAL
WITH BLACKBERRIES

Oats are a complex carbohydrate, providing slow-release
energy to keep you sustained throughout the morning.

SERVES 2 • PREP TIME: 5 MINS • COOK TIME: 8 MINS

PER SERVING:

268 cal	9g	2.9g	38g	1.5g	7.2g	11g	280mg
CALORIES	FAT	SAT FAT	CARBS	SUGAR	FIBER	PROTEIN	SODIUM

INGREDIENTS

1 cup large rolled oats
small pinch of sea salt
2½ cups cold water
3½ tablespoons heavy cream
1 tablespoon stevia
1 tablespoon pumpkin seeds
6 large blackberries, quartered

1. Put the oats and salt into a medium saucepan and pour
the water over them. Bring to a boil, then reduce the heat to
medium–low and simmer, stirring regularly, for 5–6 minutes, or
until the oats are thick but have a dense pouring consistency.

2. Stir in the cream and stevia. Spoon the oatmeal into two
bowls, top with the pumpkin seeds and blackberries, and
serve immediately.

BUCKWHEAT

Buckwheat contains a rich supply of youth-enhancing flavonoids, particularly rutin.
These help to keep your circulation flowing freely and prevent varicose veins.

MAJOR NUTRIENTS PER ⅔ CUP BUCKWHEAT

343 cal	3.4g	71.5g	10 mg	13.25g	0.43 mg	7.02 mg	1.23 mg
CALORIES	TOTAL FAT	CARBS	FIBER	PROTEIN	VITAMIN B2	VITAMIN B3	VITAMIN B5

0.21 mg	1052 mg	30 mcg	231 mg	1.33 mg	460 mg	8.3 mcg	2.4 mcg
VITAMIN B6	OMEGA-6 OILS	FOLATE	MAGNESIUM	MANGANESE	POTASSIUM	SELENIUM	ZINC

Buckwheat is technically a seed, not a grain, so it is an excellent source of fiber and energy for people who are intolerant to wheat and gluten. Whether you have an intolerance or not, reducing your wheat intake will take pressure off the body. Buckwheat is not only easier to digest than wheat but also more alkalizing, meaning that it helps all physical processes work as efficiently as possible, whatever your time of life. It is a particularly sustaining energy source and is recommended for diabetics, because it releases its sugars slowly into the bloodstream. Buckwheat, like millet, also contains substances called nitrilosides that are essential in detoxification processes, helping rid the body of harmful, aging toxins.

- Contains lecithin, which helps break down fats in the liver and in the food that you eat, aiding detoxification and reducing cravings for fatty foods.
- Magnesium and potassium work together to ensure a healthy heart and strong bones for youthful mobility.
- Selenium produces both of the rejuvenating antioxidants glutathione and coenzyme Q-10.

DID YOU KNOW?

Buckwheat is not related to wheat. It isn't even a grain, but a fruit seed, in the same family as rhubarb and sorrel.

PRACTICAL TIPS

Buckwheat may be used as an alternative to rice. It can also be bought in flakes and made into porridge. Buckwheat flour makes excellent gluten-free pancakes, which are traditional in Poland and Russia, and are also eaten in France.

BUCKWHEAT BREAKFAST BOWL

Buckwheat makes a delicious cereal and, being a source of complex carbohydrates, provides an excellent boost of energy. You'll need to allow time for the buckwheat to sprout, about 36 hours.

SERVES 4 • PREP TIME: 20–25 MINS, PLUS STANDING & SPROUTING • COOK TIME: NONE

PER SERVING:

452 cal	22.4g	17.5g	58g	22.8g	9.8g	10.1g	40mg
CALORIES	FAT	SAT FAT	CARBS	SUGAR	FIBER	PROTEIN	SODIUM

INGREDIENTS

1 cup buckwheat
2 cups cold water
1¾ cups coconut yogurt
grated zest and juice of 1 orange
3 tablespoons goji berries
¾ cup raspberries
1 Granny Smith apple, cored and diced
1 tablespoon pumpkin seeds
2 passion fruits, pulp only
2 teaspoons ground cinnamon
½ teaspoon ground turmeric
seeds of 1 pomegranate
2 tablespoons agave syrup

1. Rinse the buckwheat three times in fresh water to clean the groats. Place in a bowl with the cold water. Let stand for 30 minutes.

2. Drain and rinse the buckwheat and let stand at room temperature—in either a sprouting tray or a strainer with a bowl beneath—for 36 hours. Rinse the buckwheat if the groats look sticky, and then once again before using.

3. Rinse, drain, and divide the buckwheat among four bowls. Divide the yogurt among the bowls, sprinkle with the remaining ingredients, and serve.

VARIATION
Add your favorite berries and seeds to the buckwheat in place of the raspberries and pumpkin seeds.

MILLET

This underrated nongluten grain provides high levels of
hormone-balancing and skin-plumping omega-6 oils.

MAJOR NUTRIENTS PER ½ CUP UNCOOKED MILLET

378 cal	4.22g	72.85g	8.5 mg	11.02g	0.42 mg	0.29 mg	4.72 mg
CALORIES	TOTAL FAT	CARBS	FIBER	PROTEIN	VITAMIN B1	VITAMIN B2	VITAMIN B3

0.85 mg	0.38 mg	2015 mg	TRACE	114 mg	1.63 mg	285 mg
VITAMIN B5	VITAMIN B6	OMEGA-6 OILS	COPPER	MAGNESIUM	MANGANESE	PHOSPHORUS

Millet contains none of the sticky gluten found in wheat, oats, rye, and barley that can swamp our diets. This makes it easier to digest and less likely to set off inflammatory tendencies that cause conditions such as eczema, asthma, acne, arthritis, osteoporosis, and irritable bowel syndrome (IBS). The omega-6 oils present in millet also help to soothe and lessen these aggravating conditions. Omega-6 oils are also vitally important for digestion, immunity, detoxification, and metabolism. Eating them stops us from craving more unhealthy and aging oils, fats, and sugars, and helps maintain healthy, youthful-looking skin, hair, and nails.

- The B vitamins and magnesium support the adrenal glands and help to prevent stress aging the body prematurely.
- B3 lowers high cholesterol and keeps the brain functioning positively.
- Both copper and manganese are needed to make the large amounts of the detoxifying enzyme superoxide dismutase, which keeps the system youthful.
- Phosphorus plays a part in energy production in every cell; this enables new bone to form and fuels the DNA that drives renewal throughout the body.

DID YOU KNOW?

Millet was one of the first grains to be eaten, meaning that we are much more likely to be able to digest it and experience less intolerance.

PRACTICAL TIPS

The most common type of millet sold is the pearl, hulled type, but a millet couscous made from the cracked grain is also available from good health food stores. Millet flakes can be made into porridge or added to muesli.

SALMON PACKAGES WITH MILLET & SPINACH

Salmon is always an excellent pairing with any kind of grain. This delicious lunch or dinner dish provides essential omega-3 and omega-6 oils, together with valuable iron.

SERVES 4 • PREP TIME: 20 MINS • COOK TIME: 30 MINS

PER SERVING:

687 cal	42.5g	16.5g	33.1g	1.7g	5.2g	41.9g	440mg
CALORIES	FAT	SAT FAT	CARBS	SUGAR	FIBER	PROTEIN	SODIUM

INGREDIENTS

¾ cup millet, rinsed
½ teaspoon salt
4 salmon fillets, each about 6 ounces and 1¼ inches thick
6-inch piece leek, cut into matchsticks
1 carrot, cut into matchsticks
1 celery stalk, cut into matchsticks
1 tablespoon snipped fresh chives
6 tablespoons butter
7 cups baby spinach
salt and pepper (optional)

1. Preheat the oven to 425°F and put a baking sheet inside to heat. Cut out four 13-inch squares of parchment paper.

2. Bring a saucepan of water to a boil. Add the millet and ½ teaspoon of salt. Bring back to a boil, then reduce the heat and simmer briskly for 10 minutes. Drain and set aside.

3. Place a salmon fillet in the center of each paper square. Arrange the leek, carrot, and celery on top and sprinkle with the chives. Season with salt and pepper, if using, and dot with half the butter. Roll up the edges of the paper securely, leaving room in the package for steam to circulate.

4. Place the packages on the preheated baking sheet and bake in the preheated oven for 12 minutes.

5. Meanwhile, heat the remaining butter in a skillet over medium–high heat. Stir in the reserved millet and the spinach and heat until the spinach has just wilted. Season with salt and pepper, if using.

6. Divide the millet and spinach among four warm plates and arrange the contents of one of the packages on top of each. Serve immediately.

SPELT

The rich fiber content of spelt can help to manage weight fluctuations and keep you trim and active as you get older.

MAJOR NUTRIENTS PER ½ CUP PLUS 1 TABLESPOON SPELT

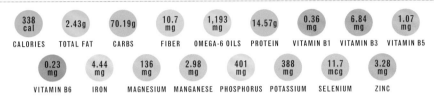

338 cal	2.43g	70.19g	10.7 mg	1,193 mg	14.57g	0.36 mg	6.84 mg	1.07 mg
CALORIES	TOTAL FAT	CARBS	FIBER	OMEGA-6 OILS	PROTEIN	VITAMIN B1	VITAMIN B3	VITAMIN B5

0.23 mg	4.44 mg	136 mg	2.98 mg	401 mg	388 mg	11.7 mcg	3.28 mg
VITAMIN B6	IRON	MAGNESIUM	MANGANESE	PHOSPHORUS	POTASSIUM	SELENIUM	ZINC

An ancient grain, spelt has not been put through the selective breeding undergone by its modern counterpart, wheat. This makes it lower in the potentially inflammatory and difficult-to-digest gluten that causes intolerances in so many people. Spelt is also higher in iron and vitamin K, both needed to ensure the health of our blood, the life force that carries oxygen and nutrients around the body to vitalize every single cell. It has higher levels of omega-6 oils, too, which keep our cells flexible and are an important contribution to youthful skin. Omega 6 also supports the nervous system to ensure quick brain and muscle reactions.

- Selenium activates the thyroid hormones that keep you burning energy and calories to help you retain a slim and youthful figure.
- Fiber slows the rate at which you break down food, so stabilizing blood sugar levels and helping you resist quick-fix foods that pile on weight.
- Manganese and vitamin B3 help to produce insulin, another vital ingredient in the management of blood sugar levels.

DID YOU KNOW?

Spelt is an ancient cousin of wheat. It was one of the first grains used to make bread and was also popular in ancient Greece and Rome.

PRACTICAL TIPS

Many spelt breads and crackers are now available in health food stores, and spelt can be used as a substitute for rice or potatoes. If you have a severe intolerance to wheat, however, it is advisable to avoid spelt, because the proteins in spelt are similar and may provoke the same reaction.

SPELT & CARROT SALAD

As with most salads, it's the dressing that makes all the difference. Here, the grains and crunchy nuts and vegetables are brought to life with the citrusy ginger dressing.

SERVES 4 • PREP TIME: 25 MINS, PLUS STANDING • COOK TIME: 15 MINS

PER SERVING:

462 cal	27.9g	3.4g	47.5g	5.3g	5.4g	8.3g	480mg
CALORIES	FAT	SAT FAT	CARBS	SUGAR	FIBER	PROTEIN	SODIUM

INGREDIENTS

1¼ cups pearled spelt, rinsed
½ teaspoon salt
2 tablespoons fresh thyme leaves
⅓ cup pine nuts, toasted
5 scallions, thinly sliced
4 carrots
3 tablespoons cress or microgreens, to serve

DRESSING

2 tablespoons orange juice
1 tablespoon lemon juice
¾-inch piece fresh ginger, squeezed in a garlic press
2 teaspoon soy sauce
⅓ cup extra virgin olive oil
salt and pepper (optional)

1. Put the spelt and salt into a saucepan with plenty of water to cover. Bring to a boil, then reduce the heat, cover, and simmer for 10 minutes, until tender but still chewy. Drain, then spread out on a tray to cool slightly. Transfer to a serving bowl while warm.

2. To make the dressing, combine the orange juice, lemon juice, and ginger in a small bowl. Add the soy sauce. Season with salt and pepper, if using. Whisk in the oil.

3. Pour the dressing over the spelt, gently mixing with a fork. Stir in the thyme, pine nuts, and scallions.

4. Using a vegetable peeler, shave the carrots into thin ribbons, discarding the woody core. Add to the spelt mixture.

5. Let stand at room temperature for 30 minutes. Sprinkle with the cress just before serving.

HINT

Letting this salad stand before serving allows time for the flavors to develop.

MISO

Miso is one of the traditional foods of Japan, where it is associated with long life and good health.

MAJOR NUTRIENTS PER 1 TABLESPOON MISO

34 cal	1.03g	4.55g	0.93g	2.01g	0.02 mg	0.04 mg	0.16 mg
CALORIES	TOTAL FAT	CARBS	FIBER	PROTEIN	VITAMIN B1	VITAMIN B2	VITAMIN B3

0.06 mg	0.03 mg	0.43 mcg	8.53 mcg	0.43 mg	0.3 mg	1.2 mcg	0.44 mg
VITAMIN B5	VITAMIN B6	VITAMIN B12	VITAMIN K	IRON	MANGANESE	SELENIUM	ZINC

Like sauerkraut, yogurt, and kefir, miso is fermented food associated with good digestive health, because it feeds the beneficial probiotic bacteria present in the body. This supports toxin elimination and the absorption of nutrients to keep you looking and feeling young and healthy. Fermented foods also help the immune system, keeping in check overreactions that can lead to multiple sensitivities and inflammation, as seen in hay fever and skin problems. The soy type of miso is a useful vegetarian protein source.

- Contains tryptophan, needed for serotonin production, which encourages good mood and restorative sleep.
- Manganese makes the detoxifying antioxidant enzyme superoxide dismutase, which helps slow down the aging process.
- Vitamin K transports calcium around the body in support of good bone health and efficient blood clotting.
- Zinc-rich food that promotes optimal immune function and rapid healing, helping your skin look more youthful.

DID YOU KNOW?

Most miso is the hatcho form made from soybeans, but it can also be produced from rice, barley, or wheat by adding a koji yeast mold that stimulates fermentation.

PRACTICAL TIPS

Miso is salty, but a little goes a long way in terms of taste and mineral content. The paste is superior to the powdered form and can be used just as easily to make an instant, simple soup when mixed with boiling water. Add miso to boiled vegetables and ginger to make a heartier broth, which you can supplement with shrimp, chicken, or tofu.

TURKEY MISO SOUP

This soup is just the thing to warm you up on a cold day. The tryptophan content of both the turkey and miso will aid your mood and encourage good sleeping patterns.

SERVES 4 • PREP TIME: 5 MINS • COOK TIME: 25 MINS

PER SERVING:

| 369 cal CALORIES | 9.8g FAT | 2.1g SAT FAT | 32.9g CARBS | 7.1g SUGAR | 7.9g FIBER | 35.7g PROTEIN | 1,200 mg SODIUM |

INGREDIENTS

8 ounces fresh udon noodles
1 tablespoon vegetable oil
1 small leek, halved lengthwise and thinly sliced
8½ cups turkey broth
3 carrots, sliced
1 teaspoon white pepper
3 cups halved sugar snap peas
2 cups shredded or chopped, cooked turkey meat
¼ cup white miso paste

1. Cook the noodles according to the package directions.

2. Heat the oil in a medium saucepan over medium–high heat. Add the leek and cook, stirring frequently, for 3 minutes, or until it begins to soften. Add the broth, carrots, and pepper and bring to a boil. Reduce the heat to low and simmer for 15 minutes, or until the carrots are just tender.

3. Add the sugar snap peas, turkey, and cooked noodles and simmer for 2–3 minutes, until heated through. Stir in the miso paste until it is dissolved.

4. Transfer the soup to warm bowls and serve immediately.

CHICKPEAS

Pale, golden chickpeas, also called garbanzo beans, are an excellent, low-cost source of protein, and they are rich in fiber, protective plant chemicals, and vitamin E.

218 cal	3.5g	37g	10.3g	12g	66 mg	232 mcg	3.9 mg	65 mg	393 mg	2g
CALORIES	TOTAL FAT	CARBS	FIBER	PROTEIN	CALCIUM	FOLATE	IRON	MAGNESIUM	POTASSIUM	ZINC

Chickpeas are a delicious protein food for vegetarians and a good source of fiber. Their insoluble fiber, which binds to cholesterol and removes it from the body, not only helps to increase stool bulk and prevent constipation but also helps prevent digestive disorders, such as irritable bowel syndrome and diverticulosis. Its soluble fiber controls and lowers blood cholesterol and helps prevent strokes and heart disease. Chickpeas are extremely high in folate and this helps lower levels of blood homocysteine, which is a risk factor for cardiovascular disease. They are also rich in magnesium, which helps to relax the arteries and helps protect against heart attacks.

- High in folate and magnesium.
- A good source of minerals, including iron, zinc, and calcium.
- High in potassium to help balance body fluids and protect against fluid retention.
- Rich in plant chemicals to fight heart disease and cancer.

DID YOU KNOW?

Cooked chickpeas are ground into a flour that is used widely in Middle Eastern and Indian cooking. It is an alternative to wheat flour in many recipes, including batters, breads, and soups.

PRACTICAL TIPS

Chickpeas need to be soaked for several hours, then boiled for at least 1½ hours. Chickpeas bought prepared in cans are excellent and still contain the important nutrients. Chickpeas are often eaten in the form of hummus, a Middle-Eastern dip, but they can also be used to replace meat or poultry in soups, stews, and casseroles.

SMOKY PAPRIKA ROASTED CHICKPEAS

Chickpeas are made up of complex carbohydrates, which take longer
for the body to digest and so give a slower release of energy.

SERVES 4 • PREP TIME: 15 MINS, PLUS COOLING • COOK TIME: 20–25 MINS

PER SERVING:

235 cal	8.3g	1g	36g	6.5g	5.7g	7.2g	320mg
CALORIES	FAT	SAT FAT	CARBS	SUGAR	FIBER	PROTEIN	SODIUM

INGREDIENTS

2 tablespoons olive oil
1 teaspoon cumin seeds, coarsely crushed
1 teaspoon smoked mild paprika
¼ teaspoon ground allspice
¼ teaspoon ground cinnamon
½ teaspoon sea salt
5 cups rinsed and drained, canned chickpeas
2 tablespoons date syrup

1. Preheat the oven to 400°F. Add the oil to a roasting pan and place in the oven to heat for 3–4 minutes.

2. Add the cumin seeds, paprika, allspice, cinnamon, and salt to a small bowl, and mix together well.

3. Add the chickpeas to the roasting pan, drizzle with the date syrup, sprinkle with the spice mix, and stir together. Roast in the preheated oven for 15–20 minutes, stirring once, until brown and crusty.

4. Spoon into a bowl and let cool before eating. Store any leftovers in a plastic container in the refrigerator.

SOYBEANS

A valuable bean, rich in minerals and disease-preventing plant chemicals, soybeans are a complete source of protein and an ideal food for vegetarians.

MAJOR NUTRIENTS PER ⅓ CUP DRIED SOYBEANS

250 cal	12g	18g	5.6g	22g	0.5 mg	0.5 mg
CALORIES	TOTAL FAT	CARBS	FIBER	PROTEIN	VITAMIN B1	VITAMIN B2

0.95 mg	166 mg	225 mcg	9.4 mg	168 mg	1,078 mg	2.9g
VITAMIN B3	CALCIUM	FOLATE	IRON	MAGNESIUM	POTASSIUM	ZINC

Soybeans have been cultivated in China for more than 10,000 years and are among the few plant sources of complete protein, containing all eight essential amino acids needed in our diet. Soy is also an excellent source of calcium, the B vitamins, potassium, zinc, and magnesium. It is a rich source of iron, although this may only be absorbed by the body if consumed with vitamin C-rich foods. Soy is rich in plant chemicals that offer protection from diseases, including breast cancer, prostate cancer, and heart disease. A regular intake of soybeans can also reduce menopausal symptoms.

- Complete source of low saturated-fat protein.
- Rich in plant compounds, which may help protect against hormone-base cancers.
- Help lower "bad" cholesterol and protect against heart disease.
- Can reduce symptoms of menopause, including hot flashes.

DID YOU KNOW?

Edamame is the name for fresh soybeans, which you can find shelled, frozen or, sometimes, fresh in delis and markets. Cook and use them as you would fava beans and other fresh legumes.

PRACTICAL TIPS

Canned soybeans are a quick and easy alternative to dried beans and contain a similar nutritional profile. Use in soups and casseroles, mash for a dip, or add to vegetable burgers. Tofu is made from processed soybeans and is a good low-fat, low-sodium alternative to meat. Some of the wheat flour in baking recipes can be replaced with soy flour to increase nutrient content.

GREEN BEAN PROTEIN BURST

This spicy bean dish is perfect when there is a surplus of beans in the summer—
served with spiced tofu, it will boost your intake of protein and fiber.

SERVES 4 • PREP TIME: 12 MINS • COOK TIME: 15 MINS

PER SERVING:

516 cal	37.9g	23.7g	21.9g	8g	9.5g	27.9g	480mg
CALORIES	FAT	SAT FAT	CARBS	SUGAR	FIBER	PROTEIN	SODIUM

INGREDIENTS

14 ounces tofu, drained
2 tablespoons soy sauce
2 garlic cloves, crushed
1¼-inch piece fresh ginger, grated
½ teaspoon crushed red pepper flakes
3 cups green beans
1⅓ cups fresh or frozen fava beans
1 tablespoon coconut oil
1 red bell pepper, seeded and chopped
1 teaspoon garam masala
1 teaspoon tomato paste
1¾ cup canned coconut milk
⅔ cup frozen edamame (soybeans), thawed
1 tablespoon lime juice
2 tablespoons salted cashew nuts
small handful of fresh cilantro

1. Cut the tofu into cubes and put into a nonmetallic bowl.

2. Mix together the soy sauce, garlic, ginger, and crushed red pepper flakes and pour the mixture over the tofu.

3. Meanwhile, trim and slice the green beans diagonally. Bring a large saucepan of water to a boil, add the fava beans and green beans, and blanch for 4 minutes. Drain.

4. Heat the oil in a wok or large skillet, add the red bell pepper, and stir-fry for 2–3 minutes.

5. Add the garam masala and tomato paste and cook for 1 minute, then pour in the coconut milk. Bring to a boil, then add the fava beans, greens beans, and edamame and simmer for 4–5 minutes, until the beans are tender.

6. Add the tofu and lime juice and cook for an additional 2–3 minutes, until the tofu is heated through.

7. Serve in four warm bowls, sprinkled with the cashew nuts and cilantro.

KIDNEY BEANS

Iron-rich kidney beans are an excellent source of good-quality protein, zinc, and fiber, and they contain compounds to help prevent blood clots.

MAJOR NUTRIENTS PER ⅓ CUP DRIED RED KIDNEY BEANS

200 cal	0.8g	36g	10g	13.7g	0.25 mg	0.9 mg	205 mcg	55 mg	3.5 mg	66 mg	640 mg	1.6g
CALORIES	TOTAL FAT	CARBS	FIBER	PROTEIN	VITAMIN B1	VITAMIN B3	FOLATE	CALCIUM	IRON	MAGNESIUM	POTASSIUM	ZINC

Kidney beans are invaluable for vegetarians, because they are high in good-quality protein and minerals. An average portion of kidney beans contains at least one-quarter of our daily iron needs to help prevent anemia and increase energy levels, while their zinc content helps boost the immune system and maintain fertility. The high degree of insoluble fiber in kidney beans helps prevent colon cancer, while for diabetics and people with insulin resistance, the total fiber content helps regulate blood sugar levels.

- Excellent source of protein, iron, and calcium for vegetarians.
- High fiber content helps regulate release of insulin and helps to prevent hunger—a good choice for dieters.
- Protects against colon cancer.
- Extremely high in potassium, which can minimize fluid retention and may help control high blood pressure.

DID YOU KNOW?

Raw kidney beans can contain high levels of potentially toxic substances, which can cause an upset stomach, vomiting, and diarrhea. To remove this risk, the beans must be rapidly boiled for at least 10 minutes before cooking.

PRACTICAL TIPS

There is little nutritional difference between cooked dried kidney beans and canned kidney beans, so, if you are short of time, use the canned beans. Red kidney beans are often added to meat dishes, such as chili con carne, or used in three-bean salad, and, when mashed with oil and lemon juice, they make a good sandwich filling or dip.

MEXICAN BEEF & BEAN BOWL

Chili con carne with extra beans for protein and fiber, plus red bell peppers for their great flavor and antioxidant content make this is a perfect dish. Make it in advance—the flavors improve with time.

SERVES 4 • PREP TIME: 10 MINS • COOK TIME: 20–25 MINS

PER SERVING:

682 cal	25.4g	8.7g	69.6g	8.7g	11.3g	37.9g	200mg
CALORIES	FAT	SAT FAT	CARBS	SUGAR	FIBER	PROTEIN	SODIUM

INGREDIENTS

1 tablespoon olive oil
1 pound 2 ounces fresh ground beef
1 onion, chopped
2 red bell peppers, seeded and sliced
2½ teaspoons chili powder
2½ cups rinsed and drained, canned red kidney beans
2½ cups rinsed and drained, canned cannellini beans
1⅔ cups canned diced tomatoes
1 tablespoon tomato paste
1¼ cups vegetable broth
1 cup basmati rice or other long-grain rice
2 tablespoons chopped fresh cilantro
2 tablespoons sour cream
¼ teaspoon smoked paprika
salt and pepper (optional)

1. Heat the oil in a large skillet, add the beef, and cook for 2–3 minutes, until brown all over.

2. Add the onion and red bell peppers and cook, stirring occasionally, for 3–4 minutes.

3. Stir in the chili powder and cook for 1 minute, then add the kidney beans, cannellini beans, tomatoes, tomato paste, and broth. Bring to a simmer and simmer for 12–15 minutes. Season with salt and pepper, if using.

4. Meanwhile, cook the rice according to the package directions.

5. Stir the cilantro into the chili and serve in warm bowls on top of the rice, along with a dollop of sour cream and a sprinkling of smoked paprika.

VARIATION

If you are trying to cut down on red meat, use fresh ground turkey in place of the beef—it is lighter and equally delicious.

LENTILS

Small, lens-shaped dried lentils are one of the legumes richest in cancer-blocking fibers called isoflavones and lignan, and they are low in fat and saturates.

MAJOR NUTRIENTS PER ⅓ CUP DRIED GREEN OR BROWN LENTILS

212 cal	0.6g	36g	18g	15.5g	0.5 mg	1.6mg
CALORIES	TOTAL FAT	CARBS	FIBER	PROTEIN	VITAMIN B1	VITAMIN B3

0.3 mg	34 mg	287 mcg	4.5 mg	73 mg	573 mg	2.9g
VITAMIN B6	CALCIUM	FOLATE	IRON	MAGNESIUM	POTASSIUM	ZINC

Lentils come in a variety of colors and include green, brown, and red. The green and brown tend to contain the highest levels of nutrients and fiber. Lentils are a rich source of fiber, both insoluble and soluble, which helps protect us against cancer and cardiovascular disease. They also contain plant chemicals called isoflavones, which may offer protection from cancer and coronary heart disease, and lignan, which has a mild estrogen-like effect that may lower the risk of cancer, minimize premenstrual syndrome, and protect against osteoporosis. Lentils are also rich in the B vitamins, folate, and all major minerals, particularly iron and zinc.

- Rich in fiber for protection from cardiovascular disease and cancers.
- High iron content for healthy blood and energy levels.
- Contain plant chemicals to help premenstrual syndrome and bone health.
- High zinc content to boost the immune system.

DID YOU KNOW?

Lentils are thought to be one of the earliest foods to have been cultivated, with 8,000-year-old seeds found at sites in the Middle East.

PRACTICAL TIPS

Lentils are one of the few legumes that don't need soaking before cooking. They are also quick to cook by simmering in water for about 30 minutes. Dried lentils cooked in broth with carrots, celery, and onion makes a quick soup. Canned lentils contain almost as many nutrients as dried ones.

LENTIL & SWISS CHARD SOUP

This vibrant soup is full of fiber for a healthy digestive system, and it also contains vital nutrients for good bones and a healthy heart.

SERVES 6 • PREP TIME: 20 MINS • COOK TIME: 55 MINS

PER SERVING:

229 cal	2.3g	0.8g	41.7g	6.5g	7.2g	13g	880mg
CALORIES	FAT	SAT FAT	CARBS	SUGAR	FIBER	PROTEIN	SODIUM

INGREDIENTS

¾ cup brown lentils
1 onion, finely diced
1¾ cups tomato puree or tomato sauce
2½–3 cups chicken broth or vegetable broth
½ teaspoon cumin seeds, lightly crushed
½ teaspoon salt
12 ounces Swiss chard (about 5¼ cups prepared)
1 cup (½-inch) potato cubes
¼ cup plus 2 tablespoons chopped fresh mint
2 whole-wheat pita breads
6 tablespoons Greek-style yogurt
salt and pepper (optional)
¼ teaspoon cumin seeds, to garnish
6 lemon wedges, to garnish

1. Put the lentils in a large saucepan with the onion, tomato puree or sauce, 2½ cups of the broth, cumin seeds, and ½ teaspoon salt. Bring to a boil, then cover and simmer over low heat for 20 minutes, until the lentils are just tender.

2. Remove the stems from the chard and thinly slice. Slice the leaves crosswise into ribbons.

3. Add the chard stems and potatoes to the lentils and cook for 10 minutes.

4. Add the chard leaves and cook for an additional 15 minutes. If necessary, add the remaining broth to thin the soup—but it should still be thick. Stir in ¼ cup of the mint and season with salt and pepper, if using.

5. Meanwhile, preheat the broiler to medium. Open out the pita breads and toast under the preheated broiler for 3 minutes, until crisp. Break into bite-size pieces and arrange around the edge of six warm soup plates.

6. Ladle the soup into the plates. Add 1 tablespoon of yogurt to each and sprinkle with the remaining mint and some cumin seeds. Garnish with the lemon wedges and serve immediately.

NAVY BEANS

High-protein navy beans are often used in canned baked beans and
are high in fiber, minerals, and the B vitamins.

200 cal	12g	37.8g	15g	0.9g	0.35 mg	0.95 mg	100 mg	3.4 mg	203 mcg	77 mg	564 mg	1.5g
CALORIES	TOTAL FAT	CARBS	FIBER	PROTEIN	VITAMIN B1	VITAMIN B3	CALCIUM	IRON	FOLATE	MAGNESIUM	POTASSIUM	ZINC

The soluble fiber in navy beans helps to lower cholesterol and prevent blood sugar levels from rising too rapidly after a meal, making these beans a good choice for dieters as well as people with diabetes, insulin resistance, and hypoglycemia. Their insoluble fiber helps to prevent constipation and reduce the severity and symptoms of digestive disorders, such as irritable bowel syndrome and diverticulosis. Navy beans are also a good source of protein and one of the best beans for supplying calcium. One portion provides one-seventh of the daily recommended intake. They are also rich in magnesium, potassium, iron, and zinc and are a good source of the B vitamins and folate.

- Rich in soluble fiber to help lower blood cholesterol and protect from cardiovascular disease.
- Insoluble fiber helps the digestive system and bowels.
- A good source of calcium for a healthy heart and strong bones.
- Rich in antioxidant minerals, such as zinc, to help prevent disease.

DID YOU KNOW?

It was early in the twentieth century when these beans were given the name navy beans, because they were a staple food for the U.S. Navy.

PRACTICAL TIPS

To prepare, soak the beans overnight, then replace the water and boil rapidly for 10 minutes before simmering for about 1½ hours, until tender. Do not add salt to beans before they are cooked, because the salt will make them tough. Cooked beans can be pureed with olive oil, salt, and pepper as an alternative to mashed potatoes.

SPANISH VEGETABLE STEW

Quick and easy to make, this comforting Spanish-inspired stew is flavored with smoked paprika for a wonderful, deep spicy flavor.

SERVES 4 • PREP TIME: 20 MINS • COOK TIME: 50 MINS

PER SERVING:

525 cal	26.1g	12.66g	62.3g	14.8g	18.5g	14.6g	720mg
CALORIES	FAT	SAT FAT	CARBS	SUGAR	FIBER	PROTEIN	SODIUM

INGREDIENTS

2 tablespoons virgin olive oil
1 onion, coarsely chopped
1 eggplant, coarsely chopped
½ teaspoon smoked hot paprika
2 garlic cloves, finely chopped
1 large red bell pepper, seeded and coarsely chopped
9 ounces baby new potatoes, unpeeled, and any larger ones halved
7 plum tomatoes (about 1 pound), peeled and coarsely chopped
2⅔ cups rinsed and drained, canned navy beans in water
⅔ cup homemade vegetable broth
2 fresh rosemary sprigs
2 zucchini, coarsely chopped
sea salt and pepper (optional)

1. Heat 1 tablespoon of the oil in a saucepan over medium heat. Add the onion and sauté for 5 minutes, or until soft. Add the remaining oil, then add the eggplant, and cook, stirring, for 5 minutes, or until just beginning to soften and brown.

2. Stir in the paprika and garlic, then the red bell pepper, potatoes, and tomatoes. Add the beans, broth, and rosemary, then season with salt and pepper, if using. Bring to a boil, cover, reduce the heat to medium–low, and simmer for 30 minutes, stirring occasionally.

3. Stir the zucchini into the stew, then cook, uncovered, for 10 minutes, or until all the vegetables are tender and the sauce has reduced slightly.

4. Ladle the stew into shallow bowls, discard the rosemary sprigs, and serve.

VARIATION
Stews are easy to vary, depending on what ingredients you have on hand. Try replacing the eggplant with mushrooms.

TOFU

Tofu, or bean curd, is made from soybeans and is widely used in Asian cooking.
It is one of the factors associated with Asians' better health in old age.

MAJOR NUTRIENTS PER 3½ OUNCES TOFU

76 cal	4.78g	1.88g	0.3g	8.08g	0.2 mg	350 mcg	0.19 mg	5.36 mg	0.61 mg	8.9 mcg	0.13g
CALORIES	TOTAL FAT	CARBS	FIBER	PROTEIN	VITAMIN B3	CALCIUM	COPPER	IRON	MANGANESE	SELENIUM	TRYPTOPHAN

Soy protein is one of the few plant sources of complete protein, which means that it contains all of the essential amino acids that you can't make in the body and must obtain through your diet. This includes the amino acid tryptophan, which is necessary for good mood and sleep, and they are crucial in combating the aging effects of daily stress, too. Soy is also a rich source of saponins and fiber and is, therefore, often recommended as part of a diet intended to lower cholesterol. Lignins in soy proteins have been found to stop the growth and spread of prostate cancer cells. They also contain phytoestrogens, specifically the isoflavones genistein and daidzein. These have been shown to reduce the incidence of hormone-related prostate and breast cancers and the rate of osteoporosis.

- Enriched with calcium for strong bones and a robust heart.
- Contains iron and copper, which is used by red blood cells to transport oxygen and renew worn-out cells.
- Copper is needed to make collagen and elastin from the enzyme lysyl oxidase, ensuring firm and flexible blood vessels, bones, and joints.

DID YOU KNOW?

Tofu was first made 2,000 years ago, in China. It was first written about in a poem called "Ode to Tofu" by Su Ping in AD 1500.

PRACTICAL TIPS

Tofu is available in three types: firm, soft, and silken. Each has a different texture and usage. Tofu can seem bland when first tried, but it soaks up other flavors wonderfully. Silken tofu also makes a good protein addition to smoothies.

TOFU PACKAGES

Served with fresh crusty bread, these little packages of flavor and goodness provide a complete and properly balanced vegetarian meal.

SERVES 4 • PREP TIME: 10 MINS • COOK TIME: 10–15 MINS

PER SERVING:

169 cal CALORIES	12.3g FAT	1.7g SAT FAT	5.8g CARBS	2.3g SUGAR	2.5g FIBER	11.6g PROTEIN	TRACE SODIUM

INGREDIENTS

2 tablespoons olive oil
1 garlic clove, crushed
9 ounces firm tofu, cut into chunks
1¾ cups cherry tomatoes, halved
1 small red onion, thinly sliced
handful of fresh basil leaves
salt and pepper (optional)

1. Preheat the oven to 425°F. Brush four 12-inch squares of double-thickness aluminum foil with oil. Mix the remaining oil with the garlic.

2. Divide the tofu, tomatoes, onion, and basil among the foil squares, sprinkle with salt and pepper, if using, and spoon over the garlic-flavored oil.

3. Fold over the foil to enclose the filling and seal firmly. Place on a baking sheet in the preheated oven and cook for 10–15 minutes, until heated through.

4. Carefully open the packages and serve.

BLACK BEANS

Shiny, oval black beans are an ideal and inexpensive addition to the diet, being rich in nutrients and cholesterol-lowering fiber as well as low in fat and saturates.

MAJOR NUTRIENTS PER ⅓ CUP DRIED BLACK BEANS

205 cal	0.8g	36.7g	13.5g	13.7g	0.4 mg	42 mg	231 mcg	109 mg	550 mg	1.7g
CALORIES	TOTAL FAT	CARBS	FIBER	PROTEIN	VITAMIN B1	CALCIUM	FOLATE	MAGNESIUM	POTASSIUM	ZINC

Black beans are a delicious addition to the diet. Nutritionally, they are high in the indigestible portion of the plant known as insoluble fiber, which can reduce cholesterol. Their extremely high magnesium content means that they are an excellent food for people at risk of developing or experiencing heart disease—an optimum intake of magnesium is linked with a reduced risk of various heart problems. Black beans are also rich in antioxidant compounds called anthocyanins, flavonoids that can help prevent cancer and blood clots. The darker the bean's seed coat, the higher its level of antioxidant activity. In addition, black beans are an excellent source of minerals and folate.

- High-fiber food to help beat some cancers and reduce cholesterol.
- Rich in anthocyanins to block cancer cells.
- Contain folate for healthy blood and development.
- A good source of vegetable protein.

DID YOU KNOW?

Black beans were native to South America, but since the fifteenth century, when they were introduced into Europe by Spanish explorers, they have been popular throughout Europe, Africa, and Asia, as well as the United States.

PRACTICAL TIPS

Buy the beans dried for long storage or cooked in cans. Be sure to rinse canned beans packed in liquid thoroughly before use. Presoaking beans reduces the raffinose-type oligosaccharides they contain—these are the sugars associated with flatulence. Black beans can be used in a range of dishes, from soups and stews to rice dishes and crepe fillings.

BRAZILIAN GREENS WITH BLACK BEANS & ORANGES

Kale and black beans play the starring role in this lively Brazilian-style dish. The beans are a good match for kale's full-bodied flavor, enhanced with orange, chile, garlic, and cilantro.

SERVES 4 • PREP TIME: 25 MINS • COOK TIME: 25 MINS

PER SERVING:

284 cal	15.7g	2.1g	26.6g	9g	13.3g	11.8g	160mg
CALORIES	FAT	SAT FAT	CARBS	SUGAR	FIBER	PROTEIN	SODIUM

INGREDIENTS

1 large orange
3 tablespoons olive oil
1 small onion, finely chopped
1 garlic clove, finely chopped
1 fresh green chile, seeded and finely chopped
1 pound 5 ounces kale, thick stems removed and leaves sliced crosswise (about 9 cups prepared)
⅓–½ cup vegetable broth or chicken broth
2½ cups rinsed and drained, canned black beans
⅓ cup chopped fresh cilantro
1 tablespoon olive oil, for drizzling
salt and pepper (optional)

1. Using a sharp knife, cut a slice from the top and bottom of the orange. Remove the peel and white pith by cutting downward, following the shape of the fruit as closely as possible.

2. Working over a bowl, cut between the flesh and membrane of each section and ease out the flesh. Slice each section in half. Squeeze the membrane over the bowl to extract the juice.

3. Heat the oil in a large skillet over medium heat. Add the onion and sauté for 5 minutes, until soft. Add the garlic and chile and sauté for an additional 2 minutes.

4. Gradually stir in the kale. Add a splash of broth, then cover and cook for 5–6 minutes, or until just wilted. Add more broth if the leaves start to look dry.

5. Stir in the orange juice and any remaining broth. Season with salt and pepper, if using, then cover and cook for 5 minutes, until tender.

6. Stir in the beans and the orange sections. Simmer, uncovered, for a few minutes to heat through. Stir in the cilantro, drizzle with a little oil, and serve immediately.

WALNUTS

Known for their unusually high content of omega-3 fat, walnuts can help prevent heart disease, cancers, arthritis, skin complaints, and nervous system disorders.

MAJOR NUTRIENTS PER ¼ CUP WALNUTS

196 cal	19.5g	4g	2g	4.5g	0.3 mg	0.16 mg	29 mg	0.9 mg	47 mg	132 mg	0.9 mg
CALORIES	TOTAL FAT	CARBS	FIBER	PROTEIN	VITAMIN B3	VITAMIN B6	CALCIUM	IRON	MAGNESIUM	POTASSIUM	ZINC

Unlike most nuts, walnuts are much richer in polyunsaturated fats than in monounsaturates. The type of polyunsaturates that walnuts contain are mostly the essential omega-3 fats, in the form of alpha-linolenic acid. Just one ¼-cup portion will provide you with more than the recommended daily intake. An adequate and balanced intake of the omega fats has been linked with protection from aging, cardiovascular disease, cancer, arthritis, skin problems, and diseases of the nervous system. For people who don't eat fish and fish oils, an intake of omega-3 fats from other sources, such as walnuts, flaxseed, and soy, is important.

- Good source of fiber and the B vitamins.
- Rich in omega-3 fats and antioxidants for health protection.
- Good source of a range of important minerals.
- Can lower "bad" cholesterol and blood pressure and increase elasticity of the arteries.

DID YOU KNOW?

The most popular type of walnut for eating is Juglans regia, the so-called "English walnut." Black and white walnuts are also edible, although their shells are difficult to crack.

PRACTICAL TIPS

The high levels of polyunsaturated fats mean that walnuts turn rancid easily. Buy nuts with their shells on, if possible, store in the refrigerator, and consume quickly. Avoid buying chopped walnuts—chopping speeds up the oxidation of the nuts. Walnuts are best eaten raw as a snack, in muesli, or sprinkled on yogurt and fruit.

CHICKPEA WALNUT PATTIES

These hearty patties are similar to falafel, but they have
the added richness and flavor of walnuts.

SERVES 4 • PREP TIME: 15 MINS, PLUS CHILLING • COOK TIME: 10 MINS

PER SERVING:	320 cal	24.7g	2.6g	18.1g	3.5g	5.2g	7g	360mg
	CALORIES	FAT	SAT FAT	CARBS	SUGAR	FIBER	PROTEIN	SODIUM

INGREDIENTS

2 garlic cloves
1 shallot
2⅔ cups drained and rinsed, canned chickpeas
⅓ cup fresh flat-leaf parsley
1 teaspoon ground coriander
1 teaspoon ground cumin
½ teaspoon salt
⅛ teaspoon cayenne pepper
2 tablespoons olive oil
2 tablespoons all-purpose flour
½ teaspoon baking powder
½ cup roasted, unsalted walnuts
2 tablespoons sunflower oil, for frying
toasted hamburger buns, lettuce, tomato, and
mayonnaise, to serve (optional)

1. Put the garlic and shallot into a food processor and pulse to chop. Add the chickpeas, parsley, coriander, cumin, salt, cayenne pepper, olive oil, and flour and pulse to a chunky puree. Add the baking powder and pulse once to incorporate. Add the walnuts and pulse once to incorporate.

2. Shape the chickpea mixture into four equal patties, about 4 inches in diameter. Chill in the refrigerator for at least 30 minutes or overnight.

3. Heat the sunflower oil in a large skillet over medium–high heat. Add the patties and cook for 4–5 minutes on each side, until golden brown. Serve hot on toasted hamburger buns, with lettuce, tomato, and mayonnaise, if using.

HINT
You can serve the patties in the same way you would falafel,
stuffed in pita breads with lettuce, tomato, and cucumber.

ALMONDS

The high vitamin E content of almonds offers protection against cancer, heart disease, heart attacks, strokes, arthritis, infertility, and skin problems.

MAJOR NUTRIENTS PER ¼ CUP ALMONDS

174 cal	15g	6g	3g	6.6g	1 mg	7.4 mg	65 mg	1 mg	43 mg	206 mg	1 mcg
CALORIES	TOTAL FAT	CARBS	FIBER	PROTEIN	VITAMIN B3	VITAMIN E	CALCIUM	IRON	MAGNESIUM	POTASSIUM	ZINC

Almonds are the seeds of a drupe fruit related to peaches and plums. They are rich in monounsaturated fats and, due to their high fat content, take a long time for the body to digest. This can help keep hunger at bay and help people watching their weight. Almonds are extremely high in vitamin E, which protects against cancer and cardiovascular diseases, helps reduce the pain of osteoarthritis, and keeps skin healthy. Vitamin E can also boost male fertility. Almonds are higher in calcium than almost any other plant food and are, therefore, an excellent addition to vegan and dairy-free diets.

- Satisfying snack to keep hunger at bay and blood sugar levels even.
- Rich in the antioxidant vitamin E.
- Good source of calcium.
- High in monounsaturated fat for arterial and heart health.

DID YOU KNOW?

There is a type of inedible almond that contains a form of cyanide, known as the bitter almond. It is poisonous and is unavailable in stores.

PRACTICAL TIPS

Buy whole almonds in their shells or, at least, still in their brown skins—these keep better than blanched, chopped, or slivered almonds. Store in a cool, dark, dry place—the refrigerator is ideal. Almonds combine well with apricots, peaches, chicken, rice, and red bell peppers.

ROASTED ALMOND GINGERSNAP BUTTER

Lightly sweetened with treacle or molasses and brown sugar, and spiced with ginger, this nutritionally loaded nut butter tastes just like gingersnaps.

MAKES 1⅓ CUPS • PREP TIME: 10 MINS • COOK TIME: NONE

PER 1⅓ CUPS:

 2204 cal CALORIES

 182.3g FAT

 14.8g SAT FAT

 110.5g CARBS

 63g SUGAR

 31.2g FIBER

 60.5g PROTEIN

600mg SODIUM

INGREDIENTS

2¼ cups roasted almonds
2 tablespoons packed light brown sugar
2 tablespoons black treacle or molasses
1½ teaspoons grated fresh ginger
½ teaspoon ground ginger
¼ teaspoon salt
2–3 tablespoons grapeseed oil
apple slices, to serve (optional)

1. Put the almonds into a food processor and process for 5–10 minutes, until smooth.

2. Add the sugar, treacle or molasses, fresh ginger, ground ginger, and salt and process until well combined. With the processor running, add the oil, a little at a time, until you achieve the desired consistency.

3. Serve immediately on apple slices, if using, or refrigerate until ready to use. Almond butter can be stored in the refrigerator for several weeks.

CASHEW NUTS

High in monounsaturated fats, cashew nuts protect the heart, and they contain a range of minerals for strong bones, improved immunity, and increased energy levels.

MAJOR NUTRIENTS PER ¼ CUP CASHEW NUTS

166 cal	13g	9g	1g	5.5g	0.1 mg	0.3 mg	0.12 mg	2 mg	88 mg	198 mg	6 mcg	1.7 mg
CALORIES	TOTAL FAT	CARBS	FIBER	PROTEIN	VITAMIN B1	VITAMIN B3	VITAMIN B6	IRON	MAGNESIUM	POTASSIUM	SELENIUM	ZINC

Cashew nuts are considerably lower in total fat than all other nuts and could be useful as a dieter's snack. Much of their fat is monounsaturated oleic acid (the type found in olive oil), which has health benefits, including protection from heart and arterial disease. Cashew nuts are also rich in important minerals, including magnesium for strong bones and heart health, immune-boosting zinc, and iron for healthy blood and energy. Like other nuts, cashew nuts are linked with protection from cardiovascular disease. People who regularly eat nuts are less likely to die from these diseases than people who never eat nuts.

- Regularly eating nuts is linked with a considerably lower risk of dying from cardiovascular diseases.
- Good source of monounsaturated fats linked to protection from disease.
- A good source of the B vitamins for brainpower and energy.
- Rich in zinc to boost the immune system.

DID YOU KNOW?

Commercially roasted cashew nuts will have lost the benefit of their unsaturated oils, which are oxidized at high temperatures, but you can roast raw cashew nuts at home in a low oven for 20 minutes.

PRACTICAL TIPS

You can use cashew nuts to make cashew nut butter at home just as you would peanut butter. Buy whole, shelled cashew nuts and store in the refrigerator. Combine cashew nuts with dried apricots for a healthy mineral-rich snack. Add a handful of cashew nuts to a vegetable stir-fry for a healthy meal.

AVOCADO & CASHEW NUT PASTA SAUCE

This unusual meatless pasta sauce is a good source of monunsaturated fats from the avocado and cashew nuts, and magnesium, zinc, and iron from the nuts.

MAKES 1¾ CUPS • PREP TIME: 20 MINS • COOK TIME: 3–4 MINS

PER 1¾ CUPS:

1666 cal	142.9g	28.4g	74.1g	9.8g	32.6g	45.7g	800mg
CALORIES	FAT	SAT FAT	CARBS	SUGAR	FIBER	PROTEIN	SODIUM

INGREDIENTS

¾ cup cashew nuts
2 garlic cloves
¾ cup fresh mint leaves
2 ripe avocados, peeled, pitted, and coarsely chopped
½ cup finely grated Parmesan cheese
2 tablespoons olive oil
juice of 1 lime
1–2 tablespoons water

1. Toast the nuts in a dry skillet over high heat for 3–4 minutes, moving the pan regularly to prevent the nuts from burning.

2. Put the nuts and garlic into a food processor and pulse until the nuts are finely chopped. Add the mint leaves, avocados, and cheese. Blend and, with the motor running, pour in the oil and lime juice. Add just enough water to make a thick sauce.

3. Use immediately or keep in the refrigerator in a covered container. The sauce will keep for up to two days. Serve mixed into pasta.

PECANS

Pecans contain the highest amount of antioxidant nutrients of any nut,
making them highly protective against aging and disease.

MAJOR NUTRIENTS PER ⅓ CUP PECANS

207 cal	21.6g	12.2g	4.15g	2.8g	2.7g	0.19 mg	0.35 mg	0.25 mg
CALORIES	TOTAL FAT	MONO UN-SATURATED FAT	CARBS	FIBER	PROTEIN	VITAMIN B1	VITAMIN B3	VITAMIN B5

295 mg	6,189 mg	12,178 mg	55 mcg	1,4 mg	36 mg	1.35 mg	32 mg	123 mg	1.35 mg
OMEGA-3 OILS	OMEGA-6 OILS	OMEGA-9 OILS	FOLATE	IRON	MAGNESIUM	MANGANESE	PHYTOSTEROLS	POTASSIUM	ZINC

Pecans don't get the attention they deserve. Studies have shown that
a handful a day can help prevent heart disease and lower cholesterol.
The amount of calories in pecans, and nuts in general, often leads to
assumptions about weight gain, but it's important to remember that this
high energy comes from the abundance of healthy oils they contain.
These oils actually help raise metabolism and stop us craving the sugary
foods that pile on the pounds and contribute to aging conditions, such
as diabetes, arthritis, and heart disease. People who eat more than two
portions of nuts a week are less prone to put on weight than those who
avoid these nutrient-rich foods.

- High levels of omega-9 oils (oleic acid) keep your skin clear and
  smooth.
- Good levels of balanced and high-quality protein ensure the necessary
  repairs are made to the body to hold back aging.
- Phytosterols work with high levels of antioxidants to discourage
  sensitivities and intolerances.

DID YOU KNOW?

*The United States grow
80–95 percent of the world's
pecans, and pecan trees can grow
and produce nuts for 300 years.*

PRACTICAL TIPS

Pecans are associated with sweet desserts, but they can be eaten on their
own or used as an interesting salad ingredient. Their rich, buttery taste
gives them a luxurious quality that feels like a treat, and they are a healthy
alternative to candy or confectionery.

COFFEE & PECAN MINI BREAKFAST MUFFINS

Sometimes you feel you need a sweet hit in the morning to get you through the first few hours. These little muffins provide that with none of the sugar highs and crashes.

MAKES 9 • PREP TIME: 25 MINS • COOK TIME: 20 MINS

PER MUFFIN:

170 cal	16.6g	3.2g	1.6g	1.1g	0.5g	3.6g	200mg
CALORIES	FAT	SAT FAT	CARBS	SUGAR	FIBER	PROTEIN	SODIUM

INGREDIENTS

⅓ cup plus 1 tablespoon coconut flour
¼ teaspoon baking powder
½ teaspoon baking soda
1 tablespoon stevia
¼ cup coarsely chopped pecans
⅔ cup sour cream
⅓ cup vegetable oil
2 extra-large eggs, beaten
⅓ cup prepared espresso or strong instant coffee
1 teaspoon rice malt syrup
sea salt (optional)

1. Preheat the oven to 325°F. Line a mini muffin pan with paper liners.

2. Put the flour, baking powder, baking soda, stevia, 2½ tablespoons of the pecans, and a small pinch of salt, if using, in a large bowl and mix well. Add the sour cream, oil, eggs, and ¼ cup of the coffee, and stir until evenly mixed. Let stand for a moment, then spoon the batter into the mini muffin liners.

3. Bake in the preheated oven for 20 minutes, or until well risen and the tops spring back when pressed with a fingertip. Let cool for 5 minutes, then transfer to a wire rack.

4. Meanwhile, put the rice malt syrup and remaining coffee into a bowl and mix. Spoon a small drizzle over each muffin. Sprinkle with the remaining nuts and serve warm.

HINT
These muffins can be stored in an airtight container for up to two days.

HAZELNUTS

Particularly rich in potassium, hazelnuts have the ability to
reduce fluid retention and lower blood pressure.

MAJOR NUTRIENTS PER ¼ CUP HAZELNUTS

188 cal	18.2g	5g	2.9g	4.5g	0.5 mg	0.16 mg	4.5 mg	34 mcg	1.4 mg	49 mg	204 mg	0.7 mg
CALORIES	TOTAL FAT	CARBS	FIBER	PROTEIN	VITAMIN B3	VITAMIN B6	VITAMIN E	FOLATE	IRON	MAGNESIUM	POTASSIUM	ZINC

Hazelnuts are a good source of protein and monounsaturated fats, which have been shown to reduce "bad" cholesterol in the blood and even slightly raise "good" cholesterol. The nuts are high in beta-sitosterol, a plant fat that can help reduce an enlarged prostate and is also a cholesterol-lowering compound. Hazelnuts are high in vitamin E, an antioxidant that maintains skin health and heart health and can boost the immune system. The high potassium content can help people with high blood pressure and is also a diuretic. The magnesium content helps heart health and can contribute to bone strength.

- High in beta-sitosterol, which may help prostate health.
- Rich in monounsaturates, which can help improve blood cholesterol profile.
- Rich in antioxidant vitamin E.
- Good source of soluble fiber for lowering "bad" cholesterol and digestive health.

DID YOU KNOW?

*Hazelnuts are also known
as filberts or cob nuts, depending
on their country of origin.*

PRACTICAL TIPS

Hazelnuts keep better than many other nuts, because they contain less fat and their vitamin E acts as a preservative. Buy whole nuts instead of chopped—chopping destroys much of their nutrient content. Store in a refrigerator. Use as a snack, or add to salads, stir-fries, breakfast cereals, and desserts.

BANANA, GOJI & HAZELNUT BREAD

On mornings when you don't have time to eat breakfast before you leave for work, wrap a slice or two of this superfood-packed bread in parchment paper to eat on-the-go.

SERVES 10 • PREP TIME: 25 MINS, PLUS COOLING • COOK TIME: 1 HOUR

PER SERVING:

 300 cal CALORIES

 12.8g FAT

 5.6g SAT FAT

 43.4g CARBS

 19.3g SUGAR

3.7g FIBER

5.9g PROTEIN

160mg SODIUM

INGREDIENTS

2 teaspoons butter, for greasing
6 tablespoons butter, softened
½ cup firmly packed light brown sugar
2 eggs
3 bananas, peeled and mashed
1 cup whole-wheat flour
1 cup all-purpose white flour
2 teaspoon baking powder
½ cup coarsely chopped, unblanched hazelnuts
⅓ cup goji berries
⅔ cup dried banana chips

1. Preheat the oven to 350°F. Grease a 9 x 5 x 3-inch loaf pan and line the bottom and two long sides with parchment paper.

2. Cream the butter and sugar together in a large bowl. Beat in the eggs, one at a time, then the bananas.

3. Put the whole-wheat flour, white flour, and baking powder into a bowl and mix well. Add to the banana mixture and beat until smooth. Add the hazelnuts and goji berries and stir well.

4. Spoon the batter into the prepared pan, smooth the top, then sprinkle with the banana chips. Bake in the preheated oven for 50–60 minutes, or until well risen, slightly cracked on top, and a toothpick inserted into the center comes out clean.

5. Let cool in the pan for 5 minutes, then loosen the edges with a blunt knife and turn out onto a wire rack. Let cool completely, then peel away the paper and serve.

HINT
This bread can be stored in an airtight container for up to three days.

PISTACHIO NUTS

Green-tinted pistachio nuts are rich in plant sterols and soluble fibers,
which can lower "bad" cholesterol and may protect against cancers.

167 cal	13.5g	8.5g	3g	6g	0.4 mg	0.5 mg	100 mcg	32 mg	1.2 mg	36 mg	308 mg	0.7 mg
CALORIES	TOTAL FAT	CARBS	FIBER	PROTEIN	VITAMIN B3	VITAMIN B6	BETA-CAROTENE	CALCIUM	IRON	MAGNESIUM	POTASSIUM	ZINC

Pistachio nuts have become widely available in recent years and make a welcome addition to a healthy diet. They are rich in beta-sitosterols, which can help lower "bad" blood cholesterol and may protect against cancer. Pistachio nuts are also a good source of fiber and soluble fiber, which offer benefits for the blood cholesterol profile, and they may help prevent certain cancers and symptoms of digestive problems, such as constipation and irritable bowel syndrome (IBS). The nuts also contain a range of minerals and the B vitamins, and are a good source of protein, being lower in fat than other types of nuts.

- High in sterols, which lower blood cholesterol and may protect against cancer.
- Rich in potassium to lower blood pressure and eliminate fluid.
- High in fiber and soluble fiber to aid the digestive system and improve blood cholesterol profile.
- Help control blood sugar levels and may be of help to diabetics and people who are insulin resistant.

DID YOU KNOW?

Pistachio nuts are one of the few nuts to contain carotenes, which are responsible for their distinctive green-colored flesh.

PRACTICAL TIPS

A dish of unshelled pistachio nuts makes a healthy predinner snack. They are easy to shell before eating and you can eat the brown skin on the nuts, which adds extra fiber and nutrients. Add pistachio nuts to grain salads, breakfast cereals, and stuffings.

PISTACHIO ICE CREAM

With no dairy and no processed sugar, this is a healthy treat. Coconut milk and almond milk are sweetened with dates, and pistachios and almond extract add extra flavor.

SERVES 6 • PREP TIME: 10 MINS • COOK TIME: NONE

PER SERVING:	195 cal	7.5g	1.8g	31.6g	25.9g	4g	3.5g	40mg
	CALORIES	FAT	SAT FAT	CARBS	SUGAR	FIBER	PROTEIN	SODIUM

INGREDIENTS
⅔ cup unsalted pistachio nuts, shelled
1½ cups coconut milk
1½ cups almond milk
8–10 Medjool dates, pitted
1 teaspoon vanilla extract
½ teaspoon almond extract

1. Put the nuts and about ½ cup of the coconut milk into a food processor and process to a smooth paste.

2. Put the remaining coconut milk, the almond milk, dates, vanilla extract, and almond extract into a blender. Process on high speed for 3–5 minutes, until pureed. Add the pistachio paste and process until well combined.

3. Transfer the mixture to the chilled container of an electric ice cream maker and freeze according to the manufacturer's directions. The ice cream can be served immediately, or you can transfer it to a freezer-proof container and freeze overnight for a more solid consistency.

PEANUTS

Rich in antioxidants and vitamin E, peanuts can improve blood cholesterol levels
and help prevent strokes, heart disease, cancers, and cognitive decline.

MAJOR NUTRIENTS PER 3½ TABLESPOONS SHELLED PEANUTS

170 cal	14.7g	4.8g	2.5g	7.7g	3.6 mg	2.5 mg	28 mg	72 mcg	1.4 mg	50 mg	212 mg	1 mg
CALORIES	TOTAL FAT	CARBS	FIBER	PROTEIN	VITAMIN B3	VITAMIN E	CALCIUM	FOLATE	IRON	MAGNESIUM	POTASSIUM	ZINC

Research has found that peanuts rival the antioxidant content of blackberries and strawberries. They are rich in antioxidant polyphenols, including coumaric acid, to help thin the blood, and resveratrol, which can protect against hardened arteries. They have high vitamin E content, an antioxidant linked with heart and arterial health, brainpower, and protection from strokes, heart attacks, and cancer. Peanuts contain mostly monounsaturated fat, which has a better effect on blood cholesterol levels than polyunsaturates. They are a good source of the amino acids tryptophan, which helps boost mood and encourages proper sleep patterns, and l-tyrosine, which is linked with brainpower.

- Rich in antioxidants, which protect against heart disease.
- High in amino acids to boost mood and brain function.
- Contain phytosterols, which may help prevent colon cancer.
- Rich in monounsaturated fats, which are linked with protection against heart disease.

DID YOU KNOW?

Peanuts, also known as groundnuts, are not, in fact, true nuts but members of the legume family, like peas or beans.

PRACTICAL TIPS

Ideally, buy peanuts in their shells, or at least in their skins—they will keep for longer. Fresh peanuts should smell fresh, not musty. Buy unsalted peanuts and store them in the refrigerator—their high oil content means that they don't last long in warm conditions. Make your own peanut butter by blending with a little peanut oil until it has a good spreading consistency.

CHICKEN & PEANUT STEW

This rich-tasting stew—a type of Asian curry—will rival any takeout dishes for flavor. It is packed with protein and antioxidants, so it will do you nothing but good.

SERVES 4 • PREP TIME: 15 MINS • COOK TIME: 20 MINS

PER SERVING:

568 cal	41.3g	21.7g	16g	8.5g	2.2g	37.1g	840mg
CALORIES	FAT	SAT FAT	CARBS	SUGAR	FIBER	PROTEIN	SODIUM

INGREDIENTS

½ cup roasted, unsalted peanuts
4 boneless, skinless chicken breasts
1 tablespoon vegetable oil
1 shallot, diced
2-4 tablespoons Thai red curry paste
1¾ cups canned coconut milk
1 tablespoon Thai fish sauce
1 tablespoon packed light brown sugar
juice of 1 lime
¾ cup chopped fresh cilantro leaves
chopped fresh cilantro, to garnish (optional)

1. Put the peanuts into a food processor and process for 2–3 minutes, until smooth.

2. Line a large steamer basket with parchment paper and place the chicken on the paper. Place the steamer over boiling water, cover, and steam for 10–12 minutes, until the chicken is tender and cooked through. Cut into the middle to check that the meat is no longer pink. Any juices that run out should be clear and piping hot with visible steam rising.

3. Meanwhile, heat the oil in a large skillet and add the shallot. Cook, stirring frequently, for 5 minutes, or until soft. Add the curry paste and cook, stirring, for an additional minute.

4. Open the can of coconut milk and scoop off the thick cream that has risen to the top. Add the cream to the pan and cook, stirring, until it begins to simmer. Add the remaining coconut milk along with the peanut butter, Thai fish sauce, and sugar. Bring to a boil, then reduce the heat to low. Simmer for 5 minutes, or until the sauce thickens.

5. Stir in the lime juice and cilantro. Serve the chicken topped with a generous amount of the sauce and garnished with chopped cilantro, if using.

BRAZIL NUTS

One of the richest food sources of the antioxidant, anticancer mineral selenium, Brazil nuts are also a good source of calcium and magnesium for healthy bones.

197 cal	19.9g	3.7g	2.3g	4.3g	1.7 mcg	48 mg	113 mg	198 mg	575 mcg	1.2 mg
CALORIES	TOTAL FAT	CARBS	FIBER	PROTEIN	VITAMIN E	CALCIUM	MAGNESIUM	POTASSIUM	SELENIUM	ZINC

Brazil nuts have a high total fat content. Much of this is monounsaturated, however, there is also a reasonable amount of polyunsaturates and a high content of omega-6 linoleic acid, one of the essential fats. When cooked at high temperatures, these fats oxidize and are no longer healthy, so Brazil nuts are best eaten raw. The nut is extraordinary in its extremely high content of the mineral selenium and, on average, just one to two nuts can provide a whole day's recommended intake. Selenium helps protect us from the diseases of aging. The nuts are also a good source of magnesium and calcium.

- Extremely rich in selenium, a mineral often lacking in modern diets.
- Antioxidant, anti-aging, and anticancer.
- High magnesium content protects heart and bones.
- A good source of vitamin E for healthy skin and healing.

DID YOU KNOW?

Brazil nuts are not actually nuts, but seeds that are enclosed in a hard fruit the size of a coconut. The trees grow wild in the Amazon rain forests of Brazil and are rarely cultivated successfully.

PRACTICAL TIPS

Keep unshelled nuts in a cool, dry, dark place for up to six months. The shells of Brazil nuts are tough to crack, so purchase a good quality nutcracker. Shelled nuts should be stored in the refrigerator and consumed within a few weeks, because their high fat content means they turn rancid quickly. They are best eaten raw as a handy snack or added to your breakfast muesli.

BERRY & BRAZIL NUT SMOOTHIE

Frozen berries are a healthy and handy standby staple. Process with
protein-boosting cashew and Brazil nuts for a delicious shake.

SERVES 4 • PREP TIME: 10–15 MINS • COOK TIME: NONE

PER SERVING:

213 cal	12.8g	2.4g	23.2g	11.6g	3.5g	4.7g	80mg
CALORIES	FAT	SAT FAT	CARBS	SUGAR	FIBER	PROTEIN	SDOIUM

INGREDIENTS

2 cups frozen mixed sliced
strawberries and blueberries
8 Brazil nuts
⅓ cup cashew nut pieces
⅓ cup rolled oats
2 cup almond milk
2 tablespoons maple syrup

1. Put the frozen berries, Brazil nuts, and cashew nuts into a
blender. Sprinkle with the oats, then pour in half the almond
milk. Blend until smooth.

2. Add the remaining milk and maple syrup, and blend again
until smooth. Pour into four glasses and serve immediately with
spoons. As the drink stands, the blueberries will almost set the
liquid, but as soon as you stir it, it will turn to liquid again.

COCONUT

Coconut is an extremely dense energy source. It boosts the metabolism and satisfies hunger, helping to maintain youthful weight levels, energy, and vitality.

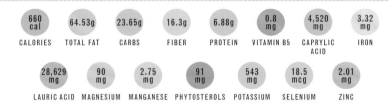

660 cal	64.53g	23.65g	16.3g	6.88g	0.8 mg	4,520 mg	3.32 mg
CALORIES	TOTAL FAT	CARBS	FIBER	PROTEIN	VITAMIN B5	CAPRYLIC ACID	IRON

28,629 mg	90 mg	2.75 mg	91 mg	543 mg	18.5 mcg	2.01 mg
LAURIC ACID	MAGNESIUM	MANGANESE	PHYTOSTEROLS	POTASSIUM	SELENIUM	ZINC

Like nuts, coconut often gets a bad press, because it is high in fat. However, this is plant fat instead of animal fat, and, therefore, it is easy for us to burn off as energy and digest. Cultures that include coconut regularly in their diets consistently show lower incidences of obesity, high cholesterol, heart disease, and diabetes. As this suggests, the anti-aging benefits of this food are vast. It has been shown to prevent tumors, regulate cholesterol, normalize blood sugar levels, and combat the aging effects of stress by nourishing tired adrenal glands.

- Good levels of phytosterols, zinc, and selenium help combat aging elements in the environment.
- Contains lauric acid, also found in human breast milk, which protects against viruses and bacterial infections.
- Caprylic acid kills off fungal infections that can upset digestion and lower immune protection.

DID YOU KNOW?

Coconut is a native plant of the tropical Pacific, but also features in Indian writings as far back as 2,000 years ago, causing much debate about its true origins.

PRACTICAL TIPS

The flesh that comes from inside the coconut may be eaten in its dry form or as milk, when the flesh has been mashed, steeped, and cooked. Dry coconut is best enjoyed unsweetened and, as a snack, will satisfy a sweet craving.

COCONUT, CACAO & HAZELNUT TRUFFLES

These power-packed little balls are just bursting with a nutritious mix of vital minerals, vitamins, protein, and raw ingredients.

MAKES 20 PIECES • PREP TIME: 25 MINS • COOK TIME: NONE

PER TRUFFLE:	46 cal	3.5g	1g	3.2g	2.1g	0.9g	1.3g	TRACE
	CALORIES	FAT	SAT FAT	CARBS	SUGAR	FIBER	PROTEIN	SODIUM

INGREDIENTS

⅔ cup unblanched hazelnuts
½ cup cacao nibs
6 dried, soft figs, coarsely chopped
⅓ cup plus 2 tablespoons dry unsweetened coconut
1 tablespoon maple syrup
finely grated zest and juice of ½ small orange
1 tablespoon cacao nibs, for coating
2 tablespoons dry unsweetened coconut, for coating

1. Add the hazelnuts and the ½ cup of cacao nibs to a food processor and process until finely chopped.

2. Add the figs, the ⅓ cup plus 2 tablespoons of coconut, the maple syrup, and orange zest and juice to the processor, and process until finely chopped and the mixture has come together in a ball.

3. Scoop the mixture out of the food processor, then cut into 20 even pieces. Roll into small balls in your hands.

4. Finely chop the extra cacao nibs, then mix with the extra coconut on a sheet of nonstick parchment paper or a plate. Roll the truffles, one at a time, in the cacao-and-coconut mixture, then arrange in a small plastic container. Store in the refrigerator for up to three days.

HINT

Although dry unsweetened coconut has a long shelf life, it is best stored in an airtight container in the refrigerator.

PINE NUTS

A source of omega-3 fats for a variety of health benefits, pine nuts are also rich in vitamin E, zinc, and cholesterol-lowering plant sterols.

MAJOR NUTRIENTS PER 2 TABLESPOONS PINE NUTS

101 cal	10g	2g	0.6g	2g	1.4 mcg	0.8 mg	38 mg	90 mg	1 mg
CALORIES	TOTAL FAT	CARBS	FIBER	PROTEIN	VITAMIN E	IRON	MAGNESIUM	POTASSIUM	ZINC

Pine nuts come from several species of pine tree. All have similar nutritional benefits, although the longer Asian types contain more oil. They are rich in polyunsaturated omega-6 fats, but they also contain some of the less widely available omega-3 fats that are important for heart health as well as brainpower. Pine nuts are rich in vitamin E and zinc, two antioxidants that help the heart, boost the immune system, and increase fertility. They also contain sterols and stanols, compounds that help lower blood cholesterol.

- High in omega-6 fats and contain omega-3s.
- Contain plant sterols for lowering cholesterol and promoting a healthy immune system.
- Rich in zinc and vitamin E.
- Good source of a range of minerals and fiber.

PRACTICAL TIPS

Pine nuts have a rich yet delicate flavor with a hint of resin. They tend to turn rancid quickly, so buy in small quantities, store in the refrigerator, and use within a few weeks. Pine nuts go well with spinach, strong cheeses, golden raisins, and oily fish. You can make a basil pesto with fresh basil, pine nuts, Parmesan, and olive oil. Lightly dry-fry the nuts to toast, but do not overcook—they can burn easily and oxidize. Pine nuts are best eaten raw.

DID YOU KNOW?

Research shows that pine nuts have been used for food since the Paleolithic period, which ended around 40,000 years ago.

SPICED COD WITH HARISSA & PINE NUT CRUST

This dish takes minutes to prepare and makes a delicious, easy, and nutritious midweek meal. The spicy, crunchy topping contrasts wonderfully with the soft fish flakes.

SERVES 2 • PREP TIME: 10 MINS • COOK TIME: 15 MINS

PER SERVING:

 334 cal CALORIES

 15.1g FAT

 1.4g SAT FAT

 10.2g CARBS

 3.7g SUGAR

 3.1g FIBER

 39.6g PROTEIN

 480mg SODIUM

INGREDIENTS

¼ cup pine nuts

⅓ cup fresh bread crumbs or 2 tablespoons dried white bread crumbs

grated zest of 1 unwaxed lemon

2 tablespoons coarsely chopped fresh cilantro

pinch of sea salt

1 teaspoon olive oil

12 cherry tomatoes (still on the vine, if available)

2 cod fillets, about 7 ounces each

2 teaspoons rose harissa

1. Preheat the oven to 400°F. Crush the pine nuts in a mortar and pestle. Transfer to a bowl, add the bread crumbs, lemon zest, cilantro, salt, and oil, and mix well.

2. Put the cherry tomatoes on a large baking sheet and add the cod fillets skin side down, arranging everything in a single layer. Spread a teaspoon of rose harissa over each cod fillet, then top with the bread crumb mixture, pressing down gently.

3. Bake in the top of the preheated oven for 15 minutes, or until the topping is crisp and golden and the fish flakes easily when pressed with a knife. Serve the cod hot with the tomatoes.

CHIA SEEDS

Mild-tasting chia seeds have become one of the most popular ingredients in superfood recipes in the past few years and even a small portion provides several health benefits.

MAJOR NUTRIENTS PER 1 TABLESPOON DRY WEIGHT CHIA SEEDS

73 cal	4.6g	6.3g	5.2g	2.5g	1.3 mg	95 mg	1.2 mg	50 mg	0.7 mg
CALORIES	TOTAL FAT	CARBS	FIBER	PROTEIN	VITAMIN B3	CALCIUM	IRON	MAGNESIUM	ZINC

Chia seeds are an excellent source of omega-3 fats—just 1 tablespoon contains about 2.6 grams, which is comparable with the amount found in 3½ tablespoons of walnuts or 8¾ ounces of salmon. They are also a good source of fiber, one-quarter of which is the soluble type that can help improve health in several ways. For example, it can improve the blood cholesterol profile, reducing total cholesterol and increasing "good" HDL cholesterol, and it helps to regulate insulin levels in the blood. Chia seeds are a useful tool for weight control, because their high fiber level and ability to absorb liquid helps prolong a feeling of fullness and prevent hunger. The seeds are one of our best plant sources of calcium as well as being a good source of iron, and they contain a range of other important minerals and antioxidants.

- Rich in omega-3 fats, which make up over half of their total fat content.
- Good plant source of calcium and iron.
- Can improve blood cholesterol profile.
- Helps regulate insulin levels in the blood.
- Useful to prevent hunger and as a weight loss tool.

DID YOU KNOW?

The first known use of chia seeds as a food was in the Mayan civilization of central America around 3,000 years ago, where the seeds were thought to be an aid to strength and stamina. The chia plant is related to sage, with pretty, long, purple flowering spikes.

PRACTICAL TIPS

The seeds can be eaten either whole or finely ground. Try adding ground seeds to your oatmeal or yogurt, salads, or smoothies, but first soak them, usually in a ratio of one part dry seeds to three parts liquid. You can stir whole seeds directly into your recipe, where they will absorb its liquid and produce a good set. Chia seeds can take from 15 minutes up to an hour or two (depending on the age of the seeds) to form a gelatinous mix with their soaking liquid. You can even make healthy preserves by adding seeds to pureed berries.

CHIA SEED & BANANA ICE POPS

Chia seeds are combined with bananas, honey, and yogurt to create
these sensational, full-of-goodness ice pops.

SERVES 6 • PREP TIME: 20 MINS, PLUS FREEZING • COOK TIME: NONE

PER SERVING:	84 cal	1.2g	0.5g	18.5g	10.6g	2.3g	1.9g	0.0g
	CALORIES	FAT	SAT FAT	CARBS	SUGAR	FIBER	PROTEIN	SODIUM

INGREDIENTS
3 large ripe bananas
3 tablespoons Greek-style plain yogurt
2 teaspoons honey
2 teaspoons chia seeds

YOU WILL ALSO NEED
6 (¼-cup) ice pop molds
6 ice pop sticks

1. Blend the bananas, Greek yogurt, and honey in a blender
or food processor until you have a thick, smooth consistency.
Stir in the chia seeds. Pour the mixture evenly into the six ice
pop molds.

2. Place an ice pop stick in the center of each mold. Place in the
freezer and freeze for 6 hours before serving.

3. To unmold the ice pops, dip the frozen molds in warm water
for a few seconds and gently release the ice pops while holding
the sticks.

PUMPKIN SEEDS

Rich in zinc, pumpkin seeds help boost the immune system and fertility. They also contain sterols linked with protection against hormone-base cancers.

MAJOR NUTRIENTS PER 5 TEASPOONS PUMPKIN SEEDS

81 cal	6.9g	2.7g	0.6g	3.7g	0.3 mg	2.2 mg	80 mg	121 mg	1.1 mg
CALORIES	TOTAL FAT	CARBS	FIBER	PROTEIN	VITAMIN B3	IRON	MAGNESIUM	POTASSIUM	ZINC

Pumpkin seeds are a nutritious snack and, even in small servings, they provide a significant amount of minerals, especially zinc and iron. Zinc is an antioxidant mineral, which boosts the immune system and, for men, improves fertility and protects against prostate enlargement and cancer. Iron is important for healthy blood cells and energy levels. High iron and zinc content make pumpkin seeds a particularly significant food for vegetarians. The seeds contain sterols, which can help remove "bad" cholesterol from the body as well as help to inhibit the development of breast, colon, and prostate cancer cells. In addition, pumpkin seeds contain some omega-3 fats, vitamin E, folate, and magnesium, which can help maintain heart health.

- Rich in zinc for fertility, immune boosting, and cancer protection.
- Rich in iron for healthy blood and to fight fatigue.
- Can help improve blood cholesterol profile.
- Good source of heart-healthy and anti-inflammatory nutrients.

DID YOU KNOW?

If you grow or buy pumpkins and squash, don't discard the seeds— make your own roasted pumpkin seeds. Wash and dry the seeds and toss in a little peanut or light olive oil. Spread out on a baking sheet and lightly roast on a low heat for 20 minutes.

PRACTICAL TIPS

Pumpkin seeds are not edible when raw and the ones sold are almost always roasted. Chew the seeds well to be sure of maximum absorption of nutrients. Add to salads, muesli, or granola, or sprinkle on breakfast cereals or yogurt. The seeds can be ground and added to vegetable, nut, and bean burgers to provide extra nutrients.

GREEK-STYLE YOGURT WITH ORANGE ZEST & SEEDS

Toasting the seeds in this recipe enhances their flavor, so they contrast wonderfully with the smooth, creamy yogurt.

SERVES 2 • PREP TIME: 5 MINS • COOK TIME: 3 MINS

PER SERVING:

172 cal	10.6g	4.3g	8.1g	4.3g	3.3g	12g	TRACE
CALORIES	FAT	SAT FAT	CARBS	SUGAR	FIBER	PROTEIN	SODIUM

INGREDIENTS

2 teaspoons flaxseed
2 teaspoons pumpkin seeds
2 teaspoons chia seeds
¾ cup Greek-style plain yogurt
grated zest of 1 small orange
1 teaspoon orange juice

1. Put a small skillet over medium heat. When it is hot, add the seeds. Toast, stirring constantly with a wooden spoon, until they start to turn brown and release a nutty aroma. Transfer to a plate and let cool.

2. Spoon the yogurt into two glass cups or serving bowls, then sprinkle the seeds on top, followed by the orange zest. Sprinkle with the orange juice and serve immediately.

SESAME SEEDS

The lignan fibers in sesame seeds help lower "bad" cholesterol, and the seeds may also have an anti-inflammatory action, reducing the pain of arthritis.

MAJOR NUTRIENTS PER 1½ TABLESPOONS SESAME SEEDS

85 cal	7.2g	3.9g	2.5g	2.5g	0.8 mg	14 mcg	20 mg	1.2 mg	52 mg	61 mg	1.5 mg
CALORIES	TOTAL FAT	CARBS	FIBER	PROTEIN	VITAMIN B3	FOLATE	CALCIUM	IRON	MAGNESIUM	POTASSIUM	ZINC

Sesame seeds contain two special types of fiber—sesamin and sesamolin—which are members of the lignans group. They can lower "bad" cholesterol and help prevent high blood pressure, which helps to protect against cardiovascular disease. Sesamin is a powerful antioxidant in its own right and has been shown to protect the liver from damage. Plant sterols contained in the seeds also have a cholesterol-lowering action. The seeds are particularly rich in copper, which may be of use to people wtih arthritis, because it is thought to have an anti-inflammatory action, reducing pain and swelling. Sesame seeds also contain the minerals iron, zinc, calcium, and potassium in varying quantities.

- Good source of plant fibers and sterols to help lower cholesterol.
- Source of the antioxidant lignan sesamin.
- High in iron and zinc.
- Contain large amounts of calcium, useful for nondairy eaters.

DID YOU KNOW?
Sesame seeds can be found in a range of colors that include pale cream, brown, red, and black; the darker the color, the stronger the flavor tends to be.

PRACTICAL TIPS
Store in a cool, dry, dark place in an airtight container. Sesame seeds can be eaten raw or lightly toasted in a low oven, but do not overcook—this destroys some healthy fats. Sprinkle the seeds on vegetables, such as broccoli or spinach, before serving, or add to grain salads. Sesame seed oil is good for stir-fries, while tahini, a sesame seed paste, can be added to hummus and other dips.

STEAK, BABY BROCCOLI & SESAME STIR-FRY

Vibrant green baby broccoli and juicy beef are the stars of this hearty vitamin- and mineral-rich stir-fry, and the sesame oil introduces a delicious nutty depth and richness.

SERVES 2 • PREP TIME: 15 MINS, PLUS MARINATING • COOK TIME: 10 MINS

PER SERVING:

366 cal	24.5g	4.8g	10.5g	2.2g	4.1g	28.6g	560mg
CALORIES	FAT	SAT FAT	CARBS	SUGAR	FIBER	PROTEIN	SODIUM

INGREDIENTS

1 tablespoon soy sauce
1 tablespoon sesame oil
7 ounces tenderloin steak, cut into strips
2 teaspoons sesame seeds
1 tablespoon peanut oil
1 large garlic clove, thinly sliced
9 ounces baby broccoli
3 tablespoons water

1. Mix the soy sauce and sesame oil in a large bowl, add the steak, and toss. Cover and let marinate for 10 minutes.

2. Toast the sesame seeds in a large dry wok over high heat until they are just beginning to brown, then transfer to the bowl with the steak and set aside.

3. Remove the wok from the heat and wipe it clean with paper towels. Return to the heat and pour in the oil. Remove the steak from the marinade and quickly cook, turning occasionally, until brown all over and cooked to your preference. Transfer to a plate and set aside.

4. If the pan is dry, add a splash more oil, then add the garlic and cook for 1 minute. Add the baby broccoli, steak marinade, and water, stir and cook for 1 minute, until the broccoli is bright green and just beginning to soften.

5. Return the steak to the wok and stir well. Divide the stir-fry between two plates and serve immediately.

HINT

If you're on a reduced-sodium diet, use low-sodium soy sauce, because regular soy sauce is salty.

SUNFLOWER SEEDS

Rich in a range of minerals and vitamin E, sunflower seeds also offer
protection from inflammation and cardiovascular disease.

MAJOR NUTRIENTS PER 5 TEASPOONS SUNFLOWER SEEDS

86 cal	7.4g	1.6g	3.4g	0.7 mg	5mg	34 mcg	17 mg	1 mg	53 mg	103 mg	9 mcg	0.8 mg
CALORIES	TOTAL FAT	FIBER	PROTEIN	VITAMIN B3	VITAMIN E	FOLATE	CALCIUM	IRON	MAGNESIUM	POTASSIUM	SELENIUM	ZINC

Sunflower seeds, usually sold shelled, are one of the world's major sources
of vegetable oil. They are rich in polyunsaturated fats. The seeds are also
rich in vitamin E, and can help protect from inflammatory conditions,
such as asthma and rheumatoid arthritis. Vitamin E is also an antioxidant,
neutralizing the free radicals that can damage the body cells and speed
up the aging process. It is also linked with a lower risk of cardiovascular
disease and with protection from colon cancer. Sunflower seeds are rich in
plant sterols, which have a cholesterol-lowering effect, as well as various
minerals, including iron, magnesium, and selenium.

- Rich in the omega-6 linoleic acid, which is an essential fat.
- High in antioxidant vitamin E, which has a range of
  health benefits.
- High in plant sterols for cholesterol-lowering effect.
- Nutrient and mineral rich.

DID YOU KNOW?

*Native to Central and South
America, sunflower seeds have
been eaten in North America for
around 5,000 years, but are now
grown all across the world for
their high oil content.*

PRACTICAL TIPS

The high polyunsaturated content of sunflower seeds means that they
spoil quickly and can turn rancid if kept in warm conditions. Shelled nuts
and seeds can be frozen and thawed at room temperature. The seeds
make a good addition to salads, muesli, granola, and oatmeal, or can be
eaten as a snack.

ZUCCHINI SPAGHETTI

Zucchini are cut into thin strips, which are then lightly cooked and tossed with pesto. Toasted sunflower seeds add crunch and some vital vitamin E, too.

SERVES 2 • PREP TIME: 30 MINS • COOK TIME: 25–27 MINS

PER SERVING:

464 cal	37.8g	9.7g	19.9g	10.9g	6g	16.7g	600mg
CALORIES	FAT	SAT FAT	CARBS	SUGAR	FIBER	PROTEIN	SODIUM

INGREDIENTS

1 cup cherry tomatoes
4 garlic cloves, sliced
1 tablespoon olive oil
⅓ cup sunflower seeds
2 large zucchini
2 tablespoons fresh pesto
½ cup crumbled feta cheese
salt and pepper (optional)
¾ cup coarsely chopped fresh basil, to garnish

1. Preheat the oven to 400°F. Cut half of the cherry tomatoes in half horizontally and leave the remainder whole. Put all the tomatoes and garlic into a small roasting pan and drizzle with the oil. Shake well to coat and place in the preheated oven for 20 minutes.

2. Meanwhile, put a dry skillet over medium heat. Add the sunflower seeds and heat for 3–4 minutes, or until the seeds are just toasted. Set aside.

3. Lay a box grater on its side, and using the wide slots grate the length of the zucchini into long strands. Try not to be firm; a loose grip makes this easier.

4. Bring a saucepan of water to a boil and add the zucchini strips. Cook for 1–2 minutes before draining thoroughly in a colander, gently squeezing any excess water away with the back of a spoon. Return the zucchini spaghetti to the pan and stir through the pesto. Season with salt and pepper, if using.

5. Stir two-thirds of the roasted tomato mixture, half the sunflower seeds, and half the cheese into the zucchini spaghetti and divide the mixture between two plates. Top with the remaining tomatoes, sunflower seeds, and cheese. Garnish with the basil and a sprinkling of pepper, if using. Serve immediately.

FLAXSEED

Golden flaxseed are one of nature's true superfoods. Soaking them bulks up the therapeutic fibers and helps you access their age-defying nutrients.

MAJOR NUTRIENTS PER 1½ TABLESPOONS GOLDEN FLAXSEED

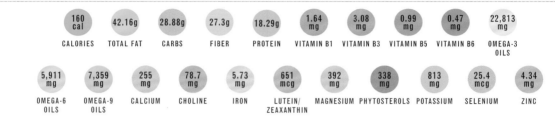

160 cal	42.16g	28.88g	27.3g	18.29g	1.64 mg	3.08 mg	0.99 mg	0.47 mg	22,813 mg
CALORIES	TOTAL FAT	CARBS	FIBER	PROTEIN	VITAMIN B1	VITAMIN B3	VITAMIN B5	VITAMIN B6	OMEGA-3 OILS

5,911 mg	7,359 mg	255 mg	78.7 mg	5.73 mg	651 mcg	392 mg	338 mg	813 mg	25.4 mcg	4.34 mg
OMEGA-6 OILS	OMEGA-9 OILS	CALCIUM	CHOLINE	IRON	LUTEIN/ ZEAXANTHIN	MAGNESIUM	PHYTOSTEROLS	POTASSIUM	SELENIUM	ZINC

Flaxseed, soaked to open up the tough outer covering and puff out the fiber inside, is an age-old way of keeping the bowels regular. They combat constipation and diarrhea and ensure the rapid removal of aging toxins before they can cause the body any damage. The seed also binds to excess cholesterol in the body, which is then removed in support of heart and brain health. Regular consumption exercises the bowel muscle, improving digestive function in the long term. The soaking process also produces a mucilage that coats the digestive wall, offering protection and healing, helping reduce food intolerances, and supporting the immune system to prevent premature aging.

- High levels of omega-3 oils prevent aging inflammation and keep the skin supple and smooth.
- Contain lignans, which are a type of phytoestrogen. Phytoestrogen regulates hormones to assist both male and female sexual health and potency.
- High in antioxidants due to the lignans, phytosterols, lutein, and selenium, which give this food an excellent anti-aging profile.

DID YOU KNOW?

Holy Roman Emperor Charlemagne (AD 742–814) popularized the use of flax as food, medicine, and cloth by making it the law to grow and eat it.

PRACTICAL TIPS

Flaxseed are either brown or golden, but the golden variety is easier to absorb. Soak for 10 minutes in warm water, then add 2 teaspoons—including the water—to oatmeal, cereal, a smoothie, or yogurt to take on their therapeutic benefits.

WALNUT & FLAXSEED CRACKERS

These crisp, nutty crackers contain ground (or milled) flaxseed as well as whole. Milling the seeds releases the nutrients—whole, unsoaked, unmilled flaxseed simply provide fiber.

MAKES 20 • PREP TIME: 20 MINS, PLUS CHILLING • COOK TIME: 20–22 MINS

PER CRACKER:

68 cal	4g	1.4g	7.6g	3.1g	1.4g	1.5g	40mg
CALORIES	FAT	SAT FAT	CARBS	SUGAR	FIBER	PROTEIN	SODIUM

INGREDIENTS

⅔ cup ground flaxseed

1¼ cups whole-wheat flour

½ teaspoon salt

2 tablespoons packed light brown sugar

6 tablespoons unsalted butter, at room temperature

1 cup raisins

½ cup milk

½ cup chopped walnuts

3 tablespoons plus 1 teaspoon whole flaxseed

1 tablespoon whole-wheat flour, for dusting

1. Preheat the oven to 350°F. Put the ground flaxseed, flour, salt, and sugar into a large mixing bowl and mix with a handheld electric mixer. Add the butter and mix on medium speed for 2–3 minutes, until coarse crumbs form.

2. Add the raisins, milk, walnuts, and whole flaxseed and mix until the dough comes together. Turn out the dough onto a piece of plastic wrap and form it into a round shape. Wrap and chill in the refrigerator for about 10 minutes.

3. Lay a large sheet of parchment paper on a work surface. Turn out the dough onto the paper and flatten it into a large rectangle with the palms of your hands. Sprinkle with a little flour, then roll out as thinly as possible (to the thickness of the chopped nuts).

4. Using a sharp knife, score the dough into 2-inch squares. Slide the paper onto a large baking sheet and bake in the preheated oven for 20–22 minutes, until the crackers are lightly browned. Remove from the oven, break apart, and let cool before serving.

HINT

These crackers make a great healthy snack that can be packed up and eaten on-the-go.

TAHINI

Tahini is a delicious way to eat large quantities of the highly beneficial and therapeutic sesame seed.

MAJOR NUTRIENTS PER 1 TABLESPOON DARK TAHINI

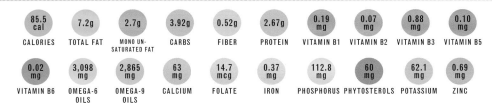

85.5 cal	7.2g	2.7g	3.92g	0.52g	2.67g	0.19 mg	0.07 mg	0.88 mg	0.10 mg
CALORIES	TOTAL FAT	MONO UN-SATURATED FAT	CARBS	FIBER	PROTEIN	VITAMIN B1	VITAMIN B2	VITAMIN B3	VITAMIN B5

0.02 mg	3,098 mg	2,865 mg	63 mg	14.7 mcg	0.37 mg	112.8 mg	60 mg	62.1 mg	0.69 mg
VITAMIN B6	OMEGA-6 OILS	OMEGA-9 OILS	CALCIUM	FOLATE	IRON	PHOSPHORUS	PHYTOSTEROLS	POTASSIUM	ZINC

Tahini is a thick paste make of sesame seeds, and these seeds contain two exclusive compounds: sesamin and sesamolin, types of lignans that offer potent heart protection by regulating cholesterol and high blood pressure. They also revitalize vitamin E in your body to increase antioxidant activity, particularly in the skin, where it helps heal scars and blemishes, and prevent age spots. Sesame seeds have the highest levels of phytosterols of any food, vital for immune function and lowering cholesterol. Sesame seeds also contain the fat-soluble nutrients beta-carotene and vitamin E, which are important antioxidants.

- High levels of vitamin B3, phosphorus and calcium keep bones strong and young.
- Sesamin helps prevent damage in the liver from the toxins it is exposed to, supporting the organ's elimination of harmful, aging waste.
- High levels of omega-6 oils and zinc promote a healthy hormone balance in women, which encourages positive mood and good bone health.

DID YOU KNOW?

Tahini is mentioned as an ingredient in hummus in a thirteenth-century Arabic cookbook, and it has become popular in recent years as an alternative to butter.

PRACTICAL TIPS

Tahini makes a versatile addition to the kitchen pantry. It may be mixed with olive oil to make a dressing, used as a spread or to make hummus, or added to falafel, as is traditional in the Middle East. The darker version is preferable, because the seeds don't have the nutritious outer hull removed, but it can be a little rich for some tastes.

BANANA FLATBREAD BITES WITH TAHINI & DATE SYRUP

Sometimes the best things are the simplest. Assembled in minutes, this speedy snack is perfect for combating the midafternoon energy slump.

SERVES 4 • PREP TIME: 15–20 MINS • COOK TIME: 5–6 MINS

PER SERVING:	354 cal	11.3g	2.5g	60g	25.4g	4.1g	9.4g	200mg
	CALORIES	FAT	SAT FAT	CARBS	SUGAR	FIBER	PROTEIN	SODIUM

INGREDIENTS

4 (8-inch) pieces whole-wheat tortillas
¼ cup tahini
3 tablespoons date syrup
4 bananas, peeled

1. Preheat a dry skillet, then add the tortillas, one by one, and warm for 30 seconds on each side.

2. Arrange the tortillas on a cutting board, thinly spread each one with tahini, then drizzle with the date syrup. Add a whole banana to each tortilla, just a little off center, then roll up tightly.

3. Cut each tortilla into thick slices, secure the bites with a toothpick, and arrange on a plate. Serve warm.

HERBS, SPICES, FLAVORINGS & OILS

MINT

Mint is a popular, often home-grown, herb that is a remedy for calming and relaxing the stomach, and it can relieve travel sickness and the congestion of colds.

MAJOR NUTRIENTS PER 12 MINT LEAVES

7 cal	TRACE	1.2g	1g	0.5g	30 mg	16 mcg	1.8 mg	9 mg	69 mg
CALORIES	TOTAL FAT	CARBS	FIBER	PROTEIN	CALCIUM	FOLATE	IRON	MAGNESIUM	POTASSIUM

For thousands of years, mint has been used for its flavor as well as its medicinal purposes. The three main types of mint commonly used are peppermint, spearmint, and apple mint. The menthol oils that they contain, particularly peppermint, are a natural remedy for indigestion, which is why mint tea is traditionally consumed after a rich meal. Menthol can also clear head and chest congestion during colds and flu, and for people who have allergic rhinitis. The oils are antibacterial and may help prevent *Helicobacter pylori,* which causes stomach ulcers, and food poisoning bugs salmonella and *E. coli,* from multiplying.

- Relieves indigestion and calms the stomach.
- Relieves nasal and chest congestion.
- Contains antibacterial properties.

PRACTICAL TIPS

Mint is best enjoyed fresh, because the dried leaves lose much of their potency. A simple way to enjoy fresh mint is to chop it finely and mix with plain yogurt to serve with lamb or eggplant. Make an easy mint sauce by combining fresh chopped mint with balsamic vinegar. You can also steep a handful of fresh leaves in boiling water for 5 minutes to make mint tea—strain before drinking.

DID YOU KNOW?

If you put a few stems of freshly picked mint in a jar of water, within a few days they will grow roots, which can be planted indoors for a year-round supply.

ORZO WITH MINT
& FRESH TOMATOES

Orzo pasta, which resembles fat grains of rice, pairs up with baby spinach, mint, and cherry
tomatoes for a palate-pleasing, digestion-calming, and fresh-tasting, meat-free side.

SERVES 4 • PREP TIME: 20 MINS • COOK TIME: 20 MINS

PER SERVING:

443 cal	11.4g	7.1g	70.9g	5.1g	5g	14g	40mg
CALORIES	FAT	SAT FAT	CARBS	SUGAR	FIBER	PROTEIN	SODIUM

INGREDIENTS

2 cups orzo
½ cup crème fraîche or Greek-style yogurt
5½ cups baby spinach
¾ cup coarsely chopped fresh mint
2 cups cherry tomatoes, coarsely chopped
salt and pepper (optional)
1 tablespoon coarsely chopped fresh mint,
to garnish

1. Bring a large saucepan of water to a boil and drop the orzo into the water. Stir vigorously to prevent them from sticking and stir occasionally during cooking. Simmer for 8 minutes, or according to package directions, until the orzo is tender but still firm to the bite. Set aside ½ cup of the cooking water.

2. Drain the orzo and return to the pan with the reserved cooking water. Put over gentle heat and add the crème fraîche and spinach. Stir until the spinach has wilted and the crème fraîche has coated the grains. Remove from the heat.

3. Stir in the mint and cherry tomatoes. Season with salt and pepper, if using. Garnish with mint and serve immediately.

ROSEMARY

Pungent fresh rosemary has strong medicinal benefits, can fight the symptoms of colds and flu, and help prevent diseases of aging.

MAJOR NUTRIENTS PER ½ CUP ROSEMARY

20 cal	0.9g	3.1g	2g	0.5g	48 mg	16 mcg	1 mg	14 mg	100 mg
CALORIES	TOTAL FAT	CARBS	FIBER	PROTEIN	CALCIUM	FOLATE	IRON	MAGNESIUM	POTASSIUM

Traditionally, rosemary has been used as a mental stimulant, memory booster, general tonic, and to aid circulation. An infusion of rosemary tea has long been recommended by herbalists to treat colds, flu, and rheumatism. Like several other herbs, rosemary has been shown to fight bacteria that can cause throat infections, such as *E. coli* and staphylococcus, so an infusion of rosemary makes a good gargle. In addition, recent research has found that rosemary is one of the leading herbs for its antioxidant activity, helping to reduce the risk of diseases and aging effects.

- Strong antioxidant activity.
- Memory and brain booster.
- Contains antibacterial properties.
- Used as a general tonic and may lift depression.

DID YOU KNOW?

In tests, rosemary extract (not fresh or dried leaves) has been found to act as a detoxifier for the liver, to help boost skin condition, and to block estrogens in the body in a similar way to antibreast cancer medicines.

PRACTICAL TIPS

Rosemary dries well and retains some of its antioxidant effects. Hang sprigs up to dry in a warm kitchen, then remove the leaves and store in an airtight container. Fresh rosemary leaves can be chopped and mixed with thyme, sage, and oregano and added to Mediterranean casseroles or omelet fillings. Use fresh sprigs with garlic to season roasted chicken, lamb, and pork. When making bread, add chopped fresh leaves to the mix.

ROSEMARY, SEA SALT & SESAME POPCORN

Forget about fat- and additive-laden potato chips—popcorn can
be cooked in a fraction of the oil for a healthier alternative.

SERVES 4 • PREP TIME: 10–15 MINS • COOK TIME: 6–8 MINS

PER SERVING:	79 cal	25.2g	3.2g	30g	1.6g	6.6g	6.4g	600mg
	CALORIES	FAT	SAT FAT	CARBS	SUGAR	FIBER	PROTEIN	SODIUM

INGREDIENTS

¼ cup sesame seeds

2 tablespoons olive oil

2 fresh rosemary sprigs, torn into large pieces

¾ cup popping corn

1 teaspoon sea salt

2 tablespoons balsamic vinegar, or to taste

1. Add the sesame seeds to a large skillet with 1 teaspoon of the oil, cover, and cook over medium heat for 2–3 minutes, shaking the pan from time to time, until the seeds are toasted golden brown and beginning to pop. Scoop out of the pan into a bowl and wipe out the pan with a piece of paper towel.

2. Add the remaining oil and the rosemary to the pan and heat gently, shaking the pan to release the rosemary's oil. Add the corn, cover with the lid, and cook over medium heat for 3–4 minutes, shaking the pan, until all the popcorn has popped. Remove from the heat and sprinkle with the toasted sesame seeds, and season with the salt and vinegar, then transfer to a serving bowl, discarding the rosemary just before eating.

BASIL

The highly fragrant, bright green leaves of basil are mildly sedative and
pain relieving, and they can help beat indigestion.

MAJOR NUTRIENTS PER ⅔ CUP BASIL

222 cal	1.8g	46g	3.6g	5g	0.2 mg	3 mg
CALORIES	TOTAL FAT	CARBS	FIBER	PROTEIN	VITAMIN B1	VITAMIN B3
0.3mg	20 mg	0.8 mg	848 mcg	19.6 mcg	86 mg	1.3g
VITAMIN B6	CALCIUM	IRON	LUTEIN/ ZEAXANTHIN	SELENIUM	MAGNESIUM	ZINC

Basil is perhaps best known as the major ingredient in the Italian sauce
pesto. Yet, the herb has been used for thousands of years in India and
the Mediterranean, has several health benefits, and has long been used
in traditional herbal medicine as a remedy for indigestion, nausea, and
stomach ache. It is mildly sedative and an infusion of basil oil can even be
used as an insect repellent and to offer sting relief. Basil contains strongly
antioxidant flavonoid compounds. The leaves contain volatile oils that have
chemicals to fight food-poisoning bacteria. The chemical eugenol, also
present, is an anti-inflammatory similar to aspirin that can help relieve the
pain of arthritis and may ease irritable bowel syndrome (IBS).

- Traditionally used in remedies for indigestion, nausea, and
  stomach ache.
- Acts as an insect repellent and has antibacterial action.
- Anti-inflammatory.
- High in lutein and zeaxanthin for eye health.

DID YOU KNOW?

*The chemical estragole, found
in basil, has been linked with
cancer in animals, but there is
no risk to humans even if huge
amounts are eaten.*

PRACTICAL TIPS

Basil is best added at the end of cooking to preserve its flavor, aroma, and
oils. Basil leaves, if large, should be torn instead of cut with a knife. To
make a quick pesto, crush basil with pine nuts, olive oil, salt, and pepper
and use to dress pasta. Sprinkle basil over a tomato and mozzarella salad.

BASIL & RAW GARLIC HUMMUS

Stomach-soothing basil makes an interesting addition to this garlicky hummus
and is a worthy replacement for the more usual cumin seeds.

SERVES 4 • PREP TIME: 15–20 MINS • COOK TIME: NONE

PER SERVING:	152 cal	7.3g	1g	15g	3.4g	5.3g	6.4g	TRACE
	CALORIES	FAT	SAT FAT	CARBS	SUGAR	FIBER	PROTEIN	SODIUM

INGREDIENTS

2½ cups rinsed and drained, canned chickpeas
3 tablespoons tahini
¾ cup coarsely chopped fresh basil
pinch of paprika
2 garlic cloves
finely grated zest and juice of 1 lemon
¼–⅓ cup cold water
salt and pepper (optional)
1 cup fresh basil sprigs, to garnish

1. Put the chickpeas, tahini, basil, paprika, garlic, and lemon zest and juice into a food processor. Process to a coarse paste.

2. With the food processor still running, slowly add the cold water until a smooth, thick paste forms, adding a little more, if needed. Season with salt and pepper, if using.

3. Garnish with basil and serve immediately or place in a covered container and keep in the refrigerator. This hummus will keep in the refrigerator for up to three days.

THYME

This herb may be tiny but, with an antioxidant action in the top ten of all herbs, it packs a huge health punch.

MAJOR NUTRIENTS PER ⅓ CUP THYME

| 15 cal CALORIES | 0.2g TOTAL FAT | 3.6g CARBS | 2.1g FIBER | 0.8g PROTEIN | 24 mg VITAMIN C | 428 mcg BETA-CAROTENE | 61 mg CALCIUM | 2.6 mg IRON | 91 mg POTASSIUM | 0.3 mg ZINC |

The evergreen leaves of thyme have a powerful, aromatic flavor and strong antioxidant action, because of the volatile oils and plant compounds they contain. The most important of these is thymol. Research on this oil has found it can boost the effects of healthy omega-3 fats on the body, for example, the omega-3 DHA found in fish oils, which has been shown to be important for healthy brain function. The oils in thyme are strongly antibacterial and can protect against food poisoning bugs, such as *E. coli*, bacillus, and staphylococcus. Finally, they are rich in flavonoids, which protect us against the diseases of aging, and they are a good source of vitamin C and iron.

- Boosts omega-3 fats' actions in the body.
- May boost brainpower.
- Strongly antiseptic and antibiotic.
- Rich in flavonoid antioxidants, vitamin C, and iron.

DID YOU KNOW?

Thyme oil has been used since the Middle Ages for its antiseptic properties, and it is often recommended by herbalists today as a treatment for bronchitis or a mouthwash.

PRACTICAL TIPS

Fresh stems can be tied with bay leaves and parsley to make a simple bouquet garni for fish soups and stews. Add chopped fresh thyme leaves, mint, and parsley to an omelet for wonderful flavor and aroma. Stuff a roasting chicken with plenty of thyme or lemon thyme. If necessary, the easiest way to remove leaves from the stems is with a fork.

ROASTED FIGS WITH HONEY & THYME

You don't need to do much with fresh figs, but roasting them is a wonderful way to bring out their flavor. You can use cream cheese or Greek-style plain yogurt instead of labneh.

SERVES 4 • PREP TIME: 10 MINS • COOK TIME: 20 MINS

PER SERVING:

220 cal CALORIES	4.8g FAT	2.8g SAT FAT	46.1g CARBS	42.9g SUGAR	3g FIBER	2.4g PROTEIN	80mg SODIUM

INGREDIENTS

8 figs
10 fresh thyme sprigs, broken into pieces
½ cup honey
½ cup labneh, to serve

1. Preheat the oven to 350°F. Using a sharp knife, cut a deep X shape through each fig, stopping just before the bottom, and stuff it with two pieces of thyme.

2. Line a small roasting pan with crumpled parchment paper, arranging it to come up the sides. Put the figs on the paper, drizzle a tablespoon of honey onto each one, then sprinkle with the remaining thyme.

3. Roast the figs for 20 minutes. Serve hot with the syrup in the parchment paper and a generous spoonful of labneh, if using.

CILANTRO

The leaves of the coriander plant (from which we get the seeds) are antibacterial and anti-inflammatory, and they can significantly improve the blood cholesterol profile.

MAJOR NUTRIENTS PER 7 CILANTRO SPRIGS

3 cal	TRACE	0.5g	0.4g	0.3g	590 mcg	10 mg	9 mcg	0.3 mg	130 mcg	78 mg
CALORIES	TOTAL FAT	CARBS	FIBER	PROTEIN	BETA-CAROTENE	CALCIUM	FOLATE	IRON	LUTEIN/ZEAXANTHIN	POTASSIUM

Cilantro has a reputation for being high on the list of the healing herbs. Research has shown that when cilantro was added to the diet of diabetic mice, it helped stimulate their secretion of insulin and lowered their blood sugar. The leaves contain the compound dodecenal, which tests show is twice as effective at killing salmonella bacteria as some antibiotics. In addition, eight other antibiotic compounds were isolated from the plant. Cilantro has also been shown to lower "bad" cholesterol and increase "good" cholesterol. It is a good source of several nutrients, including potassium and calcium, and contains high levels of lutein and zeaxanthin, which help protect our eyes and eyesight.

- Regulates blood sugars and, therefore, may help diabetics and people who are insulin-resistant.
- Anti-inflammatory and antibacterial.
- Has a positive impact on blood cholesterol levels.
- May contribute to improved eye health.

DID YOU KNOW?

Leaves of fresh cilantro bear a strong resemblance to Italian flat-leaf parsley—they both belong to the same plant family, Umbelliferae.

PRACTICAL TIPS

Use fresh cilantro, because it loses most of its aroma and flavor when dried. The leaves are delicate so store carefully, well wrapped, or use leaves from a growing plant. Fresh cilantro should be added to cooked dishes at the last minute, because it loses aroma and flavor when cooked.

TURKEY WITH CILANTRO PESTO & SOBA NOODLES

Lean, low-fat turkey and health-promoting fresh cilantro combine in a delicious and well-flavored dish that is full of goodness.

SERVES 8 • PREP TIME: 20 MINS, PLUS MARINATING & RESTING • COOK TIME: 1 HOUR

PER SERVING:

578 cal	18.9g	1.9g	50.9g	11.8g	3.3g	53.5g	1,400 mg
CALORIES	FAT	SAT FAT	CARBS	SUGAR	FIBER	PROTEIN	SODIUM

INGREDIENTS

¼ cup reduced-sodium soy sauce
2 teaspoon chili paste
3 garlic cloves, sliced
1 boneless, skinless turkey breast about 3–4 pounds
1 pound dried soba noodles

PESTO

2 cups chopped fresh cilantro
½ cup vegetable oil
¼ cup sugar
4 garlic cloves
2 tablespoons finely chopped fresh ginger
2 teaspoons chilli paste
juice of 1 lime
2 teaspoons salt

1. Combine the soy sauce, chili paste, and garlic in a bowl large enough to hold the turkey breast. Add the turkey breast and turn to coat. Cover and marinate in the refrigerator for at least 2 hours or overnight.

2. To cook the turkey, let it come to room temperature and preheat the broiler to medium. Broil for about 30 minutes on each side, until a meat thermometer inserted into the thickest part registers 165°F.

3. Meanwhile, cook the noodles according to the package directions. Drain and set aside.

4. To make the pesto, combine the cilantro, oil, sugar, garlic, ginger, chili paste, lime juice, and salt in a food processor and process until well combined.

5. Remove the cooked turkey from the broiler, loosely cover with aluminum foil, and let rest for at least 5 minutes before slicing.

6. Toss the noodles with the pesto and slice the turkey into ¼-inch slices. Serve immediately with the noodles.

SAGE

Rich in beneficial compounds, sage helps to slow down the aging process
and reduce symptoms of arthritis and asthma.

MAJOR NUTRIENTS PER ½ CUP SAGE

22 cal	0.9g	4.2g	2.8g	0.7g	244 mcg	116 mg	19 mcg	1.9 mg	30 mg	75 mg
CALORIES	TOTAL FAT	CARBS	FIBER	PROTEIN	BETA-CAROTENE	CALCIUM	FOLATE	IRON	MAGNESIUM	POTASSIUM

Native to the Mediterranean, sage has been used for thousands of years and has one of the longest histories of use of any medicinal herb. It contains a variety of volatile oils, flavonoids, and phenolic acids. Sage is in the top ten of herbs that have the most powerful antioxidant effect, neutralizing the cell-damaging free radicals that are thought to be linked with the aging process. Herbalists have long believed that sage is an outstanding memory enhancer and in trials, even small amounts significantly improved short-term recall. Sage is also antibacterial and can help reduce the number of hot flashes in menopausal women, and it is recommended for people with inflammatory conditions, such as rheumatoid arthritis and asthma.

- Strongly antioxidant, antibacterial, and preservative.
- Boosts memory.
- Reduces hot flashes in many menopausal women.
- Has anti-inflammatory properties.

DID YOU KNOW?

For a long time, herbalists have recognized sage's antioxidant qualities. The ancient Greeks used it to help preserve meat, while tenth-century physicians in Arabia believed it helped promote immortality.

PRACTICAL TIPS

Sage is an easy-to-grow, perennial hardy shrub available throughout the year. The leaves can be dried on a rack in a warm, dry place and then stored in an airtight container. Add sage to other chopped herbs for a herb omelet or stuffing. Sprinkle chopped fresh sage on pizzas and pasta.

BUTTERNUT WEDGES WITH SAGE & PUMPKIN SEEDS

Packed full of nutrition, butternut squash is one of the all-round good things about fall and winter, and roasting brings out its nutty sweetness.

SERVES 3 • PREP TIME: 20 MINS • COOK TIME: 35 MINS

PER SERVING:	259 cal	13.3g	2.1g	33.9g	6.1g	7.2g	7.8g	TRACE
	CALORIES	FAT	SAT FAT	CARBS	SUGAR	FIBER	PROTEIN	SODIUM

INGREDIENTS

1 large butternut squash
1 tablespoon olive oil
½ teaspoon chili powder
12 fresh sage leaves, finely chopped
⅓ cup pumpkin seeds
salt and pepper (optional)

1. Preheat the oven to 400°F. Prepare the butternut squash by washing any excess dirt from the skin and slicing off the top and bottom. Using a heavy, sharp knife, cut the squash into six long wedges. Scoop out any seeds and discard. Put the wedges onto a baking sheet. Brush with half the oil and sprinkle with the chili powder. Roast in the preheated oven for 25 minutes.

2. Remove from the oven and brush with the remaining oil. Sprinkle with the sage and pumpkin seeds. Season with salt and pepper, if using, and return the wedges to the oven for an additional 10 minutes. Serve immediately, garnished with extra pepper, if using.

PARSLEY

A traditional herbal remedy, parsley is strongly antioxidant and anticoagulant, and it is also rich in vitamin C and iron.

MAJOR NUTRIENTS PER 15 PARSLEY SPRIGS

5 cal	TRACE	1g	0.5g	0.5g	20 mg	758 mcg	21 mg	23 mcg	0.9 mg	834 mcg	8 mg	83 mg
CALORIES	TOTAL FAT	CARBS	FIBER	PROTEIN	VITAMIN C	BETA-CAROTENE	CALCIUM	FOLATE	IRON	LUTEIN/ZEAXANTHIN	MAGNESIUM	POTASSIUM

Flat-leaf and curly-leaf parsley both have a similar nutritional profile. Parsley sprigs are often simply used as a garnish and then discarded, which is a pity, because the leaves are a good source of several nutrients, including vitamin C and iron. Myristicin, a compound found in parsley, has a strong antioxidant action, neutralizing carcinogens in the body, such as the dangerous compounds in tobacco smoke and barbecue smoke. Parsley is also an anticoagulant and contains compounds of oils that are linked with relief from menstrual problems, such as pain, fluid retention, and cramps.

- A good source of vitamin C and iron, potassium, and folate.
- Source of lutein and zeaxanthin to prevent macular degeneration.
- A breath purifier.
- Antioxidant and anticancer action.
- Contains the essential oil apiol, used as a traditional remedy for fluid retention and menstrual disorders.

DID YOU KNOW?

Parsley is a member of the Umbelliferae family of plants and is closely related to parsnip. Hard-to-find parsley root can be used in a similar way and is popular in European cooking.

PRACTICAL TIPS

Picked parsley keeps well for several days in the refrigerator in a plastic bag. Combine plenty of chopped parsley with mint, lemon juice, and oil and toss with cooked bulgur wheat to make tabbouleh. Make a flat-leaf parsley pesto with ground walnuts and olive oil to serve with pasta.

PARSLEY PURIFIER JUICE

The strong flavors of the herbs and garlic are balanced by the natural sweetness
of the sugar snap peas and the delicate flavor of the cucumber.

SERVES 1 • PREP TIME: 10–15 MINS • COOK TIME: NONE

PER SERVING: | 152 cal CALORIES | 2.5g FAT | 0.2g SAT FAT | 22.1g CARBS | 9.7g SUGAR | 1.9g FIBER | 7g PROTEIN | 120mg SODIUM |

INGREDIENTS

2 cups sugar snap peas
small handful of fresh flat-leaf parsley
2 fresh rosemary sprigs
1 garlic clove
2 cups young spinach
½ cucumber
2 celery stalks, halved
1 teaspoon hempseed oil
chilled water, to taste
ice cubes, to serve (optional)

1. Feed the peas, parsley (reserving a sprig to garnish), rosemary, and garlic through a juicer, followed by the spinach, cucumber, and celery.

2. Pour into a glass and stir in the oil with water to taste.

3. Garnish with the reserved parsley. Serve with ice, if using.

OREGANO

Pungent oregano is the herb highest in antioxidant activity, helping to combat food-poisoning bacteria and boost the immune system.

MAJOR NUTRIENTS PER 2½ TABLESPOONS OREGANO

21 cal	0.8g	4.5g	3g	0.7g	0.4 mg	288 mcg	110 mg	3 mg	19 mcg	19 mg	117 mg
CALORIES	TOTAL FAT	CARBS	FIBER	PROTEIN	VITAMIN B3	BETA-CAROTENE	CALCIUM	IRON	FOLATE	MAGNESIUM	POTASSIUM

According to tests carried out by the United States Department of Agriculture, oregano has more antioxidant activity than any other herb. The herb has demonstrated 42 times more antioxidant activity than apples, 12 times more than oranges, and 4 times more than blueberries. The volatile oils in this spice include thymol and carvacrol, which have both been shown to strongly inhibit the growth of bacteria, including *Staphylococcus aureus*. Oregano is a good source of several nutrients, including calcium, potassium, iron, and magnesium. It is also high in dietary fiber and may help lower "bad" cholesterol.

- One of the most powerful antioxidant plants.
- Antibacterial and may relieve the symptoms of colds.
- Rich in minerals.
- High in fiber and may aid digestion.

DID YOU KNOW?

When replacing fresh oregano with dried leaves in a recipe, reduce the amount you use by about half.

PRACTICAL TIPS

Oregano is an easy-to-grow herb and can be kept in a flowerpot on the windowsill. The leaves dry well and can be stored in an airtight container. Replace dried oregano at least every three months, because it loses its aroma and flavor over time. Oregano is one of the traditional herbs to include in mixed herbs and herbes de Provence. Oregano marries particularly well with eggs, tomatoes, lamb, and chicken.

CAPER & OREGANO VINAIGRETTE

Extra virgin olive oil, which is naturally high in healthy monounsaturated fat and
low in saturated fat, is the best oil to use for this herb-packed vinaigrette.

MAKES ½ CUP • PREP TIME: 15 MINS • COOK TIME: NONE

PER ½ CUP:	519 cal	54.4g	7.5g	11.6g	3.8g	1.5g	1.1g	240mg
	CALORIES	FAT	SAT FAT	CARBS	SUGAR	FIBER	PROTEIN	SODIUM

INGREDIENTS

juice of 2 lemons
1 tablespoon finely chopped capers
2 tablespoons finely chopped fresh oregano
2 garlic cloves, crushed
¼ cup extra virgin olive oil
pinch of brown sugar
salt and pepper (optional)

1. Simply squeeze the lemon juice into a small bowl and stir in the capers, oregano, garlic, oil, and brown sugar. Whisk well and season with salt and pepper, if using.

2. Serve immediately or transfer to a covered container and keep in the refrigerator for up to one month. This vinaigrette goes well with any salad or drizzled over mozzarella cheese.

CHILES

Fiery chiles pack a nutritional and flavorful punch and research shows that they are one of the healthiest spices available.

MAJOR NUTRIENTS PER 1 OUNCE CHILE

12 cal	TRACE	2.6g	0.4g	0.5g	0.4 mg	43 mg	160 mcg	0.4g	0.3 mg	213 mcg	97 mg
CALORIES	TOTAL FAT	CARBS	FIBER	PROTEIN	VITAMIN B3	VITAMIN C	BETA-CAROTENE	FOLATE	IRON	LUTEIN/ZEAXANTHIN	POTASSIUM

The heat that chiles add to a dish comes from a compound called capsaicin, which is known to relieve the pain and inflammation associated with arthritis. Capsaicin also appears to block production of cancerous cells in prostate cancer and to act as an anticoagulant to help protect against blood clots, which can cause heart attacks or strokes. Red chiles also contain high levels of carotenes. Chile consumption helps reduce the amount of insulin required to lower blood sugar after a meal and thus could be of help to diabetics and people with insulin resistance. Chiles may also increase the metabolic rate slightly, which could help with weight loss.

- Contain capsaicin, which can relieve pain and inflammation associated with arthritis.
- Strongly antioxidant to help beat the effects of aging diseases.
- Help lower "bad" cholesterol and reduce risk of blood clots.
- Rich in vitamin C and carotenes to boost the immune system.

DID YOU KNOW?

Chiles are said to improve psoriasis and shingles when topically applied in a cream.

PRACTICAL TIPS

There are hundreds of types of chiles in various shapes, colors, and degrees of heat. Don't rub your eyes when preparing chiles—you can wear thin disposable gloves when handling. Dried peppers and chili powders should be kept in a dark, airtight jar.

TABBOULEH-STUFFED JALAPEÑOS

Jalapeño chiles are small in size but are loaded with flavor and nutrition. These little chiles derive their heat from a natural compound called capsicum.

SERVES 4 • PREP TIME: 22 MINS • COOK TIME: 10–12 MINS

PER SERVING:	331 cal	18.4g	2.5g	40.3g	9.5g	15.5g	8.6g	200mg
	CALORIES	FAT	SAT FAT	CARBS	SUGAR	FIBER	PROTEIN	SODIUM

INGREDIENTS

½ cup quinoa
2 cups chopped fresh parsley
2½ cups chopped fresh mint
2½ cups chopped fresh cilantro
1 preserved lemon, chopped
1 tablespoon walnuts, chopped
seeds from 1 pomegranate
24 jalapeño chiles, halved and seeded
2 avocados, peeled, pitted, and sliced
juice of 1 lemon
salt and pepper (optional)

1. Cook the quinoa according to the package directions. Drain and refresh under cold water, then drain again and put into a large bowl.

2. Add the parsley, mint, cilantro, preserved lemon, walnuts, and pomegranate seeds and mix thoroughly. Season with salt and pepper, if using.

3. Spoon the tabbouleh into the chiles. Top each one with a couple of slices of avocado, then squeeze over the lemon juice to serve.

HINT

If you really want to turn up the heat, don't seed the chiles, because the seeds are where most of the heat resides.

GINGER

The plant compounds in fresh ginger have a powerful cancer-destroying action,
are anti-inflammatory, and can calm nausea and aid digestion.

MAJOR NUTRIENTS PER ⅜-INCH PIECE GINGER (½ OUNCE)

19 cal	0.3g	3.8g	0.7g	0.5g	0.4 mg	0.6 mg	10 mg	73 mg
CALORIES	TOTAL FAT	CARBS	FIBER	PROTEIN	VITAMIN B1	IRON	MAGNESIUM	POTASSIUM

For thousands of years, ginger has been considered a healthy food and recent research has borne this out. The main active compounds are terpenes and gingerols, which have anticancer properties and have been shown to destroy colon, ovarian, and rectal cancer cells. Gingerols also have a powerful anti-inflammatory action and ginger has been shown to improve pain and swelling in up to 75 percent of people with arthritis—it also improves mobility. It may also ease migraine tension. Ginger has long been used as a remedy for nausea and to aid digestion, relaxing the intestines and helping to eliminate flatulence.

- As effective as prescription medicine in beating motion sickness without drowsiness.
- Proven relief from the pain of arthritis.
- Digestive aid.

DID YOU KNOW?

Ginger is a type of root known as a rhizome and grows underground in tropical climates.

PRACTICAL TIPS

Try to buy fresh ginger instead of other forms of ginger, such as ground or preserved, because it contains the highest levels of beneficial compounds. Fresh ginger can be stored in the refrigerator and peeled, chopped, or grated as required. Make a soothing ginger drink by combining freshly grated ginger, lemon juice, honey, and hot water.

GINGER, GARLIC & SOY DRESSING

Widely regarded for its anti-inflammatory properties, fresh ginger adds
a wonderful aromatic, spicy flavor to this Chinese-style dressing.

MAKES ⅔ CUP • PREP TIME: 10 MINS • COOK TIME: NONE

PER ⅔ CUP:

400 cal	40.5g	5.6g	8.6g	4.8g	0.4g	2.4g	1,800 mg
CALORIES	FAT	SAT FAT	CARBS	SUGAR	FIBER	PROTEIN	SODIUM

INGREDIENTS

2¼-inch piece fresh ginger, grated,
juices reserved
2 garlic cloves, crushed
2 tablespoons rice vinegar
2 tablespoons dark soy sauce
1 teaspoon sugar
3 tablespoons olive oil
2 tablespoons water

1. Put the ginger into a screwtop jar with any juices. Add the garlic, vinegar, soy sauce, sugar, oil, and water. Shake well until thoroughly combined.

2. Chill and store in the refrigerator until ready to use. This dressing improves with age, so prepare the day before it is needed, if possible. It goes well with a Chinese noodle salad or chopped Chinese greens.

CINNAMON

Sweet cinnamon is an anti-inflammatory, antibacterial spice that can help relieve bloating and heartburn, and it offers protection against strokes.

MAJOR NUTRIENTS PER 2 TABLESPOONS CINNAMON

18 cal	TRACE	5.5g	3.7g	TRACE	84 mg	2.6 mg	287 mcg	34 mg
CALORIES	TOTAL FAT	CARBS	FIBER	PROTEIN	CALCIUM	IRON	FOLATE	POTASSIUM

Cinnamon contains several volatile oils and compounds, including cinnamaldehyde, cinnamyl acetate, and cinnamyl alcohol, which have a variety of beneficial actions. Cinnamaldehyde has an anticoagulant action, meaning that it can help to protect against strokes, and is also anti-inflammatory, relieving the symptoms of arthritis and asthma. The spice is a digestive aid, relieving bloating and flatulence, and it can reduce the discomfort of heartburn. Cinnamon has antibacterial action that can block the yeast fungus candida and bacteria that can cause food poisoning. In one study, cinnamon was shown to lower blood sugars and blood cholesterol.

- Helps to beat indigestion and bloating.
- Antibacterial and antifungal.
- Helps prevent blood clots.
- May lower "bad" cholesterol and blood sugars.

DID YOU KNOW?

True cinnamon is the inner bark of an evergreen tree of the Laurel family native to Sri Lanka, and cassia is another variety native to China. Both are widely available, but it is not always possible to know which one you are buying.

PRACTICAL TIPS

Whole bark cinnamon sticks will retain their flavor and aroma for a year, while the ground dried spice will last for about six months. You can tell if ground cinnamon is still fresh by sniffing it—if it has lost its aroma, then you should discard it. Whole or part sticks can be added to apple or pear fruit compotes and mulled wine. Ground cinnamon is a good addition to a baked goods and Indian- and Middle Eastern-inspired stews.

APPLE & CINNAMON CHIPS

Crisp and crunchy, without the fat, salt, and strong flavors of potato chips,
these make a much healthier alternative for all the family.

SERVES 4 • PREP TIME: 20–25 MINS • COOK TIME: 1 HOUR 30 MINS–2 HOURS

PER SERVING:	72 cal	0.2g	TRACE	19.1g	14.2g	3.4g	0.3g	280mg
	CALORIES	FAT	SAT FAT	CARBS	SUGAR	FIBER	PROTEIN	SODIUM

INGREDIENTS

4¼ cups water
1 tablespoon sea salt
3 sweet, crisp apples, such as Braeburn or Gala
pinch of ground cinnamon

1. Preheat the oven to 225°F. Put the water and salt into a large mixing bowl and stir until the salt has dissolved.

2. Thinly slice the apples, one at a time, with a sharp knife or mandoline slicer, leaving the skin on and the core still in place, but removing any seeds. Add each apple slice to the water. Turn to coat in the salt water, which will help prevent discoloration.

3. Drain the apple slices in a colander, then lightly pat dry with a clean dish towel. Arrange in a thin layer on a large roasting rack. Place in the preheated oven so that the heat can circulate under the slices as well as over the tops.

4. Bake for 1½–2 hours, until the apple slices are dry and crisp. Loosen with a spatula and transfer to a large plate or cutting board, then sprinkle with cinnamon. Let cool completely, then serve.

HINT
To store, pack into a plastic container, seal, and keep in the refrigerator for up to two days.

BLACK PEPPER

Black pepper kick-starts our enjoyment of the foods it garnishes, and it stimulates revitalizing beta-endorphins, with a positive effect on mood and immunity.

MAJOR NUTRIENTS PER 2 TABLESPOONS BLACK PEPPERCORNS

38 cal	0.48g	9.72g	3.98g	1.64g	3.15 mg	85.2 mg	TRACE	29.1 mg	0.84 mg	189 mg
CALORIES	TOTAL FAT	CARBS	FIBER	PROTEIN	VITAMIN C	CALCIUM	CHROMIUM	MAGNESIUM	MANGANESE	POTASSIUM

The spicy taste of black pepper comes from piperine, which has recently been understood to assist in the absorption of nutrients, such as the energizing B vitamins and the immune-supporting antioxidants selenium and beta-carotene. It also supplements the anti-inflammatory and anticancer actions of the chemical curcumin, found in turmeric, by making it easier to absorb. The essential oils in black pepper are made of terpenes, such as limonene, also found in citrus fruits, and pinene, found in pine trees, that help prevent cancer, regulate heartbeat, and are antibacterial.

- Source of the mineral chromium, which promotes blood sugar balance and good weight management.
- Strengthens membranes to help prevent varicose veins and keep skin firm and young.
- Believed to have antidepressant qualities, so encouraging a youthful, positive, and motivated attitude.

DID YOU KNOW?

Black peppercorns are not in the same family as sweet peppers or chile, but the explorer Christopher Columbus assumed that this was the case when he came across them in Haiti.

PRACTICAL TIPS

Black peppercorns have more nutrients than white peppercorns. Both are prepared from unripe pepper berries, but the white peppercorns have their skins removed. Buy the whole corns and invest in a good grinder for freshly ground and best-tasting pepper. Keep in a sealed glass container in a cool, dark place.

T-BONE STEAK WITH PEPPERCORN SAUCE

It's the peppercorns that make this classic dish so appetizing—and they have the added advantage of being really beneficial for your health.

SERVES 4 • PREP TIME: 10 MINS • COOK TIME: 20 MINS

PER SERVING:

870 cal	56.1g	26.4g	4.9g	1.3g	0.9g	68.8g	1,400 mg
CALORIES	FAT	SAT FAT	CARBS	SUGAR	FIBER	PROTEIN	SODIUM

INGREDIENTS

4 T-bone steaks, each weighing 10½ ounces
1 teaspoon salt
1 teaspoon pepper
2 tablespoons olive oil

PEPPERCORN SAUCE

1 tablespoon olive oil
1 tablespoon butter
2 shallots, finely chopped
2 garlic cloves, crushed
½ cup brandy
1 cup heavy cream
1 tablespoon Dijon mustard
1 teaspoon salt
1 tablespoon mixed cracked peppercorns

1. To make the peppercorn sauce, heat a saucepan over medium–low heat, add the oil and butter, and then cook the shallots and garlic for 5–10 minutes, or until translucent.

2. Add the brandy and flambé. Add the cream and cook until reduced by half. Then add the mustard, salt, and cracked peppercorns. Set aside and keep warm.

3. Season the steaks with the salt and pepper, and rub with the oil.

4. Preheat a ridged grill pan over high heat and cook the steaks for 5 minutes on each side for medium-rare, or until cooked to your preference. Cook the steaks in batches, if necessary.

5. Set aside to rest for 5 minutes before serving with the peppercorn sauce.

VARIATION

This peppercorn sauce would work well with other cuts of steak—choose your favorite or ask your butcher for advice.

NUTMEG

Compounds in nutmeg are sedative, anaesthetic, and antibacterial. The fruit also contains monoterpenes, which can help prevent cardiovascular disease.

MAJOR NUTRIENTS PER 2¼ TABLESPOONS NUTMEG

12 cal	0.8g	1g	0.5g	TRACE	4mg	4mg	8mg
CALORIES	TOTAL FAT	CARBS	FIBER	PROTEIN	CALCIUM	MAGNESIUM	POTASSIUM

Nutmeg is the fruit of an evergreen native to Indonesia, now grown in several countries. The spice is made from the seed of this fruit. The fruit contains the compounds myristicin and elemicin, which are mildly sedative and anesthetic. It also contains monoterpenes, which are believed to have anticoagulant action and may help prevent cardiovascular disease. Like many other spices, nutmeg has antibacterial action and can help to protect us from food poisoning bacteria, such as *E. coli*. Nutmeg has also been used to treat Crohn's disease, an inflammatory condition of the bowel, and it is said that the essential oil of the fruit can help painful gums.

- Mildly sedative.
- Helps prevent blood clots and cardiovascular disease.
- Antibacterial.
- May be anti-inflammatory.

DID YOU KNOW?

Nutmeg is a hallucinogenic and is toxic in large quantities, so use it sparingly. A teaspoonful or less in a recipe will be sufficient.

PRACTICAL TIPS

Nutmeg is best used freshly grated from a whole dried fruit—ground nutmeg quickly loses its aroma and flavor. Nutmeg goes well with cooked fruits, such as apples, and with milk desserts, such as rice pudding. Nutmeg can also be used in savory dishes, such as game casseroles, meat sauces, and stews. A little nutmeg can be stirred into spinach and carrots toward the end of cooking time.

SPINACH & NUTMEG BAKED EGGS

Nutrient-rich fresh spinach adds delicious flavor and color to this popular egg dish, lightly seasoned with ground nutmeg.

SERVES 4 • PREP TIME: 20 MINS • COOK TIME: 20–30 MINS

PER SERVING:

| 235 cal CALORIES | 16.5g FAT | 4.2g SAT FAT | 7.5g CARBS | 1.6g SUGAR | 1.1g FIBER | 14.2g PROTEIN | 160mg SODIUM |

INGREDIENTS

1 tablespoon olive oil, for brushing
1 tablespoon olive oil, for frying
4 shallots, finely chopped
3 garlic cloves, sliced
3½ cups baby spinach
8 eggs
½ teaspoon ground nutmeg
salt and pepper (optional)

1. Preheat the oven to 350°F. Lightly brush the insides of four 1-cup ramekins (individual ceramic dishes) with oil.

2. Heat the oil in a skillet. Once hot, add the shallots and garlic and sauté over medium heat for 3–4 minutes, or until soft. Add the baby spinach and stir for 2–3 minutes, or until just wilted. Season with salt and pepper, if using.

3. Spoon the spinach mixture into the bottoms of the prepared ramekins and crack 2 eggs into each. Sprinkle with the nutmeg and place the ramekins in a roasting pan. Fill the roasting pan with boiling water until the water reaches halfway up the ramekins—this creates a steamy environment for the eggs so there is no chance of them drying out.

4. Carefully transfer the roasting pan to the preheated oven for 15–20 minutes. Let the ramekins cool slightly, then serve.

VARIATION

Serve with your favorite kind of toasted bread for a wholesome breakfast or brunch.

PAPRIKA

Paprika is dried and powdered capsicum (sweet pepper). It offers the same circulation-enhancing action as chile, helping your skin to stay looking young.

MAJOR NUTRIENTS PER 2 TABLESPOONS GROUND PAPRIKA

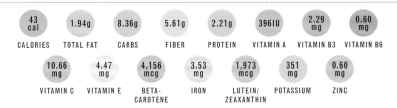

43 cal	1.94g	8.36g	5.61g	2.21g	396IU	2.29 mg	0.60 mg
CALORIES	TOTAL FAT	CARBS	FIBER	PROTEIN	VITAMIN A	VITAMIN B3	VITAMIN B6

10.66 mg	4.47 mg	4,156 mcg	3.53 mg	1,973 mcg	351 mg	0.60 mg
VITAMIN C	VITAMIN E	BETA-CAROTENE	IRON	LUTEIN/ZEAXANTHIN	POTASSIUM	ZINC

Paprika has been used traditionally to promote heart health, and it has been shown to reduce "bad" cholesterol/LDL. It is said to create heat in the body without burning or irritating, which improves circulation and ensures that invigorating oxygen and nutrients are distributed effectively around the whole body, including the heart. Like turmeric and cumin, paprika is high in salicylic acid, which forms the basis of aspirin. A single highly spiced stew can actually provide more than is contained within an aspirin pill. This explains the anti-inflammatory actions of these spices, which help keep joints mobile and the skin clear.

- Contains more protective vitamin C than lemon juice by weight, which is retained during drying and cooking.
- Increases saliva production, so promoting good digestion and the absorption of nutrients that fight aging.
- Helps reduce the bacterial infections that put stress on the body and age us prematurely.

DID YOU KNOW?

Paprika has been used as a coloring in cosmetics for centuries, and some zoos have been known to add it to the flamingo food to enhance their pink color.

PRACTICAL TIPS

Store paprika away from light and only get it out of the pantry when you need to use it, because it loses color and flavor quickly when exposed. This also applies to the cooking process, so add it as close to the end of cooking as possible (unless making goulash). Don't be fooled by its mild taste in the package; paprika increases in strength and flavor when heated.

PAPRIKA TURKEY STRIPS

Turkey has the reputation of being bland and boring, although it is high in nutrition.
The addition of paprika to this dish really adds that vital zing.

SERVES 4 • PREP TIME: 10 MINS • COOK TIME: 7–10 MINS

PER SERVING:	454 cal	10.5g	1.4g	54.7g	1.4g	2.1g	34.7g	320mg
	CALORIES	FAT	SAT FAT	CARBS	SUGAR	FIBER	PROTEIN	SODIUM

INGREDIENTS

1 pound 2 ounces turkey breast cutlets
1 tablespoon paprika
1 teaspoon crushed coriander seeds
½ teaspoon garlic salt
¼ teaspoon pepper
2 tablespoons olive oil
1 red onion, sliced
3 tablespoons chopped fresh cilantro
3½ cups cooked rice, to serve

1. Cut the turkey into long strips, about ½ inch thick.

2. Put the paprika, coriander seeds, garlic salt, and pepper into a large bowl and mix together. Stir in 1 tablespoon of the oil. Add the turkey strips and turn to coat evenly in the mixture.

3. Heat the remaining oil in a large skillet or wok, add the onion, and stir-fry for 1 minute. Add the turkey strips and stir-fry over fairly high heat for 6–8 minutes, until cooked through.

4. Sprinkle with the fresh cilantro and serve with the rice.

CARDAMOM

Like ginger, cardamom has a strong, soothing effect on the digestive tract. It helps you to digest a meal completely and receive all of its rejuvenating nutrients.

MAJOR NUTRIENTS PER 2 TABLESPOONS CARDAMOM SEEDS

47 cal	1g	10.27g	4.2g	1.614g	3.15 mg	57.45 mg	2.09 mg	34.35 mg	4.2 mg	167.85 mg
CALORIES	TOTAL FAT	CARBS	FIBER	PROTEIN	VITAMIN C	CALCIUM	IRON	MAGNESIUM	MANGANESE	POTASSIUM

The strong aromas of herbs and spices are testament to the medical strength of their volatile oils. Many cultures have long relied on their inclusion in the diet to ward away illness and promote longevity. Generally speaking, they achieve this by helping circulation, cleansing, and digestion and contributing to blood sugar balance. Cardamom has a particularly cleansing effect on the digestive tract, and it is traditionally used to treat stomach gripes and pains, dysentery, and the constipation that can lead to toxic buildup, as well as for high cholesterol and hormonal problems.

- The oils help clear mucus from the throat, nose, and chest that can lead to aging inflammation.
- Helps clear out the kidneys to reduce fluid retention and maintain a clear, youthful-looking complexion.
- Chewing cardamom helps prevent the infections of teeth and gums that are linked to heart disease.

DID YOU KNOW?

Cardamom has been used as an antidote for scorpion and snake bites in South Asia, where it is a common flavoring. It is also used frequently in Nordic cuisine and in Middle Eastern confectioneries, coffee, and tea.

PRACTICAL TIPS

Cardamom pods can be added to sweet and pungent dishes, but use only a few, because their strength can be overwhelming. Tea made from the crushed seeds (you can reuse ones that you have cooked with) is a traditional remedy for depression, and they can be combined with cinnamon to help alleviate a sore throat or hoarseness. The oil of cardamom is recommended for massaging away muscle tension.

CARDAMOM, FENNEL & GINGER TEA

Get your day off to a great start with this fragrant and
soothing low-sugar tea, infused with spices.

MAKES 4¼ CUPS • PREP TIME: 10 MINS • COOK TIME: NONE

PER 4¼ CUPS:	2 cal	0g	0g	0.5g	0g	0.1g	0.1g	0g
	CALORIES	FAT	SAT FAT	CARBS	SUGAR	FIBER	PROTEIN	SODIUM

INGREDIENTS

10 green cardamom pods
1 teaspoon fennel seeds
3¼-inch piece fresh ginger, sliced
4¼ cups boiling water

1. Put the cardamom pods onto a heavy chopping board and gently bruise each pod with a rolling pin.

2. Put the crushed pods into a teapot. Add the fennel seeds and fresh ginger. Pour over the boiling water and steep the tea for 5–6 minutes, or to taste.

3. Pour the tea into cups or mugs through a tea strainer and serve immediately.

TURMERIC

The warm spice turmeric contains healing properties as powerful as modern medicines in the fight against inflammatory diseases, such as arthritis.

MAJOR NUTRIENTS PER 2 TABLESPOONS TURMERIC

24 cal	0.7g	4.4g	1.4g	0.5g	225 mcg	2.8 mg	13 mg	172 mg
CALORIES	TOTAL FAT	CARBS	FIBER	PROTEIN	FOLATE	IRON	MAGNESIUM	POTASSIUM

Turmeric comes from the orange-fleshed root of a plant native to Indonesia and southern India. Its volatile oils and curcumin, the yellow/orange pigment, have been proved to offer protection comparable to that of modern medicines against inflammatory diseases. Curcumin is thought to be the main health-promoting compound in turmeric, and studies have shown that it is also a powerful antioxidant. Turmeric can help prevent colon cancer and inhibit the growth of certain types of cancer cells, such as breast and prostate cancers. The compound is also able to lower "bad" cholesterol and increase "good" cholesterol.

- Powerful anti-inflammatory.
- Contains anticancer properties.
- Improves blood cholesterol profile.
- May slow progression of Alzheimer's disease and multiple sclerosis.

DID YOU KNOW?

Turmeric was traditionally called Indian saffron because of its deep yellow color, and it has been used throughout history as a textile dye as well as a spice. It is also, unsurprisingly, hard to remove turmeric stains from clothing.

PRACTICAL TIPS

You can usually find only ground turmeric in stores. Store it in an airtight container. Make your own curry blend with four parts turmeric, one part chili powder, one part cumin seed, and one part coriander seed. Add a little turmeric to lentils when cooking them, or to yogurt for a healthy dip. Stir-fry vegetables, such as cauliflower or green beans, in oil with turmeric added.

ROASTED CAULIFLOWER, KALE & CHICKPEA BOWL

This bowl is packed with goodness and, as well as having numerous health benefits, the spices help to make it feel really nourishing.

SERVES 4 • PREP TIME: 20 MINS • COOK TIME: 40 MINS

PER SERVING:

406 cal	19.5g	4.2g	41.4g	10.7g	12.2g	19.5g	360mg
CALORIES	FAT	SAT FAT	CARBS	SUGAR	FIBER	PROTEIN	SODIUM

INGREDIENTS

1 teaspoon turmeric
1 teaspoon mustard seeds
½ teaspoon cumin seeds
½ teaspoon ground ginger
½ teaspoon ground coriander
½ teaspoon ground cinnamon
1 head of cauliflower, broken into florets
1⅔ cups rinsed and drained, canned chickpeas
2 red onions, thickly sliced
2 tablespoons olive oil
3 cups shredded kale
2 cups fresh whole-wheat bread crumbs
3 tablespoons chopped walnuts
2 tablespoons slivered almonds
⅔ cup freshly grated Parmesan cheese

1. Preheat the oven to 400°F.

2. Dry-fry the turmeric, mustard seeds, cumin seeds, ginger, coriander, and cinnamon in a small skillet for 2 minutes, or until the mustard seeds start to pop.

3. Put the cauliflower florets, chickpeas, and onion slices into a large roasting pan. Sprinkle with the spices and toss well together. Drizzle with the oil and toss again.

4. Roast in the preheated oven for 20 minutes.

5. Stir the kale into the roasted vegetables, and roast for an additional 10 minutes, until the vegetables are tender and slightly charred.

6. Mix the bread crumbs, walnuts, almonds, and cheese together and sprinkle them over the vegetables. Roast for an additional 5–8 minutes, until golden.

7. Divide among four bowls and serve immediately.

CLOVES

Cloves are associated with infusing the cold winter with warmth. Their warming property is the key to their ability to relieve aches and pains in the muscles and joints.

MAJOR NUTRIENTS PER 3 TABLESPOONS CLOVES

48.5 cal	3.04g	9.18g	5.13g	0.89g	12.12 mg	22.27 mcg	96.9 mg	13 mg	4.5 mg	165 mg
CALORIES	TOTAL FAT	CARBS	FIBER	PROTEIN	VITAMIN C	VITAMIN K	CALCIUM	IRON	MANGANESE	POTASSIUM

Cloves contain the active compound eugenol in sufficient quantities to be effective in detoxifying the harmful and aging pollutants that we take on from the environment. This is the substance used in dental preparations, such as mouthwashes, throat sprays, and toothpastes, because it both reduces bacteria in the mouth and has a mildly anesthetic effect on the sensitivities that cause pain. Because mouth infections are associated with heart disease, this is an important anti-aging consideration. Studies have also shown that eugenol can reduce inflammation. If you eat cloves as part of an existing healthy diet, you will be helping to combat inflammatory symptoms, such as joint pain, skin flareups, and headaches, and reducing the level of "bad" cholesterol/LDL in your body.

- The flavonoids kaempferol and rhamnetin offer youth-retaining antioxidant properties.
- Clove oil is used traditionally to treat acne and rashes, and to heal scars after burns and injuries, keeping skin looking young.

DID YOU KNOW?

Cloves are pressed into oranges at Christmas to make fragrant pomanders, and they have also been used in incense.

PRACTICAL TIPS

Cloves are included in the curry spice mixture known as garam masala and in the spiced tea chai. They are often mixed with cinnamon and cumin to provide warmth and comfort, especially in winter. Cloves can be added to hot water, honey, and lemon to make a delicious drink that is also an effective remedy for colds or flu. To spice it up, add ginger and cinnamon.

VIETNAMESE NOODLES WITH BEEF

Transport your taste buds across the world and enjoy the enticing fresh and clean flavors of this popular Vietnamese beef and noodle dish.

SERVES 4 • PREP TIME: 20–25 MINS • COOK TIME: 40 MINS

PER SERVING:

 411 cal CALORIES

 3.7g FAT

 1.3g SAT FAT

 47.1g CARBS

 4.4g SUGAR

 2.5g FIBER

 46.1g PROTEIN

1,840 mg SODIUM

INGREDIENTS

6¾ cups beef broth

1½-inch piece fresh ginger, sliced

1 star anise or ½ teaspoon five-spice powder

2 cinnamon sticks

5 cloves

3 tablespoons Thai fish sauce

1 red chile, finely sliced

7 ounces vermicelli rice noodles

12 ounces sirloin steak, very finely sliced

1 cup finely sliced snow peas

⅓ cup bean sprouts

¾ cup coarsely chopped fresh cilantro, to garnish

¾ cup coarsely chopped fresh Thai basil, to garnish

1 tablespoon finely sliced red chile, to garnish

1. Pour the broth into a large saucepan. Add the ginger, star anise, cinnamon sticks, cloves, fish sauce, and chile to the pan and place over high heat. Bring to a boil, then reduce the heat and simmer over low heat, covered, for 30 minutes.

2. Meanwhile, put the dry noodles into a large bowl and pour boiling water over the top. Let stand for 3–4 minutes, or according to package directions, until they are completely softened. Drain, return to the bowl, cover, and set aside.

3. Add the steak strips to the beef broth and poach for 2–3 minutes. Remove the ginger slices, star anise, cinnamon sticks, and cloves from the broth with a slotted spoon.

4. Divide the noodles among four deep bowls. Add a handful of raw snow peas and bean sprouts, then ladle the hot broth mixture over them. Garnish with the cilantro, Thai basil, and sliced red chile and serve immediately.

VARIATION
Sprinkle some toasted sesame seeds over the top of the soup for some extra crunch.

MACA

Maca is a herbaceous plant of the broccoli family, native to the mountains of Peru, and it is commonly used there as a root vegetable.

MAJOR NUTRIENTS PER 1 TEASPOON DRIED MACA POWDER

12 cal	TRACE	2.4g	0.6g	0.6g	0.4g
CALORIES	TOTAL FAT	CARBS	FIBER	PROTEIN	IRON

The turnip-like maca root has been used as a herbal health tonic for many years in Peru. Scientific trials have found that the root may help ease anxiety and depression and may also help to improve libido and sexual function. The plant has also traditionally been used to treat fatigue, loss of energy, lack of stamina, high blood pressure, osteoarthritis, and stress and also to boost the immune system. The plant contains glucosinolates and isothiocyanates, compounds known to help prevent cancers. Maca has been shown to improve prostate health, and some studies have found that the plant can help improve brainpower and bone density, too. The root is a good source of some minerals, especially iron.

- May ease anxiety and depression.
- May help beat fatigue, lack of stamina, and act as a general body tonic.
- High in a range of minerals and in cancer-fighting plant chemicals.

DID YOU KNOW?

Maca is sometimes known as "Peruvian ginseng," and in Peru the fresh plant is often eaten baked or roasted, made into a soup, or used in the fermented drink maca chicha. Maca is a relative of radish and turnip, and some people think it has a sweet odor similar to butterscotch.

PRACTICAL TIPS

Maca is hard to find outside Peru as a fresh vegetable, so it is usually bought as a supplement —in pill or powder form. Powdered maca can be added to smoothies, juices, yogurt, or soups. A typical daily dose of the dried root is up to 3 grams.

GRAPEFRUIT CRUSH JUICE

This fresh and cooling juice is mixed with coconut water, which is packed
with electrolytes and minerals to help counter dehydration.

SERVES 1 • PREP TIME: 10–15 MINS • COOK TIME: NONE

PER SERVING:	185 cal	1.2g	0.1g	43.5g	28.7g	3g	4.7g	160mg
	CALORIES	FAT	SAT FAT	CARBS	SUGAR	FIBER	PROTEIN	SODIUM

INGREDIENTS

½ cucumber, coarsely chopped
½ pink grapefruit, zest and a little pith removed,
seeded and coarsely chopped
2 kiwis, peeled and coarsely chopped
2 celery stalks, coarsely chopped
1 teaspoon maca powder
¼ cup coconut water
1 pink grapefruit section, to garnish
crushed ice, to serve (optional)

1. Feed the cucumber, grapefruit, kiwis, and celery through a juicer.

2. Stir through the maca powder and coconut water until combined.

3. Pour the beverage over crushed ice, if using, garnish with a grapefruit section, and serve immediately.

GREEN TEA

The Chinese and Japanese have long understood the health attributes of green tea,
and they view it as an important part of their heart, energy, and skin routines.

MAJOR NUTRIENTS PER 1 CUP GREEN TEA

approx* 2cal	0g	Negligible	0g	0g	3.75g
CALORIES	TOTAL FAT	CARBS	FIBER	PROTEIN	CATECHINS

*CAN VARY GREATLY BETWEEN VARIETIES AND STRENGTH OF BREW

The leaves of the tea plant *Camellia sinensis* are loaded with catechins, which have been found to have natural antioxidant, antibacterial, and antiviral properties, thereby protecting against cancer and helping to lower cholesterol and regulate blood clotting. One such compound, epigallocatechin gallate (EGCG), is able to penetrate the cells and protect the crucial DNA that the body relies on to replicate cells and combat the damage caused by aging. EGCG also prevents cancer cells from forming and can help reduce the severity of allergies by blocking the body's response.

- Green tea may also act as a weight loss aid by helping to burn fat and regulate blood sugar and insulin levels.
- Contains quercetin, a bioflavonoid (plant chemical) that reduces inflammation and helps control food allergies.
- Catechins promote liver detoxification, so assisting in the removal of aging toxins and promoting glowing skin.

DID YOU KNOW?

Green tea leaves are the dried leaves of the tea plant, while black "normal" tea is fermented. The fermentation process makes black tea much higher in caffeine: about 50 mg a cup compared to 5 mg for green tea.

PRACTICAL TIPS

Changing from black tea or coffee to green tea, which will still give you a boost, will lower your total intake of caffeine with its aging effects. Different varieties have different strengths and flavor. Genmaicha is a particularly palatable Japanese blend, with a nutty taste from the toasted brown rice that has been added to it.

GREEN TEA FRUIT SALAD

Bursting with vitamins and antioxidants, this multicolored fruit salad makes a light and delicious dessert. Pistachios and pomegranate seeds add a final flourish of goodness.

SERVES 4 • PREP TIME: 25 MINS, PLUS BREWING, COOLING, AND CHILLING • COOK TIME: NONE

PER SERVING:	258 cal	3.5g	0.4g	59.5g	45.3g	8.4g	4.1g	TRACE
	CALORIES	FAT	SAT FAT	CARBS	SUGAR	FIBRE	PROTEIN	SALT

INGREDIENTS

2 teaspoons green tea
1 cup boiling water
1 tablespoon honey
½ small watermelon, cut into cubes
1 large mango, cut into cubes
1 papaya, seeded and cut into cubes
2 pears, cut into cubes
2 kiwis, cut into cubes
2 tablespoons coarsely chopped fresh mint
seeds of ½ pomegranate
2 tablespoons coarsely chopped pistachio nuts

1. Put the tea into a heatproof pitcher or teapot, pour over the boiling water, and let brew for 3–4 minutes. Strain into a small bowl, stir in the honey, and let cool.

2. Put the watermelon, mango ,and papaya into a large serving bowl, then add the pears, kiwis, and mint. Pour the cooled green tea over the fruit and gently stir everything together.

3. Cover with plastic wrap and chill in the refrigerator for 1 hour. Stir gently to mix the tea through the fruit.

4. Spoon the fruit salad into four bowls. Serve immediately, sprinkled with the pomegranate seeds and pistachio nuts.

HONEY

Raw honey is one of nature's oldest known antibacterial products. It destroys harmful invaders, keeping you young both inside and out.

MAJOR NUTRIENTS PER 1 TABLESPOON HONEY

45.5 cal	0g	12.36g	0.03g	0.04g
CALORIES	TOTAL FAT	CARBS	FIBER	PROTEIN

Honey is created when the saliva of bees meets the pollen they collect from flowers, so the properties of a particular honey will reflect those of the flowers the bees have visited. In its raw state, it contains an array of antioxidants, such as chrysin and vitamin C, to help you stay young, but these properties are destroyed when it is excessively heated or processed. Manuka honey from New Zealand is the only honey that has been tested for its ability to destroy harmful bacteria, and batches of this are given a Unique Manuka Factor (UMF), according to strength. Manuka has been shown to be twice as effective as other honeys against the *E. coli* and *Staphylococcus* bacteria, which commonly infect wounds.

- Raw honey contains propolis, which helps reduce inflammation and premature aging.
- Good-quality honey contains probiotic beneficial *Lactobacillus* and *Bifidobacterium* bacteria to support youth-protecting immunity.
- When applied to the skin, it helps heal acne, burns, cuts, and sores that can age your appearance.

DID YOU KNOW?

When mixed with water, honey creates antiseptic hydrogen peroxide, which can be applied directly to wounds to dry them out and keep them free from infection while they heal.

PRACTICAL TIPS

Choose good-quality honey. Look for local, raw, and unprocessed varieties from farm stores. Darker kinds, such as buckwheat and sage, contain the most antioxidants, and the honey produced by flower-fed bees in the summer contains more beneficial bacteria. Use in place of sugar, but sparingly, or you will set off sugar cravings.

HONEY SALMON
WITH COUSCOUS

Loaded with beneficial nutrients, this light yet substantial meal
makes a great quick-and-easy midweek meal for two.

SERVES 2 • PREP TIME: 15 MINS • COOK TIME: 15 MINS

PER SERVING:

711 cal	27.4g	5.7g	83g	35g	4.3g	35.2g	880mg
CALORIES	FAT	SAT FAT	CARBS	SUGAR	FIBER	PROTEIN	SODIUM

INGREDIENTS

2 salmon fillets, about 4½ ounces each
⅔ cup couscous
1 cup vegetable broth
1 tablespoon vegetable oil, for drizzling
2 scallions, chopped
salt and pepper (optional)
4 steamed baby zucchini, to serve

SAUCE

¼ cups honey
2 tablespoons Dijon mustard
2 tablespoons lukewarm water
2 teaspoons soy sauce
1 teaspoon olive oil

1. To make the sauce, heat the honey, mustard, water, soy sauce, and oil in a saucepan over low heat for 5 minutes, stirring occasionally. Place the salmon fillets on a sheet of aluminum foil and season with salt and pepper, if using. Brush generously with some of the sauce. Preheat the broiler to high.

2. Put the couscous into a heatproof bowl. Pour the broth over the couscous, cover, and let stand for 10 minutes. Meanwhile, cook the salmon fillets under the preheated broiler for 4 minutes, then turn them over, brush with more sauce, and cook for an additional 4 minutes, or until cooked through.

3. Drizzle the couscous with a little oil and run a fork through it. Brush the salmon with the remaining sauce and sprinkle with the chopped scallions. Serve the salmon with the couscous and steamed baby zucchini.

VARIATION
The honey-and-mustard sauce could also be served with broiled or baked chicken or pork.

CHIVES

Chives belong to the allium family and provide the same protective sulfur compounds as garlic and onion. These foods work hard to keep you detoxified.

MAJOR NUTRIENTS PER ⅓ CUP CHIVES

30 cal	0.73g	4.35g	2.5g	3.27g	4353 IU	58.1 mg	212.7 mcg	2612 mcg	323 mcg
CALORIES	TOTAL FAT	CARBS	FIBER	PROTEIN	VITAMIN A	VITAMIN C	VITAMIN K	BETA-CAROTENE	LUTEIN/ZEAXANTHIN

Chives have the same health benefits as garlic, but are slightly weaker. They contain the same potent sulfur substance sulfoquinovosyl diacylglycerol, which is also found in spinach, parsley, green tea, and carrots, and which has been shown to stop the action that makes cancer cells proliferate. These foods also have antifungal and antibacterial properties, which help keep your digestive tract free from the elements affecting health and digestion, so preventing debilitating gas, bloating and constipation. Because they are antiviral, too, they reduce the viral load that threatens the body's stocks of youthful energy and vitality.

- Contain the energy-producing nutrients vitamin C, citric acid, malic acid, and glutamic acid.
- Immune-supporting antioxidant power comes from vitamin C, beta-carotene, quercetin, and ferulic acid.
- Aid circulation in support of heart health so that it can pump revitalizing nutrients to all parts of the body.

DID YOU KNOW?

Chives are grown in yards to repel unwanted insects that feed off plants and also to attract the bees that pollinate them.

PRACTICAL TIPS

Chives are easy to grow. Keep a plant handy on a kitchen windowsill so you can add them to fish, potatoes, and soups. Because they have a mild flavor, they can be easier to include in the diet than their cousin garlic. They are particularly tasty with soft cheeses and herring, or other cured fish.

THREE HERB & RICOTTA OMELET

Vibrant green mixed herbs add plenty of wonderful natural flavor and color to this appetizing omelet. Served with fresh bread, it's a satisfying breakfast or lunch for two.

SERVES 2 • PREP TIME: 15 MINS • COOK TIME: 8 MINS

PER SERVING:

390 cal	32g	10g	2.8g	0.7g	0.2g	21.7g	240mg
CALORIES	FAT	SAT FAT	CARBS	SUGAR	FIBER	PROTEIN	SODIUM

INGREDIENTS

4 extra-large eggs
2 tablespoons finely snipped fresh chives
2 tablespoons finely chopped fresh basil
2 tablespoons finely chopped fresh parsley
⅔ cup crumbled ricotta cheese
2 tablespoons olive oil
salt and pepper (optional)

1. Crack the eggs into a small mixing bowl and lightly beat with a fork. Stir the herbs and cheese into the bowl and season with salt and pepper, if using.

2. Heat the oil in a nonstick skillet over high heat until hot. Pour in the egg mixture and, using a spatula, draw the outside edges (which will cook more quickly) toward the gooey center. Let any liquid mixture move into the gaps. Continue with this action for 4–5 minutes. The omelet will continue to cook once the pan is removed from the heat.

3. Cut the omelet in half and divide between two plates. Serve immediately.

COCONUT WATER

Refreshing and with a sweet taste, coconut water makes an ideal drink for rehydration at any time of day because it is isotonic, meaning it is readily utilized by the body.

MAJOR NUTRIENTS PER 1 CUP COCONUT WATER

43 cal	0.4g	8.3g	2.5g	1.6g	5.4 mg	54 mg	0.65 mg	0.2g	56 mg	562 mg	236 mg
CALORIES	TOTAL FAT	CARBS	FIBER	PROTEIN	VITAMIN C	CALCIUM	IRON	LAURIC ACID	MAGNESIUM	POTASSIUM	SODIUM

Not to be confused with coconut milk, coconut water is the clear liquid that is extracted from the center of the coconut when it is young and green. This liquid contains easily digested sugars, and electrolytes—the minerals calcium, magnesium, potassium, and sodium, which are essential to health because they govern electrical impulses and the balance of fluid in our bodies. Coconut water is a useful tool for those wanting to lose weight, because it is low in calories and naturally fat and cholesterol free. It also contains some protein, vitamin C, fiber, and iron, and plant chemicals called cytokinins, which appear to have anti-aging and anticancer properties.

- An isotonic drink ideally suited to rehydrating the body after exercise.
- Low in calories and ideal as part of a weight loss plan.
- Contains cytokinins, which may help prevent the signs of aging.
- A source of protein, vitamin C, fiber, and iron.

DID YOU KNOW?

Coconut water is often called "Mother Nature's sports drink," because of its rehydrating ability and favorable electrolyte profile. Coconut water contains a small amount of lauric acid, a saturated fat that may help to reduce calorie consumption in dieters, some research has found.

PRACTICAL TIPS

While coconut water can be syphoned from young green coconuts, it is widely available to purchase in bottles and cartons. It is best drunk chilled and is an ideal addition to smoothies, frozen tropical fruit sorbets, and granitas.

MELON BREEZE SOUP

Unlike winter soups, which warm your insides, this soup will cool you down—perfect for a summer appetizer or as part of your lunch.

SERVES 1 • PREP TIME: 10 MINS • COOK TIME: NONE

PER SERVING:

134 cal	1.1g	0.4g	27.9g	20.6g	6.6g	4.8g	280mg
CALORIES	FAT	SAT FAT	CARBS	SUGAR	FIBER	PROTEIN	SODIUM

INGREDIENTS

2 cups diced green melon
2½ cups diced cucumber
¼ cup chopped fresh mint,
plus a sprig to garnish
1 cup chilled coconut water

1. Put the diced melon and cucumber into a blender.

2. Add the mint, pour in the coconut water, and blend until smooth and creamy.

3. Serve immediately or chill in the refrigerator and stir just before serving. Garnish with a sprig of mint.

CHOCOLATE & COCOA POWDER

Not just an indulgent treat, the cocoa bean contains
flavonoids, magnesium, and iron for protection from heart disease.

34 cal	2g	8g	5g	3g	19mg	2mg	22mg	229mg	1mg
CALORIES	TOTAL FAT	CARBS	FIBER	PROTEIN	CALCIUM	IRON	MAGNESIUM	POTASSIUM	ZINC

Chocolate is made from cocoa beans, which are rich in antioxidant flavonoids, fiber, and minerals. The chocolate-making process also provides procyanidins, which have an anti-inflammatory action. For better or worse, chocolate contains caffeine, and a 3½-ounce bar of semisweet chocolate has about as much as a cup of coffee. Cocoa powder is a relatively low-fat, high-fiber source of minerals and antioxidants, and for chocolate lovers watching their fat intake, a cocoa drink made with skim milk is a good choice.

- Antioxidant content can have an anticoagulant action and protect against the oxidation of cholesterol in our bodies.
- Magnesium content protects the heart.
- Iron content can keep blood healthy and maintain energy levels.
- Contains the stimulant theobromine, which is a diuretic.

PRACTICAL TIPS

Generally, the more cocoa solids chocolate contains, the more antioxidants and minerals it has. This means that dark bittersweet chocolate with 70 percent cocoa solids is a good source, while a lighter milk chocolate is not. Cocoa butter is high in total fat and saturated fat, so dark chocolate should be consumed in moderate amounts. White chocolate is a mixture of cocoa butter and milk solids and has negligible amounts of healthy nutrients.

DID YOU KNOW?

Cocoa beans grow on cocoa trees, which are now mainly grown in South America and Africa. They were first imported to Europe by Christopher Columbus in the early sixteenth century.

SUPERFOOD CHOCOLATE BARK

This pretty chocolate bark is a delicious way to eat healthy nuts and berries.
It comes together quickly and makes a useful, nutritious snack.

SERVES 6 • PREP TIME: 15 MINS, PLUS COOLING • COOK TIME: 5 MINS

PER SERVING:

227 cal	15.7g	5.3g	17.7g	10.2g	5.1g	5.1g	0.0g
CALORIES	FAT	SAT FAT	CARBS	SUGAR	FIBER	PROTEIN	SODIUM

INGREDIENTS

3½ ounces bittersweet chocolate, broken into pieces
⅔ cup coarsely chopped mixed Brazil nuts,
unblanched almonds, and pistachio nuts
2 tablespoons coarsely chopped dried goji berries
2 tablespoons coarsely chopped dried cranberries
1 tablespoon chia seeds

1. Put the chocolate into a heatproof bowl set over a saucepan of gently simmering water and heat for 5 minutes, until melted.

2. Line a large baking sheet with nonstick parchment paper. Stir the chocolate, then pour it onto the paper and spread to an 8 x 12-inch rectangle.

3. Sprinkle the nuts, berries, and chia seeds over the top, then let set in a cool place or the refrigerator.

4. To serve, lift the chocolate off the paper and break into coarse shards. Store in a plastic container in the refrigerator for up to three days.

CUMIN SEEDS

With its antiseptic action, cumin offers sore throat relief. It also helps
the digestive system to work efficiently.

MAJOR NUTRIENTS PER 2½ TABLESPOONS CUMIN SEEDS

23 cal	1g	2.6g	0.6g	1g	56 mg	4 mg	22 mg	107 mg
CALORIES	TOTAL FAT	CARBS	FIBER	PROTEIN	CALCIUM	IRON	MAGNESIUM	POTASSIUM

Small, brown cumin seeds are harvested from a herb belonging to the
parsley family. Its flavor is warm and spicy but not too hot. The spice has
been used since ancient times—the Romans used it as an appetizer
and digestive. Research has shown that cumin stimulates the secretion
of pancreatic enzymes necessary for efficient digestion and nutrient
absorption. Currently, cumin is being investigated for its antioxidant
powers and it may help to block cancer growth. The seeds are rich in iron.
Cumin is an antiseptic, so an infusion of cumin seeds with honey makes an
ideal beverage for people with a sore throat.

- Aid digestion.
- May help prevent cancers.
- Contain antiseptic properties.
- Rich in iron for healthy blood.

DID YOU KNOW?

*Cumin seeds are native to the
Middle East but have been
cultivated in India and China
for thousands of years,
and they are one of the key
ingredients in curry blends.*

PRACTICAL TIPS

Buy whole seeds, because these retain their aroma longer than ground
cumin. All dried spices are best kept in airtight containers in cool, dry,
dark conditions. Use opaque containers to store spices, because they
deteriorate rapidly in light. Add lightly ground cumin seeds to brown rice
and chopped dried fruits and nuts for a delicious salad. Cumin also goes
well with legumes, such as lentils and chickpeas, as well as with kidneys or
other beans in chili.

FEEL-THE-HEAT
HARISSA SAUCE

Depending on the chiles used, the color of this hot sauce will range from red to brownish red. After several days, the covering oil will have absorbed some of the heat and can be used in salad dressings.

MAKES ¾ CUP • PREP TIME: 5 MINS, PLUS SOAKING AND STANDING • COOK TIME: 1–2 MINS

PER ¾ CUP:

 1,422 cal CALORIES

 139.3g FAT

 17.3g SAT FAT

 47.4g CARBS

 29.3g SUGAR

 24.8g FIBER

 11.7g PROTEIN

80mg SODIUM

INGREDIENTS

12 hot dried red chiles,
such as aji, guajillo, New Mexican, or pasilla,
or a combination
1 tablespoon Aleppo crushed red pepper flakes
½ cup olive oil, plus extra if needed
1 teaspoon caraway seeds
1 teaspoon cumin seeds
½ teaspoon fennel seeds
2 red jalapeño chiles, finely chopped
salt and pepper (optional)

1. Put the dried chiles into a heatproof bowl, pour over boiling water to cover, and let stand for 15 minutes. Drain well and pat dry. When cool enough to handle, remove the stems and finely chop the chiles.

2. Transfer to a bowl and add the crushed red pepper flakes and oil. Set aside for 1 hour.

3. Meanwhile, heat a dry skillet over medium–high heat. Add the caraway seeds, cumin seeds, and fennel seeds and dry-fry for 1–2 minutes, or until aromatic. Transfer the seeds from the pan to a mortar, then finely grind with a pestle.

4. Transfer the soaked chile mixture, seeds, and chopped chiles to a small food processor or blender. Season with salt and pepper, if using, then puree. Adjust the seasoning, if necessary. Slowly add more oil, if necessary, to make a thick sauce and serve.

HINT
Store with a layer of olive oil poured over the surface in an airtight container in the refrigerator for up to two weeks.

WASABI

Wasabi is a strong natural antiparasitic, which helps us to enjoy omega-3-rich oily fish without the damaging consequences of a parasite infection.

MAJOR NUTRIENTS PER 1 TEASPOON WASABI PASTE

5.5 cal	TRACE	1.18g	0.39g	0.24g	2.09 mg	28.4 mg
CALORIES	TOTAL FAT	CARBS	FIBER	PROTEIN	VITAMIN C	POTASSIUM

Wasabi is a hotter, Asian version of horseradish. The hot vapors come from the isothiocyanates it contains. Its pungency is the secret weapon that can kill off a whole host of microbes, which we ingest perfectly naturally along with the various foods that we eat. Because these microorganisms can compromise our digestion, immune system, and nervous system—potentially affecting all the systems of the body—to stay youthful and vibrant we need to employ continual defenses from nature's clever chemical pantry, such as wasabi.

- Related to broccoli, cabbage, and horseradish, with the same power to help the liver eliminate aging toxins.
- The isothiocyanates support youthful heart health, helping to reduce the risk of stroke and heart attack.
- Anti-inflammatory action boosts the youthful functioning of the joints and lungs.

DID YOU KNOW?

Wasabi and its pungent vapors are at the center of research into the development of a sensory fire alarm for the deaf.

PRACTICAL TIPS

Dyed horseradish is sometimes served in Japanese restaurants in place of wasabi. It will contain the beneficial properties of horseradish, but also the potentially unhealthy chemicals of the green dye. Check that you are being served the real thing, and buy good-quality wasabi for use when cooking at home. Always use fresh wasabi and store it carefully, because it will lose color and pungency quickly when exposed to air.

RAINBOW SALAD WITH WASABI DRESSING

A salad doesn't need to be complicated to be good. This bright, healthy
salad is an easy and exciting way to eat more vegetables.

SERVES 4 • PREP TIME: 10–15 MINS • COOK TIME: 5 MINS

PER SERVING:	119 cal	8.3g	0.8g	8.2g	3.7g	1.8g	3.4g	600mg
	CALORIES	FAT	SAT FAT	CARBS	SUGAR	FIBER	PROTEIN	SODIUM

INGREDIENTS

1 tablespoon sunflower oil
¼ cup sunflower seeds
2 tablespoons soy sauce
1½ cups rainbow Swiss chard, shredded
1½ cups rainbow Swiss chard, cut into strips

DRESSING

1 teaspoon wasabi paste
1 tablespoon mirin
juice of 1 small orange
pepper (optional)

1. Heat the oil in a covered skillet over medium heat. Add the
sunflower seeds, cover, and cook for 2–3 minutes, shaking
the pan so they don't stick, until you hear them begin to pop.
Remove the pan from the heat, add the soy sauce, cover,
and let cool.

2. To make the dressing, put the wasabi paste, mirin, and orange
juice in a screw-top jar, season with a little pepper, if using,
screw on the lid, and shake well.

3. Put all the Swiss chard leaves in a salad bowl. Drizzle with
the dressing, then toss gently together. Sprinkle with the
toasted sunflower seeds and serve.

HINT

*Any type of greens would work well in this recipe—try adding
a mixture such as mizuna, radicchio, or frisée.*

COCONUT OIL

Cooking with coconut oil is a sure way to reduce your exposure to the aging free radicals that are produced when roasting, frying, and baking.

MAJOR NUTRIENTS PER 1 TABLESPOON COCONUT OIL

129 cal	15g	0g	0g	0g	270 mg	870 mg	1.125g	6.69g	2.5g
CALORIES	TOTAL FAT	CARBS	FIBER	PROTEIN	OMEGA-6 OILS	OMEGA-9 OILS	CAPRYLIC ACID	LAURIC ACID	MYRISTIC ACID

Whenever we cook with oil, the heat causes some damage to the oil's fat molecules, which has a knock-on effect in our bodies. The free radicals produced can damage our body tissues and make us more susceptible to cancer, heart disease, and osteoporosis. Of all the saturated fats, coconut oil is the least prone to damage by heat, light, and oxygen, and it can be heated to temperatures as high as 375°F. Because it is so stable, it keeps for a long time. Coconut oil contains about 60 percent medium-chain triglycerides (MCTs), plant-base oils that raise metabolism and cannot be stored as fat in our bodies. Researchers have found that in countries where breast milk is high in MCTs, the population as a whole demonstrates a better quality of aging.

- The fats in coconut oil help feed the lining of the digestive tract, ensuring good digestion and the elimination of aging toxins.
- Has been shown to assist thyroid function and regulate metabolism and mood, keeping us both trim and happy.

PRACTICAL TIPS

Coconut oil, which becomes a clear liquid when heated, can be used in all kinds of cooking and doesn't retain any of the coconut flavor from the flesh. It does behave differently from other oils, however, so a little experimentation may be necessary. Choose an unprocessed type, and avoid any that have been hydrogenated or contain preservatives.

COCONUT QUINOA BOWL

This high-protein, low-sugar quinoa granola is served on a creamy coconut-and-banana porridge, with lots of omega-3 fats from walnuts and pecans.

SERVES 4 • PREP TIME: 20 MINS • COOK TIME: 15 MINS

PER SERVING:

746 cal	43.1g	26g	84.7g	31.3g	11.3g	11.8g	40mg
CALORIES	FAT	SAT FAT	CARBS	SUGAR	FIBER	PROTEIN	SODIUM

INGREDIENTS

½ cup coconut oil
1 tablespoon honey
2 tablespoons packed dark brown sugar
1 cup quinoa flakes
1⅔ cups rolled oats
3 tablespoons dry unsweetened coconut
½ teaspoon ground cinnamon
1 tablespoon dried cranberries
1 tablespoon chopped pecans
2 bananas, peeled and chopped
½ cup walnuts
1 cup coconut milk
1 teaspoon ground cinnamon, to sprinkle
¾ cup raspberries
small handful of mint leaves
2 tablespoons maple syrup

1. Preheat the oven to 350°F. Put the coconut oil, honey, and sugar into a saucepan over low heat and heat, stirring, until the sugar has dissolved.

2. Remove from the heat and stir in the quinoa flakes, ⅔ cup of the oats, 2 tablespoons of the coconut, the cinnamon, cranberries, and pecans. Mix well to combine.

3. Spread the mixture over a baking sheet and bake in the preheated oven for 15 minutes, stirring halfway through the cooking time.

4. Remove from the oven, spoon into a bowl, and let cool.

5. Meanwhile, put the bananas, the remaining oats, the walnuts, and coconut milk into a food processor and process until almost smooth.

6. Pour into four bowls and add the granola. Top with the cinnamon, raspberries, mint, the remaining dry coconut, and a drizzle of maple syrup.

OLIVE OIL

Well known for being high in heart-protective monounsaturates, virgin olive oils also contain a range of antioxidant plant compounds and vitamin E.

MAJOR NUTRIENTS PER 1 TABLESPOON OLIVE OIL

 130 cal
CALORIES

 15g
TOTAL FAT

 2.1g
VITAMIN E

The main type of fat in olive oil is monounsaturated, which helps prevent cholesterol being deposited on artery walls and, therefore, helps protect us from cardiovascular disease and strokes. In addition, early pressings of the olives (as in extra virgin olive oil, particularly "cold pressed") produce an oil that is rich in beneficial plant compounds. These can protect against cancer and high blood pressure, and lower cholesterol. The compound oleocanthal is an anti-inflammatory with similar action to ibuprofen. Finally, olive oil is a good source of vitamin E.

- Helps improve blood cholesterol profile and protect us from cardiovascular disease.
- Rich in polyphenols to protect against colon and other cancers.
- Can help prevent *Helicobacter pylori*, which can lead to stomach ulcers.
- Antibacterial and antioxidant.

DID YOU KNOW?

Researchers in Italy have found that light destroys many of the disease-fighting compounds in olive oil. Studies showed that after a year, oils stored in clear bottles under store lighting showed at least a 30 per cent decrease in antioxidants.

PRACTICAL TIPS

Olive oil should be stored in the dark and used within one to two months. Buy olive oil from a source with a high turnover where the oil is kept in dimly lit conditions. For its full benefit, eat it cold in salad dressings or drizzled on bread or vegetables. Don't use extra virgin olive oil for cooking at high temperatures, otherwise the beneficial chemicals will be destroyed.

BEEF CARPACCIO

Loaded with essential protein, minerals, and beneficial plant compounds, this traditional Italian appetizer also makes a good light lunch or supper, served with plenty of crusty bread.

SERVES 2 • PREP TIME: 5 MINS, PLUS FREEZING AND CHILLING • COOK TIME: NONE

PER SERVING:	766 cal	70g	11.5g	3.9g	1.6g	1.3g	32.8g	120mg
	CALORIES	FAT	SAT FAT	CARBS	SUGAR	FIBER	PROTEIN	SODIUM

INGREDIENTS

9 ounces excellent-quality beef, such as filet mignon
½ cup extra virgin olive oil
¼ cup pine nuts
5 cups arugula
2 tablespoons Parmesan cheese
salt and pepper (optional)

1. Put the beef into the freezer for 1 hour before use so it is firm for slicing. Trim any fat or sinew from the beef, then cut the filet into slices as thinly as possible.

2. Lay a slice of beef on a cutting board and, using a flat, broad knife, press against the meat, pushing down hard and pulling across the beef in a spreading motion. Repeat with all the beef slices.

3. Pour a little pool of oil into a wide dish. Place a layer of beef on the oil, lightly season with salt and pepper, if using, and pour over some more oil. Repeat until all the beef has been seasoned in this way.

4. Chill in the refrigerator for at least 30 minutes, or for up to 2 hours. Meanwhile, toast the pine nuts in a dry skillet over medium heat until lightly browned, then set aside.

5. Pile a bed of arugula onto two serving plates, remove the beef slices from the marinade, and divide evenly between the plates.

6. Sprinkle with the pine nuts, shave the Parmesan cheese over the top using a vegetable peeler, and serve.

CANOLA OIL

This is one of the healthiest oils, rich in monounsaturates and omega-3 fats to protect against cancers, heart disease, and other ailments.

MAJOR NUTRIENTS PER 1 TABLESPOON CANOLA OIL

130 cal	15g	2.6 mg
CALORIES	TOTAL FAT	VITAMIN E

Canola oil had been neglected as a health-giving oil until recently, when farmers began producing it as a competitively priced alternative to olive oil. In fact, canola oil in many ways has an even better "health profile" than its rival does. It has nearly as high a content of monounsaturated fat as olive oil and contains higher amounts of the essential omega-3 fat alpha-linoleic acid than any other oil used in quantity for culinary purposes. Canola oil also has a perfect balance between omega-6 and omega-3 fats and is lower in saturated fat than all the other commonly used oils. It is also a good source of vitamin E.

- Excellent balance of essential fats in line with recommended guidelines.
- Low in saturated fat.
- Good source of the antioxidant vitamin E.
- High in omega-3 fats, which have a variety of health benefits when eaten regularly.

DID YOU KNOW?

Canola oil is an annual plant and a member of the Brassica (cabbage) family. It has bright yellow flowers in summer and turns many fields golden.

PRACTICAL TIPS

Refined canola oil is a good choice for cooking, because it doesn't degrade when heated. Cold pressed or extra virgin canola oil is a great choice for salad dressings and drizzling. Its nutty flavor is particularly good drizzled over artichoke hearts or asparagus. It is ideal for mayonnaise, because it has a milder flavor than olive oil.

GARLIC & CHILI DIPPING OIL

This golden flavored oil will add life and heat to your favorite dipping ingredients—
it is quick and easy to make and is a great standby to have in the refrigerator.

MAKES ABOUT 1 CUP • PREP TIME: 15 MINS, PLUS COOLING • COOK TIME: 1½–2 HOURS

PER 1 CUP:	1,989 cal	225g	16.6g	0g	0g	0g	0g	TRACE
	CALORIES	FAT	SAT FAT	CARBS	SUGAR	FIBER	PROTEIN	SODIUM

INGREDIENTS

5 garlic cloves, halved lengthwise
2 tablespoons seeded and chopped jalapeño chiles
1 teaspoon dried oregano
1 cup canola oil

1. Preheat the oven to 300°F. Combine the garlic, chile, and oregano with the oil in an ovenproof glass bowl.

2. Place on a glass pie plate in the center of the oven and heat for 1½–2 hours. The temperature of the oil should reach 250°F.

3. Using thick oven mitts, carefully remove the bowl from the oven, let cool, then strain through cheesecloth into a clean jar. Store in an airtight container in the refrigerator for up to one month. You can also keep the garlic and chile pieces in the oil and strain before using.

FLAXSEED OIL

Flaxseed oil is one of the best plant sources of anti-inflammatory omega-3 oils. These balance with the omega-6 oil content to create a superior anti-aging ingredient.

MAJOR NUTRIENTS PER 1 TABLESPOON FLAXSEED OIL

132 cal	0.43g	4.63g	11.58g	0.5g	1.19g	0.05 mg	0.04 mg	0.64 mg	0.21 mg	0.06 mg	0.05 mg
CALORIES	TOTAL FAT	MONO UN-SATURATED FAT	CARBS	FIBER	PROTEIN	VITAMIN B1	VITAMIN B2	VITAMIN B3	VITAMIN B5	VITAMIN B6	VITAMIN C
7,995 mg	1,905 mg	3,029 mg	9.9 mg	27.6 mcg	0.74 mg	31.5 mcg	24 mg	0.9 mg	69 mg	2.7 mcg	0.75 mg
OMEGA-3 OILS	OMEGA-6 OILS	OMEGA-9 OILS	CALCIUM	FOLATE	IRON	LUTEIN/ZEAXANTHIN	MAGNESIUM	MANGANESE	POTASSIUM	SELENIUM	ZINC

Most modern diets are much higher in omega-6 oils than omega-3. This can cause health problems and the dry skin and poor concentration associated with omega-3 oil deficiency. The omega oil ratio in flaxseed oil provides the optimum support for heart, joint, and brain function. Flaxseed oil is also rich in lignans, renowned for their antioxidant, antiviral, antibacterial, and anticancer actions. Lignans help regulate sex hormones and combat premenstrual syndrome, menopausal symptoms, prostate problems, and hormone-sensitive cancers, such as breast and prostate. Flaxseed contain by far the highest amount of these valuable substances—ten times more than any other seed, grain, or vegetable.

- Important rejuvenating food for people who do not get their essential omega-3 oils from oily fish.
- Excellent digestive-healing action that stops harmful elements entering the bloodstream and prevents inflammatory food intolerances.
- High in heart-revitalizing oleic acid (omega-9 oil), the same as is found in olive oil.

DID YOU KNOW?

Also known as linseed oil, flaxseed oil hardens on exposure to air. This is why it is used to mix oil paints and to create a hard, glossy surface.

PRACTICAL TIPS

Flaxseed oil is easily damaged by heat, light, and oxygen. To preserve its benefits, it needs to be stored in dark glass bottles and cannot be used for any type of cooking. It makes a healthy base for salad dressings, and can also be added to juices or smoothies, slowing the release of sugars into the bloodstream.

RUBY COUSCOUS SALAD WITH GRILLED CHICKEN

This salad looks good—and it does you good, too. The beets turn everything a deep vibrant red and the whole plate glistens, jewel-like, with the pomegranate seeds.

SERVES 4 • PREP TIME: 10–15 MINS • COOK TIME: 20–30 MINS

PER SERVING:

517 cal	18.6g	2.4g	53.8g	16g	8.1g	36.2g	80mg
CALORIES	FAT	SAT FAT	CARBS	SUGAR	FIBER	PROTEIN	SODIUM

INGREDIENTS

1 cup Israeli (pearl) wholewheat couscous
1 cup diced cooked beets (in natural juices)
1 small red onion, finely chopped
8 cherry tomatoes, halved
1 pomegranate, halved, seeds reserved
juice of 2 lemons
2 tablespoons flaxseed oil
2 tablespoons olive oil
4 teaspoons tomato paste
2 tablespoons coarsely chopped fresh mint
1 teaspoon black peppercorns, coarsely crushed
1 pound 2 ounces chicken breast strips
salt and pepper (optional)

1. Bring a saucepan of water to a boil. Add the couscous, bring back to a boil, then simmer for 6–8 minutes, or according to package directions, until just tender. Drain through a strainer, rinse with cold water, then transfer to a salad bowl. Add the beets, onion, tomatoes, and pomegranate seeds.

2. To make the dressing, put the juice of 1 lemon, the flaxseed oil, half the olive oil, and half the tomato paste into a screw-top jar, season with salt and pepper, if using, screw on the lid, and shake well. Drizzle the dressing over the salad, then sprinkle with the chopped mint and toss together.

3. Put the remaining lemon juice, olive oil, and tomato paste and the crushed peppercorns into a clean plastic bag, twist, and shake well. Add the chicken, seal the bag, then shake until the chicken is evenly coated.

4. Preheat a ridged grill pan over high heat. Cook the chicken (in batches, if necessary) in the hot pan for 10 minutes, turning once or twice, until cooked through. Cut through the middle of a slice to check that the meat is no longer pink and that any juices run clear and are piping hot. Arrange over the salad and serve.

GLOSSARY

ALLERGIES Immune system reactions that set off inflammation and can be triggered by foods or environmental factors.

ALPHA-LINOLENIC ACID A polyunsaturated fat; one of the omega-3 group of essential fats that we need to consume for health, because our bodies can't manufacture it. Can be converted into EPA and DHA within the body.

AMINO ACIDS The "building blocks" of protein contained in many foods in varying combinations and amounts. Only nine are indispensable (essential) for adults and, when a food contains all nine in good proportion, that food is often described as a "complete protein."

ANTHOCYANIN An antioxidant—see bioflavonoids.

ANTI-INFLAMMATORY DIET Inflammation is the body's natural immune reaction to stress and illness and is thought to be linked to health problems, such as heart disease and arthritis. An anti-inflammatory diet is said to reduce inflammation.

ANTIOXIDANT Antioxidants are phytochemicals, vitamins, and other nutrients that protect our cells from damage and aging caused by free radicals. Antioxidants should be consumed in foods instead of as dietary supplements.

"BAD" LDL CHOLESTEROL Low-density lipoproteins transport cholesterol from the liver to the heart. If LDL is higher than "good" HDL cholesterol, then the risk of heart disease increases.

BIOFLAVONOID/FLAVONOID A group of several thousand antioxidant compounds found in fruits, vegetables, and other plant foods, and including rutin, anthocyanins, catechins, and quercetin.

CARBOHYDRATE A carbohydrate can be in the form of sugars, starches, or fiber and is usually the main source of energy in the human diet. It is present in most foods and in largest quantity in cereals, root vegetables, beans, fruits, and vegetables, as well as in milk and most dairy produce.

CAROTENES Yellow, red, or orange pigments found in foods, such as carrots, with several health benefits, including protection from cancers. Carotenes include alpha and beta, lutein, lycopene, zeaxanthin, cryptozanthin and betacryptoxanthin—these are some of the most researched and beneficial.

CHOLESTEROL A fatty substance present in many foods of animal origin and manufactured in humans in the liver, it is essential in the body but under certain circumstances can also encourage the development of coronary artery disease. See HDL and "bad" LDL.

CIRCULATION The system by which blood is pumped by the heart around the body, delivering oxygen and nutrients to all cells.

DETOXIFICATION The process in the liver and all individual cells by which harmful and aging toxins are broken down and eliminated.

DHA FATS Docosahexaenoic acid—a "long-chain" omega-3 fatty acid found only in fish, particularly oily fish, with several health benefits.

DIGESTION The process by which we break down, absorb, and assimilate the food we eat to derive the nutrients we need.

ENZYMES Proteins that act as catalysts to bring about biochemical reactions. The human body contains thousands of different enzymes vital for digestion and metabolism of food, for example.

EPA FATS Eicosapentaenoic acid—a "long-chain" omega-3 fatty acid found only in fish, particularly oily fish, with several health benefits.

ESSENTIAL FATTY ACIDS/EFAS Essential fats—linoleic acid and alpha-linolenic acid—which must be provided in the diet in balanced and adequate amounts for good health.

FATS One of the major sources of calories in the human diet as well as providing vitamins. Some also provide phytochemicals including antioxidants.

FREE RADICALS Highly reactive, unstable atoms or molecules in the body that are a normal by-product of metabolism but are believed, in excess, to be a factor in onset of disease and the aging process.

GLUCOSINOLATES A group of sulfur-base plant compounds, including indoles and isothiocyanates, found in brassicas, such as cabbage and kale, which support immune function and can help prevent cancers.

GLYCEMIC INDEX A system of ranking carbohydrate foods according to their effect on blood sugar levels.

"GOOD" CHOLESTEROL/HDL High-density lipoproteins that bind to cholesterol and carry it through the blood to help keep arteries clear and protect against cardiovascular disease.

HOMOCYSTEINE An amino acid that can build up in the blood. High levels are a strong risk factor for cardiovascular disease.

HYPOALLERGENIC Relating to food, an item unlikely to cause an allergic reaction.

IMMUNE SYSTEM Body system responsible for protection against bacteria, viruses, disease, and other potentially harmful pathogens.

INDOLES see Glucosinolates.

INSOLUBLE FIBER The indigestible portion of plant foods that moves all the way through the digestive system, absorbing water, increasing stool bulk, and helping satiety. It can help prevent disorders of the bowel.

INSULIN A hormone produced by the pancreas that regulates blood sugar levels. In insulin resistance, the insulin doesn't work effectively and can lead to type-2 diabetes.

INTOLERANCES Food intolerances are nonallergic food hypersensitivity. They are an adverse reaction to a food (or component of food) or beverage that produces unwanted symptoms in the body without being an allergy.

LIGNAN One of a range of plant chemicals with estrogen-like effects, thought to be of benefit in hormone-related health issues, including breast cancer, prostate cancer, menopause symptoms, and heart disease. Other estrogenic plant chemicals include coumestrol and daidzein.

L-TYROSINE An amino acid that can help improve brain function and energy levels and is found in a variety of high-protein foods.

METABOLISM The chemical reactions that occur in the body to maintain life, during which food and drink are broken down and their nutrients used for body repair, maintenance and energy.

MINERALS Natural inorganic chemicals, around 20 of which are vital for the body's health and cannot be made in the body, so they are supplied via food and beverages.

MONOUNSATURATED FAT A type of fat found in most foods but in high quantities in a few, such as olive oil, avocados, and some nuts, which has a beneficial effect on cholesterol levels, cardiovascular disease, and other health problems.

OLEIC ACID A type of omega-9 monounsaturated fat found in high amounts in olive oil, avocado, and canola oil, for example. Thought to be helpful in diabetes and insulin resistance because it can improve blood glucose levels, insulin sensitivity, and blood circulation.

OMEGA-3 Polyunsaturated fats that help prevent and minimize inflammation and disease; necessary for strong immune and heart function.

OMEGA-6 Polyunsaturated fats found in a wide variety of plant foods, the most common of which is linoleic acid, one of the essential fatty acids.

OMEGA-9 A group of monounsaturated fats, of which oleic acid is the most common.

ORAC Stands for Oxygen Radical Absorbance Capacity and is an international scale of measurement of antioxidant capacity of foods.

PHYTOCHEMICALS/PHYTONUTRIENTS see plant compounds

PLANT COMPOUNDS Natural chemicals or compounds found in plants thought to be largely responsible for the health protective effects plants offer when consumed.

PHYTOSTEROLS A group of plant compounds, including beta-sitosterol, that have a cholesterol-lowering effect when eaten regularly.

POLYPHENOL/PHENOLS/PHENOLIC COMPOUNDS A large category of antioxidant plant compounds, including anthocyanins, ellagic acid, resveratrol, and tannins, strongly linked with the prevention of heart disease.

POLYUNSATURATED FAT Type of fat high in omega-6 and which also includes the omega-3 fatty acids.

PREBIOTICS Types of fiber, including inulin, oligofructose, and oligosaccharides, found in plant foods, that act as food for beneficial bacteria (probiotics) in the intestines.

PROBIOTICS Beneficial bacteria, such as *Lactobacillium* and *Bifidobacteria* bacteria, which are present in the digestive system and help to support digestion, immunity, and detoxification, as well as help to reduce allergies, intolerances, and inflammation.

PROTEIN A macronutrient that the body needs to make and maintain lean tissue (muscle) and for a variety of other functions. See also amino acids.

SAPONINS Plant compounds found, for example, in oats, soybeans, and yams, with a unique foaming ability that can help prevent colon cancer and can block the body's absorption of cholesterol.

SATURATED FAT Fats that are found in largest quantities in foods of animal origin and remain solid at room temperature. High consumption has long been associated with increased risk of heart disease and other health problems but further research needs to be done. One type of saturated fat—lauric acid, found mainly in coconuts, is thought to have positive health benefits, being easy to digest and of possible help in cholesterol-lowering and weight loss.

SOLUBLE FIBER Various types of soluble fiber include pectin, oligosaccharides, and beta-glucans, which not only have a beneficial effect on digestive health but can also help reduce cholesterol as well as control blood sugar levels by slowing sugar absorption.

STEROLS see phytosterols

SULFIDES Antioxidant and immune-stimulating plant compounds found for example in onions, garlic, and leeks.

SULFORAPHANE Found in cruciferous vegetables, such as cauliflower, broccoli, and Brussels sprouts, this compound, a member of the glucosinolate family, has anticancer and antidiabetic properties.

TRYPTOPHAN An amino acid that enables relaxation and improves mood and sleep by promoting the secretion of the brain chemical serotonin.

VITAMIN A group of organic substances essential to metabolism in small quantities and found in minute amounts in food. A deficiency can lead to a variety of health problems and diseases.

INDEX